Fundamental Curriculum Decisions

Prepared by the
ASCD 1983 Yearbook Committee

Fenwick W. English, Chairperson and Editor

**Association for Supervision
and Curriculum Development**
225 North Washington Street
Alexandria, Virginia 22314

Editing:
Ronald S. Brandt, ASCD Executive Editor
Nancy S. Olson, Senior Editor

Stock number: 610-83290
Library of Congress Catalog Card Number: 82-074237
ISBN 0-87120-117-8

Contents

Foreword

W e practitioners in the curriculum enterprise confront only a few curriculum problems. We are aware of many other problems, but they are confronted by others and resolved some distance from the arena of our own practice. Indeed, taking the form of legislation, criticism, agency directives and regulations, textbook publication and marketing, and proposals touted in the media, these remote resolutions affect us. They constrain or free us to act in our individual settings, but they are typically not the problems we encounter. Our curriculum problems are different and local, and we come almost to believe that they are just ours and unlike those faced by practitioners elsewhere.

If nothing else—and it does more— this Yearbook reminds us that our local curriculum problems are similar to those known by other local curriculum workers. They are similar and they can be approached from common bases. We must make our individual and local curriculum decisions. Yet, the decision making across districts can be informed and guided by shared elements of curriculum development processes. The yield, even so, likely will be different from site to site.

These are worthy reminders.

During the past two decades, standard curriculum decisions laid siege to American schools. The alphabet-labeled curricula were accompanied by legions of standardized prescriptions. Local problems, we were told, were not merely local; they could be solved by a standard and universal practice. Objectives developed, say, in Rochester and computer-accessed in Los Angeles could be effectively applied in Lometa and Kent and Orlando. Materials developed in Cambridge or San Francisco could be used as effectively and without adaptation in Atlanta and Ozona and Provo. Standard curriculum decisions were the victors. But victory was hollow. The standard curriculum decisions were adopted in policy and abandoned in practice.

Now, with the necessity of local curriculum work legitimated, we still have our local problems. We also are beset by other and fierce realizations. Two merit our public acknowledgment if for no other reason than that they are implicitly assumed by this Yearbook Committee. And these two are not lightly dismissed.

One is the awareness that school faculties are suspicious of anyone bearing curriculum gifts—proposals for change. This uneasiness is easy to understand. Teachers endured the recent curriculum reform era or have heard the war stories of the old-timers in countless faculty lounges. SMSG or AAAS Science or structural linguistics or the New Social Studies. Inquiry learning and mastery learning. Modules and packages. And years of missed time for teaching or reading or planning consumed in meetings to list and assemble compendia of objectives—now forgotten. Also, teachers now have agendas for themselves.

A second realization is that many curriculum leaders truly do not understand the processes or possess skills necessary for local curriculum development. We have largely accepted the rhetoric and practices of industrial management and have not inherited the rich experience of our predecessors in curriculum development. In fact, too many of us do not distinguish decision making about curriculum matters from curriculum development. We need help. We need more and different help with concepts and understanding. We also need to focus on our own behaviors as helpers as well as managers.

This Yearbook constitutes one tangible resource for us in these circumstances. It is not a handbook of ready solutions and lists of tools. It is one major resource offered by our Association. And it should be useful to many.

Assertedly practical, this Yearbook emphasizes technical solutions to local problems. It acknowledges other philosophic positions, but it admits and consistently advocates processes in the positivist tradition. It does not include everything, even as much as some of us need. Its choices have been calculated. It constitutes a thoughtful explication of conventional curriculum making.

I am pleased to invite reflective attention to this Yearbook. Much of it I find comfortable and, thus, I can think easily with and away from the concepts and positions. Several of the authors are close professional colleagues, ones from whom I have continued to learn throughout my career and ones with whom I have profited from conversation and, occasionally, sharp dissent and vigorous debate. Other authors are new acquaintances whose ideas I expect to enjoy as we engage in dialogue. But reading and studying come before sharing in discussion—with the authors themselves—and with local colleagues. The Yearbook can become for many of us another setting for engagements of our minds and exploration for improvement of school programs for children and youth.

I also invite critique and commentary of this Yearbook. Not every book is so honored. Indeed, many are not taken thoughtfully, even if seriously. This Yearbook's ideas merit lively exchange.

Preparation of an ASCD Yearbook is not a short-time activity hastily completed. Like its predecessors in this distinguished series, this Yearbook represents several years work by committed, knowledgeable curriculum workers. It is not the book that any one of them would have written. It is the result of intense interactions, mindful considerations, and reasonable compromises. I have the privilege on behalf of all ASCD members of thanking Fenwick English, editor, and his collaborators for their labors and their product.

O. L. DAVIS, JR.
ASCD President, 1982-83

Introduction

E very field of human endeavor has its recurring problems, issues, and decisions. Curriculum development and curriculum as a field of study are no exception.

This Yearbook was commissioned by ASCD to provide a readable, usable, and practical summary of the most commonly applied elements of curriculum development on the contemporary scene.

Each chapter presents a perspective of that topic or area, highlights the most important contributions, and comments on those contributions of continuing worth.

Authors were encouraged to present their views of solutions to problems along with the major references that a person in the curriculum field should be familiar with in order to practice his or her craft.

The Yearbook is not exhaustive. It is hoped that it is broad, analytic, and reflective. At the outset the 1983 ASCD Yearbook Committee rejected the idea of a "cookbook" as being unworthy of serious use by either practitioners or scholars. Rather, the chapters are grouped into two parts. The first seven chapters deal with activities the curriculum practitioner would undertake to get ready to develop curriculum. The second group of chapters deals directly with implementation.

The Yearbook Committee was composed of eight professors, all of whom have written about and thought deeply about curriculum matters, some for more than four decades. The remainder of the Committee comprised a variety of practitioners with much experience in the curriculum field, including a past ASCD President.

Curriculum development and thought continue to be controversial. The lack of a definitive base in theory is a major barrier to improving practice. The Committee approached the task respectfully, without rancor, but not without firm opinions grounded in their own experience and practice.

We view the final product as a compilation, a distillation of contemporary thought, and as a place from which to begin other efforts that will go even further. To this end we offer the 1983 Yearbook to the members of the Association and to all who are committed to improving the craft of curriculum development in schools and other educational settings.

FENWICK W. ENGLISH
Chairperson and Editor
1983 ASCD Yearbook

Chapter 1

Contemporary Curriculum Circumstances

Fenwick W. English

Today's curriculum practice is peculiar to our times and, in some ways, universal to any time. Even curriculum events that appear unique to our times will be viewed by some as cycles of recurring responses to iterative challenges. The purpose of this chapter is to provide a framework for examining circumstances in which contemporary curriculum practice is carried on in the schools.

Curriculum practice may be viewed as involving issues that are
- ideological
- technical
- operational.

Ideological curriculum problems center on a discussion of values and the selection of values from a sociopolitical perspective. Technical issues largely center on design questions. Obviously, design issues have ideological roots. Operational issues are essentially delivery/management issues. However, what is delivered in the way of curriculum also reflects one's view of what "should be" in a curriculum (a value question), and how it "should be implemented" to fulfill its purpose (a design matter).

Each of these three broad types of issues has both a practical and a theoretical dimension. Figure 1 indicates the issues and these dimensions in schematic form.

What is a Curriculum?

Perhaps the first question to address is "what is a curriculum?" When does a person know that he or she has a curriculum? Does a curriculum exist when a school district produces a curriculum guide or scope and sequence chart? Some would aver that the presence or absence of a curriculum guide has nothing to do with whether or not one has a curriculum. Some view the "curriculum" as simply the total of the experiences a student may have in a school. Others would say that a curriculum exists only when it contains a series of essential references

1

Figure 1. Issues and Dimensions of Contemporary Curricular Circumstances

	Ideological (concerned with values and selection of values)	Technical (concerned with design)	Operational (concerned with delivery and management)
Theoretical	A	B	C
Practical	D	E	F

about content and how that content is to be addressed in a planned, explicit way.[1]

The point of view developed here is that a curriculum comes into being when school people adopt a set of recurring responses to a set of recurring circumstances in schools. When it becomes necessary for political, instructional, social, or managerial reasons to commit those responses to paper for whatever reason, the curriculum becomes a document. All that has occurred is a move from an implicit response to an explicit statement. The pressures to develop explicit statements about organizational behavior, whether in schools or other institutions, come from three generic sources:

- selection (choice of values creating priorities)
- scarcity of resources
- rules.

Choice of Values

Organizations must be selective about their activities. Without a focus it becomes impossible to cluster resources to accomplish anything. This fact of life requires decisions about what is most important to include in a scope of work and what to eliminate. It requires a boundary.

Decisions about boundaries are political, social, and economic. They are culturally embedded and rarely value free. Priorities reflect values and choices about values. Even a decision not to select a value is a decision and represents a value.

At the present time there is considerable discussion about the values selected to be in school curricula. Some critics maintain that curriculum developers have been too acquiescent about accepting values that merely reflect the dominant class structure. Viewed in political terms, if this is true, the curriculum is a form of oppression and control.[2] These critics have forced a re-

[1]Frank L. Steeves and Fenwick W. English, "Curriculum Evaluation," in *Secondary Curriculum for a Changing World* (Columbus: Charles E. Merrill, 1978), pp. 295–318.

[2]Michael W. Apple, "The Hidden Curriculum and the Nature of Conflict," in *Curriculum Theorizing*, ed. W. Pinar (Berkeley: McCutchan, 1975), pp. 95–119.

examination of the question of which values are consciously or unconsciously selected to be part of school curriculum.

Scarcity of Resources

Few human organizations have unlimited resources. Limitations of staff, time, and physical materials force organizations to cluster and select activities that will lead to maximization of outcomes, or at least to the accomplishment of as much as possible.

The curriculum not only represents a selection of values but a conscious effort to effectively use school, staff, and student time. In short, schools need to select among competing (or possible) things to do. Schools must then bring to bear their resources to ensure that those things legitimized in the curriculum are attained (or at least effort is made to attain them).

Rules

Since most human organizations exist within a society that must either distribute its resources or allow competition for them, almost all have had to resort to some regulation or organizational activity. Schools have historically been regulated by state legislatures and local boards of education and more recently by federal law and the federal courts.

Sweeping rules or complex regulation require planning. When a PL 94-142 requires placing children "in the least restrictive environment" and developing an individualized educational plan (IEP), this has an impact on curriculum development. The presence of regulation can be a dynamic force for the development of an explicit plan; that is, a curriculum.

A curriculum is the name educators have given to an explicit plan or document in response to one or more of the three generic situations confronting all human organizations in more or less advanced cultures. The more technologically advanced the culture, the more explicit the curriculum or document tends to become.

The Contemporary Issues

The Ideological Issues

An ideology is a "systematic body of concepts about human life or culture," or "a manner or the content of thinking characteristic of an individual, group, or culture." It is also "the integrated assertions, theories, and aims that constitute a sociopolitical program."[3]

For many decades curriculum development, as an embodiment of administrative science applied to schooling, held that the tenets of its basic existence

---

[3]*Webster's Seventh New Collegiate Dictionary* (Springfield, Mass.: G. and C. Merriam, 1971), p. 413.

were or should be couched with "natural phenomena and their properties and relations as verified by the empirical sciences."[4]

Beginning with the seminal work of Franklin Bobbitt,[5] a long line of curriculum thinkers such as W. W. Charters,[6] Harold Rugg,[7] Ralph Tyler,[8] B. O. Smith,[9] and George Beauchamp[10] outlined the prevailing ideology of thinking about curriculum. The tradition of thinking about curriculum has been called *positivism*.

Positivism is a theory that theology and metaphysics were earlier and imperfect modes of knowledge. The "best" knowledge was that which was verifiable and quantifiable. The development of our current language base regarding curriculum development can be largely attributed to the assumptions of logical positivism. What was "real" was that which was capable of being demonstrated, evaluated, and related to the ends of schooling, which had to be (and were) more precisely stated than ever before. A practitioner grounded in the ideology of positivism was faced with the problem of translation and of knowing the proper "mix" of variables from which to derive the best results under sets of varying circumstances in the schools.

A brief picture of the tenets of logical positivism applied to curriculum development might be these assumptions:

- One must deal with facts and facts are objective
- Means and ends can be separated and clearly cast
- Curriculum is a means to specified ends (schooling outcomes)
- Solutions in schools (of which the curriculum is one) should be selected on empirical data and be verified on how well a desired set of results are attained
- A logical and rational curriculum was one that was designed to attain specified ends and could be evaluated as an effective tool as such. The curriculum is a causal agent, a planned intervention in what might be an otherwise haphazard process.

The challenge to logical positivism has taken three forms as theoretical positions. First, positivism has been criticized as embodying a set of values that are as subjective and imperfect as those it sought to replace.

When we examine those empirical theories that have been advanced, we discover again and again they are not value-neutral, but reflect deep ideological biases and secret controversial value positions. It is a fiction to think that we can neatly distinguish the

    [4]Ibid., p. 662.
    [5]Franklin Bobbitt, *The Curriculum* (Boston: Houghton Mifflin, 1918).
    [6]W. W. Charters, *Curriculum Construction* (New York: Macmillan, 1923).
    [7]Harold Rugg, *The Foundations and Technique of Curriculum Construction*, 26th Yearbook of the National Society for the Study of Education, Parts I and II (Bloomington, Ill.: Public Schools Publishing Company, 1927).
    [8]Ralph W. Tyler, *Basic Principles of Curriculum and Instruction* (Chicago: University of Chicago Press, 1950).
    [9]B. Othanel Smith, William O. Stanley, and J. Harlan Shores, *Fundamentals of Curriculum Development* (Yonkers-on-Hudson: World Book Company, 1957).
    [10]George A. Beauchamp, *Curriculum Theory* (Wilmette, Ill.: The Kagg Press, 1975).

descriptive from the evaluative comments of these theories, for tacit evaluations are built into their very framework.[11]

Second, there are other ways of "knowing" that are not as quantifiable as some current notions of "good research" would dictate. As an alternative to the derivation of empirical theories and the customary development of linear hypotheses to be tested, the critics of positivism offer the scholarly tradition of phenomenology.

Phenomenology is based on the assumption that all "codified knowledge," including that which comprises science, is derived from and contingent on a prior level or realm that is preconceptual or pre-ideational in nature. This is the fundamental substratum of knowledge, and gaining access to and describing this layer is the proper objective of "pure science."[12]

The search for a "purer form" of knowledge than that found in logical positivism has led curriculum thinkers into several European schools of thought, among them the works of Jurgen Habermas, a colleague of Horkheimer, Adorno, and Marcuse at the Marxist Frankfurt School. Habermas proposes to discover a "theory of verifiable norms" not sanctioned on the legitimacy of the state, but upon a universal morality in which one form lies in undistorted discussion and consensus. This search for "universal pragmatics" lies in probing the common aspects of human speech, comprehensibility, truth, truthfulness, and rightness.[13] These norms in turn are "like true sentences; they are neither facts nor values."[14]

While some of the critics have chosen to attack the dominant positivistic ideology in the curriculum field and its accepted version exemplified by the Tyler Rationale,[15,16] they cease to have much unity in prescribing a methodology in which the tenets of phenomenology could be utilized as a practical scholarly substitute in research, nor in the preparation of curriculum personnel who work in the schools.

Philip Jackson candidly pointed out that the proposed alternative approach advanced by some of the contemporary ideological critics contained a paradox:

One of the things that troubles me most is that some extreme advocates of the antiscientific or antiempirical position continue to make claims about educational matters whose truth value could only be established, it seems to me, by using the methodology

---

[11]R. J. Bernstein, *The Restructuring of Social and Political Theory* (New York: Harcourt, Brace, Jovanovich, 1976), cited by William P. Foster, "Administration and the Crisis of Legitimacy: A Review of Habermasian Thought," *Harvard Educational Review* 50, 4 (1980): 496–505.

[12]William Pinar, "Search for a Method," in *Curriculum Theorizing*, pp. 415–426.

[13]Jurgen Habermas, *Communication and the Evolution of Society* trans. T. McCarthy (Boston: Beacon, 1979).

[14]Jurgen Habermas, *Legitimation Crisis* trans. T. McCarthy (Boston: Beacon, 1975), cited by Foster, "Administration," p. 503.

[15]Herbert M. Kliebard, "Reappraisal: The Tyler Rationale," in W. Pinar, "Search for a Method," pp. 70–83.

[16]"Is the Tyler Rationale a Suitable Basis for Current Curriculum Development?" *ASCD Update* 22, 6 (December 1980).

being rejected. . . . Empirical claims demand empirical support. If the latter cannot be provided, the former should not be made.[17]

The third challenge to positivism assumes that the curriculum is an agent of social control and that curriculum development is an inherently political activity in this respect. From this perspective and through the lenses of socialistic and Marxist ideology the functions of schooling have been criticized. One socialist critic observed: "The historical record of the rhetoric of public school leaders is an embarrassing testimony to this limitless capacity for self-deception."[18]

Broadly stated, the anti-positivistic critics hold that its traditions have distorted the real purpose of schools, which ought to be emancipatory but have instead focused on control issues in curriculum. In turn, that control has and is aimed at maintaining the existing class structure in the United States, which protects its privileges and, despite its rhetoric to the contrary, does not intend to liberate those persons who occupy the bottom rungs in our society.

Thus in examining two curricular documents produced by the National Institute of Education regarding current issues, problems, and concerns in curriculum development,[19] Michael Apple averred that their shortcomings revolved around the fact that research supported by NIE was, in bulk, "empirically, and especially conceptually, unsophisticated," and the lack of any attention to the linkages between curricular decisions and compromises and the existing social and economic institutions and ideologies. Apple felt that the reports drew attention away from:

. . . the actual exercise of power and the complex relationships that exist between schools and the class and economic structure in which they exist. This is not an inconsequential point. We are beginning to understand more clearly how cultural and economic apparatuses are linked in such a way that cultural and educational institutions act as means in the social reproduction of an unequal society.[20]

Another widely quoted piece of research on school effectiveness, the book *Fifteen Thousand Hours* by Michael Rutter and others,[21] was criticized because the researcher (Rutter) "cannot grasp the school as a cultural system. . . . insofar as the problem is approached, the complex task of analyzing social and historical processes is collapsed into picking and choosing from a shopping list of variables."[22]

Rutter's positivist conceptualization makes it impossible for him to understand the

[17]Philip W. Jackson, "Curriculum and Its Discontents," *Curriculum Inquiry* 10:2 (Summer 1980): 159–171.

[18]William A. Profriedt, "Socialist Criticisms of Education in the United States: Problems and Possibilities," *Harvard Education Review* 50, 4 (November 1980): 467–480.

[19]National Institute of Education, *Current Issues, Problems, and Concerns in Curriculum Development*, 1976, and *N. I. E.'s Role in Curriculum Development*, 1977.

[20]Michael W. Apple, "Politics and National Curriculum Policy," *Curriculum Inquiry* 7, 4 (Winter 1977): 355–361.

[21]Michael Rutter, Barbara Maughan, Peter Mortimore, Janet Ouston, and Alan Smith, *Fifteen Thousand Hours* (Cambridge: Harvard University Press, 1979).

[22]Dean Ashenden, "To the Editors," *Harvard Educational Review* 50:4 (November 1980): 558–560.

school as a political system, and prevents him from tracing its complex relations with the political and cultural system beyond.[23]

The critic then states,

. . . we should help working-class schools find ways of turning around and confront the task that has been set for them. Whatever the new answer to the old question, "What is good schooling for working-class people?"—it won't look like the kind of schooling that Rutter endorses, and it won't be found in his way of looking."[24]

One of the areas of greatest ferment entering the decade is the theoretical/ideological arena. According to the critics, the expressed dissatisfaction with previous approaches to thinking about curriculum issues can be summarized by saying they were:

● too simple; overly concerned with rational, empirical approaches that were quite arbitrary and "falsely" scientific in that they pretended to be devoid of values when the "scientific" approach is a value position itself

● excessively linear and one-dimensional, forcing what could be viewed as a multidimensional process into a rigid mold of means-ends contrasts

● reinforcements to a political and social system that does not appear to be liberating for all concerned, but centered on issues of control of one class by another.

Practical/Theoretical Issues

A common approach to the selection of values used in curriculum development has been that of needs assessment. Kaufman's chapter in this Yearbook provides a more detailed and extensive review of this process as the basis for the selection of values from which a curriculum is constructed.

"Needs assessment is an empirical process which is carried out to determine what goals should be addressed by a project or an organization."[25] While needs assessment is employed within a culture, it can be used to question the values of that culture and those selected to be emphasized in schools. Kaufman has called this type of radical point of departure an "Alpha needs assessment"[26]

Almost anything may be changed and questioned, there are no "sacred cows," even laws can be added, deleted, modified, organizations may be challenged, disassembled, rebuilt, or eliminated.[27]

The Alpha assessment involves a search for an external referent to help decide what values to select for schools and for curriculum. Kaufman and

[23]Ibid.
[24]Ibid.
[25]Walter Dick, "Instructional Design Models: Future Trends and Issues," *Educational Technology* 21, 7 (July 1981): 30.
[26]Roger A. Kaufman, "Toward a Taxonomy of Needs Assessments," Instructional Systems Development Center, The Florida State University, No. 1, Tallahassee, Florida, March 25, 1977.
[27]Ibid.

others[28] have suggested that this referent be the "value added" to a society as the result of the efforts of schools. The "value added" referent would consist of constructing for the learner as a client of the system an "independent survival point" as a societal participant after the schooling process has formally ended.

Macdonald indicates that there are at least three positions regarding values that can be taken and will influence what values are subsequently included in a curriculum: "It makes a considerable difference in curriculum decisions whether one is a behaviorist, a gestaltist, a psychoanalyst, or a third force psychologist (self-realization). These are value positions that affect curriculum thinking."[29] These value positions lead to approaches to curriculum development that are centered in control, consensus, or emancipation. The results are a model of curriculum that is either based on expertise, consensus, or a dialogical process. The latter model is based on the work of Paulo Freire in South America.[30]

The selection of values as goals in a curriculum is influenced by what the educator wants to accomplish and what he or she believes the curriculum is. For example, if an educator wants to develop a curriculum by consensus and believes that it consists of identifying the content-independent cognitive skills applicable to a variety of situations, then an approach to developing a curriculum will consist of organizing a committee of colleagues (as opposed to identifying some experts) and listing those skills that appear to be independent of any particular content area. These will then be provided to the instructional staff to teach.

Any a priori position regarding an approach to curriculum thinking that would not include an analysis of the value positions selected irrespective of the approach would be classified in Kaufman's terms as a "Beta assessment."[31] The "Beta assessment" begins with a set of assumptions or at least an outlook that would preclude some outlooks, assumptions, or values to be selected at the outset. In this respect they become ideologies because as models, approaches, or constructs they cannot be challenged.[32]

The discussion so far regarding cells A and D in Figure 1 has centered on a theoretical and practical approach to dealing with ideologies in contemporary curricular circumstances. Much of the criticism of traditional curriculum thinking has challenged its theoretical underpinnings as ideological. Some engaging in this debate have been called reconceptualists, though that name does not include all of them by any means.[33]

Some practical approaches to questioning the initial value position or

[28]Roger Kaufman, Robert Corrigan, and Don Johnson, "Toward Educational Responsiveness to Society's Needs, A Tentative Utility Model," *Journal of Socio-Economic Planning Sciences*, August 1969.

[29]James B. Macdonald, "Curriculum and Human Interests," in *Curriculum Theorizing*, pp. 283–298.

[30]Paulo Freire, *Pedagogy of the Oppressed* (New York: Seabury, 1970).

[31]Roger A. Kaufman and Fenwick W. English, "Conducting the Beta Needs Assessment," in *Needs Assessment: Concept and Application* (Englewood Cliffs, N.J.: Educational Technology Publications, 1979), pp. 221–240.

[32]Elliot W. Eisner and Elizabeth A. Vallance, *Conflicting Conceptions of Curriculum* (Berkeley: McCutchan, 1974).

[33]William Pinar, "Reply to my Critics," *Curriculum Inquiry* 10,2 (Summer 1980): 199–206.

constructs would challenge an ideological position taken, but could not be classified as a theoretical position. For example, Kaufman's needs assessment approach is not a theory but a procedure for dealing with an ideological position as contained in his idea of the "Alpha assessment."[34,35]

From this discussion it ought to be clear that those thinking and acting on curriculum matters in schools begin the process from varying points of view. Some appear content to engage in thinking about how people think about curriculum. Others appear not to be interested in their initial assumptions so much as in how to implement their particular approach. Different positions or assumptions will take the curriculum thinker and developer down different roads. The purpose of this initial section regarding ideologies and theory/practice has been to highlight some of these points of view.

The Technical Issues

Technical issues in the curriculum field are those concerned with design. Theoretical issues that relate to technical matters are concerned with what theory to select from which to derive a plan or design for the curriculum. Practical references are those concerned with some orderly approach to curriculum design without a full consideration of alternative theories from which to select a design.

Beauchamp has defined the full range of theoretical considerations by indicating that, "The subject matter of curriculum theory may be the events associated with decisions about a curriculum, the use of a curriculum, the development of a curriculum, curriculum design, curriculum evaluation, and so forth."[36]

Gold sketches out an approach to designing a curriculum for instructional purposes by using Pascual-Leone's neo-Piagetian theory of intellectual development.[37] This theory begins with a model representing the basic unit of what is considered knowledge as a *scheme*. A scheme represents facts or states, operations or transformations of other facts or states, or may specify a series of operations.

The Pascual-Leone theory also develops tenets regarding an individual's intellectual development. From a study of these tenets various principles of design are formulated. For example, the first principle is to "precede instructional design with a step-by-step description of both the correct strategy to be taught and incorrect strategies that children may apply to the task spontaneously."[38] These principles would be of assistance to the curriculum developer as various

---

[34]Roger Kaufman and Robert G. Stakenas, "Needs Assessment and Holistic Planning," *Educational Leadership* 38,8 (May 1981): 612–617.

[35]Daniel L. Stufflebeam, "Working Paper on Needs Assessment in Evaluation," Unpublished paper, AERA Evaluation Conference, San Francisco, September 23, 1977.

[36]George A. Beauchamp, *Curriculum Theory* (Wilmette, Ill.: Kagg, 1975), p. 58.

[37]Allan P. Gold, "A Technology of Instruction Based on Developmental Psychology," *Educational Technology* 21,7 (July 1981): 6–13.

[38]Ibid. See J. Pascual-Leone, "A Theory of Constructive Operators, a Neo-Piagetian Model of Conservation, and the Problem of Horizontal Decalages," (Unpublished manuscript, York University, 1973).

sequences of instruction came to be specified in the body of the curriculum being developed.

When curriculum design issues are not related to some other theory such as Pascual-Leone's or Piaget's, then the principles of design may be derived from considerations of various types of operational procedures that could be employed. For example, Pratt[39] uses Hall's[40] text on systems engineering to indicate what the key elements of a design are. From this perspective a design:

- focuses attention on goals
- increases the probability of success
- economizes time and effort
- facilitates communication and coordination
- reduces stress.

Beauchamp specifies two fundamental dimensions of curriculum design:

The first has to do with the total substance, the elements, and the arrangement of the document. We may speak of these as the contents of a curriculum in the same sense that we use a table of contents in a book to specify the titles of the various chapters. The second is the mode of organization of the various parts of a curriculum, particularly the culture content. Both of these dimensions circumscribe subordinate parts.[41]

McNeil[42] offers a similar vision of curriculum design by speaking of an organizational design in general as containing "a statement of the relationships among purposes (functions, domains, goals, or objectives); organizing structures (subjects, courses, topics, etc.); organizing elements (skills, values, concepts, etc.); specific learning opportunities or activities; and the principles to be followed in order that learning opportunities have a cumulative effect (simple to complex, etc.)"[43]

We have examined cells B and E in Figure 1. The trend has been for design issues to be not very well linked to specific theories of cognition or learning, if at all. This is not to say that design matters have not been researched or tested.[44] It does mean that, in general, curriculum design has been influenced by logical plans of which individual parts may have been researched, but which have not been generally derived from a larger theoretical base.

Operational Issues

Operational issues in curriculum are delivery issues and these tend to be concerned with management and control. The functions of management are:

- defining objectives/selecting a mission

---

[39]David Pratt, *Curriculum: Design and Development* (New York: Harcourt Brace Jovanovich, 1980).

[40]Arthur D. Hall, *A Methodology for Systems Engineering* (New York: Van Nostrand, 1962), cited by Pratt, ibid, p. 9.

[41]Beauchamp, *Curriculum Theory*, p. 102.

[42]John D. McNeil, *Curriculum: A Comprehensive Introduction* (Boston: Little Brown, 1977).

[43]Ibid., pp. 168–169.

[44]J. H. Block, ed., *Mastery Learning* (New York: Holt, Rinehart and Winston, 1971).

• ensuring a consistent and reliable expenditure of resources to attain the mission (objectives)

• utilization of feedback from evaluation to make adjustments in mission selection or resource flow.[45]

The curriculum is a basic management tool because it includes or requires objectives (is mission dependent), is a method for scheduling or configuring resources (people, time, materials), and acts as a mechanism to monitor/direct/evaluate teacher performance against its stated purpose/objectives. In this respect it is an agent of quality control by requiring conformance to its design specifications, however stated or implied.[46]

English and Steffy[47] have noted a comparison of corporate policy development and tactics to the process of curriculum development in the schools:

> The curriculum is a management tool of strategic importance because it is a response to a mission statement for the entire system, it implements policies adopted by boards of education, and it serves to ensure the public and the board of consistency in the implementation of the overall policies of the district as they are translated into teaching activities and pupil outcomes. It does this by forcing the system's resources to flow in specified directions.[48]

English and Steffy aver that curriculum is both tactics (the delineation of a specific curriculum for a separate program, a school, or a specific instructional station) and strategy (the development of master policy). Curriculum is both tactics and strategy, "how one looks at it is not as much a matter of taste or philosophy, as a matter of the organizational level at which the curriculum issues are being considered."[49] Figure 2 separates curriculum development in a management sense between strategy and tactics.

Another major management issue concerned with curriculum is how content is selected and organized. This can be approached either theoretically or practically by adding three perspectives to Cells C and F in Figure 1. These are delineated in Figure 3.

The first approaches to selecting and organizing content are those that are independent of the learner. Such approaches present a rationale for selecting the disciplines to be studied and determining the proper "mix" between them. This approach is perhaps best exemplified in the work of Philip Phenix.[50] Another approach not dependent on the learner is that described by Schwab when he proposed that the inherent structure of the discipline or content itself forms the base for selecting and organizing curriculum content.[51] A practical basis for

[45]Fenwick W. English, "Management Practice as a Key to Curriculum Leadership," *Educational Leadership* 36,6 (March 1979): pp. 408–413.

[46]Fenwick W. English, *Quality Control in Curriculum Development* (Arlington, Va.: American Association of School Administrators, 1978), 62 pp.

[47]Fenwick W. English and Betty E. Steffy, "Curriculum as a Strategic Management Tool," *Educational Leadership* 39,4 (January 1982): 276–278.

[48]Ibid.

[49]Ibid.

[50]Philip H. Phenix, *Realms of Meanings* (New York: McGraw-Hill, 1964).

[51]Joseph J. Schwab, "Problems, Topics, and Issues," in *Education and the Structure of Knowledge*, (ed. S. Elam) (Chicago: Rand McNally, 1964), pp. 4–43.

Figure 2. Curriculum Development Continuum

	Strategy	Tactic
Scope	Systemwide, all levels	Program, school, or classroom specific
Specificity	Low level of detail	Higher level of detail
Delineation of Instructional Methods	Broad or nonexistent	Embedded and more specific, closer to the classroom
Organization, Location of Decision	Highest levels of management/policy	Much lower level, building, classroom
Risk Involved	High risk, more uncertainty	Lower risk, much less uncertainty
Assessment	Broadly indicated as a requirement upon which to make decisions and re-examine policy	Specifically delineated by objective, type, expected standards of achievement for groups of students
Consideration of Alternatives	Broad, conceptual	Narrow, operational

ordering curriculum is the use of chronological order in teaching history.

The second approach to selecting and ordering curriculum content is to "fit" the content to the learners.[52] The idea is to break curriculum content into manageable pieces, following any implicit pattern inherent in the content area and matching it to the learner's patterns. When a pattern is taught to a learner so as to facilitate the acquisition of content, the principle of "scaffolding" has been followed.[53] The process of "hierarchical analysis" in design is also an attempt to make content easier to acquire by the learner.[54]

Those approaches dependent on the learner to organize curriculum content are based on schema theory[55,56,57]; that is, that learners possess methods or structure to order content independent from the content per se of curriculum.

[52]Robert M. Gagné and Leslie J. Briggs, *Principles of Instructional Design* (New York: Holt, Rinehart, and Winston, 1979).

[53]D. P. Ausubel, *Educational Psychology: A Cognitive View* (New York: Holt, Rinehart, and Winston, 1968).

[54]Doris T. Gow, "A Curriculum Analysis of Individualized Science," (Monograph of the Learning Research and Development Center, University of Pittsburgh, 1977), 107 pp.

[55]R. C. Anderson, "The Notion of Schemata and the Educational Enterprise," in *Schooling and the Acquisition of Knowledge*, eds. R. C. Anderson, R. J. Spiro, and W. E. Montague (New Jersey: Erlbaum, 1977), pp. 415–431.

[56]U. Neisser, *Cognition and Reality: Principles and Implications of Cognitive Psychology* (San Francisco: Freeman, 1976).

[57]Jean Piaget, "Genesis and Structure in the Psychology of Intelligence," in *Six Psychological Studies*, ed. D. Elkind (New York: Random House, 1967).

Figure 3. Three Generic Approaches to Selecting and Organizing Curriculum Content

	Content Selection and Organization Not Dependent on the Learner	Content Selection and Organization Should "Fit" the Learner	Learners Supply the Order to Selecting the Content
Theoretical	• Order based on rationale or logical argument/model	• Learning theory S-R	• Schema theory
Practical	• Order based on apparent criterion such as chronology, specificity	• Scaffolding • Hierarchical analysis	• Use of algorithms or models based on schema theory

These structures or "schema" must be accounted for in presenting content to be learned. A practical approach derived from this position is the use of algorithms or models of thinking as ways to order content prior to its being taught to learners.[58,59]

Other Operational Issues/Curriculum Alignment

Another operations area of concern for those working with curriculum in the schools is how to improve learner achievement by changing the design of the curriculum or by more closely aligning teaching content (time on task) to the prescribed curriculum and the testing program.[60,61]

One procedure for aligning the curriculum has been called "curriculum mapping."[62] Mapping is a technique for recording time on task data and then analyzing this data to determine the "fit" to the officially adopted curriculum and the assessment/testing program. Mapping provides curriculum planners and evaluators with the means to adjust the "fit" over time by providing a data base that links teaching, testing, and curriculum development. Mapping is not dependent on any particular viewpoint of how the existing curriculum content

---

[58]L. N. Landa, *Algorithmization in Learning and Instruction* (Englewood Cliffs, N.J.: Educational Technology Publications, 1974).

[59]William Winn, "The Meaningful Organization of Content: Research and Design Strategies," *Educational Technology* 21,8 (August 1981): 7–11.

[60]Fred Niedermeyer and Stephen Yelon, "Los Angeles Aligns Instruction with Essential Skills," *Educational Leadership* 38,8 (May 1981): 618–620.

[61]Fenwick W. English, *Improving Curriculum Management in the Schools* (Washington, D.C.: Council for Basic Education, 1980), 26 pp.

[62]Fenwick W. English, "Curriculum Mapping," *Educational Leadership* 37,7 (April 1980): 558–559.

was derived, but is a monitoring technique to determine teaching to any selected design.[63]

Conflict with the Community

Conflict in operational settings between communities and school curriculum people rarely develops over theory directly. More often than not it represents a clash over the selection of specific content or a book in an instructional program or school library.

Conflict occurs when the value orientation of a community or a sub-public is not in harmony with the content of the curriculum selected.[64] Rising problems of censorship over library books and textbooks in schools, the adoption of "scientific creationism," and the rejection of so-called "humanistic" curriculum by some religious leaders of the Far Right, continue to punctuate school problems in curriculum at the operational level.[65]

Classifying Contemporary Curriculum Questions

When Ralph Tyler asked the question, "What educational purposes should the school seek to attain?"[66] he was posing a practical/ideological (Cell D in Figure 1) question. Tyler was seeking a resolution to the selection of possible values that should be embraced by formalized schooling. Purposes are statements of values. Values possess an idiomatic base. The scarcity of time requires a decision in formalized schooling.

It is important to note what Tyler *did not ask*. He didn't begin by asking, "How should educators *think about* purposes?" or even, "What *are* purposes?" He began by assuming that:

- Purposes exist apart from the school
- Schools must be selective about which purposes to embrace
- Some purposes are better than others.

Tyler's approach dealt with the immediately practical problems of selection followed by questions of design and control:

"What educational experiences can be provided that are likely to attain these purposes?" (Cell E in Figure 1)

"How can these educational experiences be effectively organized?" (Cell E in Figure 1)

---

[63]Peat, Marwick, Mitchell and Co., "An Analysis and Review of the Curriculum and Organizational and Administrative Structure of Worthington High School," Washington, D.C., December 1, 1980.

[64]Fenwick W. English, "The Dynamics of School-Community Relationships," in *Considered Action for Curriculum Improvement*, ed. W. Foshay (Alexandria, Va: ASCD, 1980), pp. 1–18.

[65]Arthur Steller, "Curriculum Development as Politics," *Educational Leadership* (November 1980): 161–164.

[66]Ralph Tyler, *Basic Principles*.

"How can we determine whether these purposes are being attained?"[67] (Cell F in Figure 1).

Tyler's approach was not theoretical. It did not probe deeply into the question of the roots of purposes; that is, the theoretical/ideological underpinning of schooling our society. As Apple has noted:

. . . one cannot comprehend what schools do by thinking of them as black boxes, in input/output terms. This neglects the cultural forms and meanings that actually exist in schools. It ignores the importance of an analysis of the ways our educational institutions contribute to the creation of ideological hegemony. For schools do more than simply "process people"; they help create and make legitimate (sometimes in contradictory and paradoxical ways) forms of consciousness that are dialectically related to a corporate society like our own.[68]

To assist those asking questions about curriculum in contemporary circumstances, some common questions about curriculum practice are listed in Figure 4. Each question is followed by a reference to the cells that may be involved in answering it.

For example, the first question, "What are types of curricular goals/objectives?" might involve:

● *Cell A* if what was desired was a discussion or review of a theory of values or value formulation with a point of view about which theory to utilize in selecting values, or

● *Cell E* if a set of categories is desired by which to classify types of goals/objectives on such criteria as source, subject, clarity, specificity, and so on.

If all of the responses are summed, it can be seen that two cells (B and C) include about 49 percent of all of the questions and E and F, 41 percent. These four cells account for 90 percent of all the references. This may illustrate that most of our contemporary curriculum questions are concerned with technical-managerial issues and few appear to be concerned with ideological matters of a theoretical or practical nature. This has been alleged as a shortcoming of contemporary curriculum practice.[69,70]

While many of the issues of the decade are old ones re-emerged, such as the mood of political conservatism, both fiscally and educationally,[71,72] the new issue is the challenge to positivism. This challenge has been raised by curriculum theorists and thinkers who appear to have a different agenda for the schools. Their ideology is one that is a familiar cry to the romantics of the 60s as

[67]Ibid.

[68]Michael W. Apple,"Analyzing Determinations: Understanding and Evaluating the Production of Social Outcomes in Schools," *Curriculum Inquiry* 10,1 (Spring 1980): 55–76.

[69]Herbert M. Kliebard, "Bureaucracy and Curriculum Theory," in *Freedom, Bureaucracy, and Schooling* (Washington, D.C.: ASCD, 1971), pp. 74–94.

[70]Dwayne Heubner,"Curricular Language and Classroom Meanings," in *Language and Meaning* (Washington, D.C.: ASCD, 1966), pp. 8–26.

[71]James W. Guthrie, "Emerging Political Economy of Educational Policy," in *The Future of Education*, ed. K. C. Coles (Beverly Hills: Sage, 1981).

[72]Frederick M. Wirt, "Neoconservatism and National School Policy," *Educational Evaluation and Policy Analysis* 2,6 (November–December 1980), pp. 5–18.

Figure 4. Classifying Some Contemporary Curricular Questions

Question	Relevant Cells
What are types of curricular goals/objectives?	A,E
How can a curriculum be evaluated?	E,F
What forms can curriculum assume?	B,C
What are the essential parts of a curriculum unit?	B,E
How does one select the proper curriculum?	A,D
How is curricular scope defined?	B,E
What is a curricular concept?	B,C,E,F
What is articulation in curriculum?	B,C,E,F
What is the best curricular organization?	B
How is a behavioral hierarchy defined?	E
How does one select the appropriate curriculum setting?	C,F
What are the structures of the disciplines?	B,C
How are instructional strategies selected?	C,F
How can linkage to life experience be attained?	B,C,E,F
How can the real world be blended into classroom use?	B,C,E,F
What is the nature of linking concepts to pupil needs?	B,C,E,F
What is the role of pupil choice in studying curricular concepts/units?	C,F
What are the essential elements of a curriculum guide?	B,C,D,E,F
How can the effectiveness of learning activities be optimized?	B,C,E,F
Who should be involved in curriculum development?	F
What is a "need"?	B,E
What values should be inherent in designing a curriculum?	A,D
Are curricular outcomes (results) means or ends?	B,C
Are curricular outcomes capable of being taught in the schools?	B,C,E,F
What is the nature of knowledge?	A,B
What are the forms of content?	B,C

embodied in the works of Kohl,[73] Holt,[74] and Goodman.[75] It is different in its emphasis on a Marxist dialectic as a model from which schooling and larger societal reforms can be considered. As such it is far more than a cry against

[73] Herb Kohl, *The Open Classroom* (New York: Vintage, 1969).
[74] John Holt, *How Children Fail* (New York: Pitman, 1964).
[75] Paul Goodman, *Compulsory Mis-education and the Community of Scholars* (New York: Vintage, 1962).

certain schooling rituals. That earlier challenge was wiped out in all but a few places in the nation's schools in the late 70s. The frontal attack on the underpinnings of the concept of a science of education and particularly of curriculum construction is far more powerful because it is almost an entirely professional dialogue; that is, the battle is with those armed with some knowledge about curricular matters. It is being fought in scholarly circles and journals, conventions, private conferences, personal reflection and letters, and the libraries of the academy. It is a re-establishment of the traditions of the liberal arts. For the public at large and for many teachers, curriculum workers, and school administrators, the issues seem more concerned with academic posturing and esoteric forays into existentialism and philosophy than those they feel are real as they confront the everyday issues involved with curriculum development.

The currency of curriculum practice is founded on a base of ideas; that is, *an idiom*. An idiom provides meaning to practice. It provides perspective and a filter to process actions into some sort of larger picture that resolves practical problems and makes some sense of them. The context of practice is almost always ideological. The ideology of positivism has provided a context for curriculum thinking for over five decades. Now a new idiom is being proposed that portends the development of a new currency with a different set of values, and one that may ultimately re-define what is "good practice."

While it appears doubtful that the idiom of positivism will be totally abandoned, the growing movement to move away from its concepts may place it into a larger perspective in which its traditions are considered less demanding and appropriate for all circumstances than would otherwise have been the case. However, at midpoint in the decade, curriculum practice is still carrying on with the traditions and dominant perspective of positivism as the idiom in which what is "good practice" is defined and esteemed.

To the largest extent, this Yearbook is a compilation of the best of the positivistic tradition in curriculum thinking and practice. It is a distillation and extension of this tradition in schooling and in curriculum development in the schools.

Chapter 2

Curriculum Thinking

George A. Beauchamp

T he curriculum field is fraught with communication problems. There are both communication problems among curriculum scholars as well as problems in communication between curriculum scholars and curriculum practitioners. These are the result of thinking differently about curriculum or of using language that is ambiguous or confusing in the curriculum field.

This chapter will explore communication problems by analyzing the scope of the field as revealed through principal writings on curriculum as presented in curriculum texts, by looking at curriculum influences and substitutes, by distinguishing between administrative and conceptual levels of curriculum development, and by examining some of the language of explanation and persuasion commonly used in the literature. Finally some of the problems and issues raised for curriculum developers will be mentioned.

The Scope of the Field

One way to look at the scope of the curriculum field is to observe the contents of textbooks written on the subject of curriculum. It will not be possible here to give a complete and specific analysis of textbook contents, but we can illustrate certain categories of content and comment about their significance in communicating about curriculum matters.

Most textbook writers present definitional structures for the word *curriculum*. For example, Smith, Stanley, and Shores (1957) defined the curriculum as follows: "A sequence of potential experiences is set up in the school for the purpose of disciplining children and youth in group ways of thinking and acting. This set of experiences is referred to as the curriculum" (p. 3). Ragan and Shepherd (1977) viewed "the elementary school curriculum as including *all the experiences of children for which the school accepts responsibility*" (p. 2). Johnson (1977) referred to curriculum "as a structured series of intended learning outcomes" (p. 6). Saylor and Alexander (1974) defined curriculum as "a plan for providing sets of learning opportunities to achieve broad goals and related specific objectives for an identifiable population served by a single school center" (p.6).

In their analysis of various curriculum conceptions, Saylor and Alexander observed that the term is used in two distinct ways. One is as something intended, and the other is as something actualized (p.3). This distinction in definition is interesting because it points up vividly a sore spot among curriculum writers; namely, whether we should distinguish between curriculum and instruction in our thinking. So much of this hinges upon the use of the word *experience*. The most commonly used definition of curriculum states something to the effect that the curriculum consists of all of the experiences of children and youth under the auspices of the school. For some, the experiences are planned for in the form of educational opportunities or intended cultural structures. These elements are planned by organized groups prior to instruction. For others, the experiences are meant to be learning experiences that may take place at any time including during periods of instruction. This distinction poses a real dilemma in curriculum communication.

There are really only three legitimate uses of the word "curriculum." One is to speak of *a curriculum*. This is the substantive, or content, dimension of curriculum. A second is to speak of *a curriculum system*. A curriculum system encompasses the activities of curriculum planning, implementing, and evaluating; these constitute the process dimension of curriculum. A third use is to speak of *curriculum as a field of study*. The latter, of course, consists of study of the first two plus associated research and theory-building activities. It should be noted that all curriculum meanings hinge upon what one refers to when speaking of *a curriculum*.

A second rather consistent body of content included in curriculum textbooks is a discussion of topics emanating from philosophical, social and cultural, historical, and psychological foundations of education. The purpose for including these topics is to draw from those areas basic data, or principles, for determining educational goals, the selection of culture content for the curriculum, and the organization of that content. Three things appear to dominate that process. One is to establish the role of the school in society as background for determining what to teach. The second is to make clear basic information about the characteristics and habits of potential school students. A third is to help with the complicated process of content selection and organization in light of the first two plus information about past experience in curriculum affairs. Although virtually all curriculum textbooks contain such information in one form or another, some deal with the subjects to a greater extent than others. For example the books by Smith, Stanley, and Shores (1957), Zais (1976), and Taba (1962) contain extended discussions of the import of educational foundations for curriculum work. In many respects, some of the best knowledge in the curriculum field is derived from these foundations.

Techniques for curriculum planning are a third area of discussion in curriculum textbooks. Here writers tender advice to those who would plan curricula. A good way to illustrate this type of advice is to cite the scheme outlined by Taba (1962):

Step 1: Diagnosis of needs
Step 2: Formulation of objectives
Step 3: Selection of content
Step 4: Organization of content
Step 5: Selection of learning experiences
Step 6: Organization of learning experiences
Step 7: Determination of what to evaluate and of ways and means of doing it (p. 12).

Most such advice is reasonable and can be followed by curriculum planners if they wish to do so. We have had a great deal of experience with the process of curriculum planning in the United States, and most of it has been done at the school or school district level. Curriculum planning along with implementation and evaluation may be thought of as the process dimension of the curriculum field.

A fourth substantive area discussed by curriculum textbook writers is the subject matters to be included in curricula. Authors who address themselves to this area of curriculum usually divide according to whether they are writing books about elementary or secondary school curricula, and these are quite different from books principally addressed to techniques of curriculum planning or curriculum foundations and principles. Although some space may be allocated to foundations or planning techniques, sizable amount of space is devoted to chapters on individual school subjects.

For example, Ragan and Shepherd (1977) devote six of their 14 chapters to subjects taught in the elementary school. Tanner (1971) devoted eight of 11 chapters to secondary school subjects. The purpose of such writing is to convey to readers the trends in content selection and organization as these writers see them. Although the subjects undertaken by writers as discussed here are unique, their purpose in writing is quite consistent (and perhaps complementary) with those writers who spend most of their time and space on techniques of curriculum planning. They render advice about what to do once curriculum planners get around to the task of writing the curricula, but concerns about curriculum content and organization are more appropriately thought of as the substantive dimension of the curriculum field.

A few books that may be viewed as textbooks are devoted to the subject of curriculum theory. Writers in this area of curriculum are concerned predominately with the development of rational explanation for curriculum phenomena. So far, writers have not come up with formulations that might be labeled as curriculum theories but, nonetheless, the area is being explored. Two authors have spoken of their works as the development of conceptual systems rather than theories even though much theoretical effort must have gone into their development. Johnson (1977) developed a conceptual model for curricular and instructional planning and evaluation. A distinguishing feature of Johnson's writing about curriculum has been his insistence upon distinguishing between curricular and instructional planning and products. Goodlad (1979) has developed a conceptual system for guiding curriculum practice and inquiry. The heart of Goodlad's conceptualization consists of four decision levels or domains: societal, institutional, instructional, and personal/experiential. Unruh (1975) developed a series of propositions and constructs as theoretical bases for the direction of curriculum development. Beauchamp (1981) presented an analysis of the conditions and circumstances under which curriculum theory might be built, reviewed past developments in curriculum theory, and pointed up need for further advancements in this area.

The scope of the basic literature of the field then may be described as consisting of meanings attached to basic concepts and constructs, curriculum foundations, the process dimension of curriculum (including planning, implementing, and evaluating), the substantive dimension of curriculum (including content and design), and theory development. Diversity of opinion among writers in each of these areas abounds. Such diversity supports the contention that there are too few areas of substantive agreement among curriculum scholars, which means they have failed to generate an appreciable amount of knowledge that may be said to be indigenous to the curriculum field.

Curriculum research as well has failed to produce results that would help alleviate the above conditions. Repeatedly, curriculum research has been criticized for dealing with inconsequential problems, for inappropriate designs and techniques, and for not being theory-oriented. The paucity of theory-oriented research is a major contributor to the failure to develop substantive knowledge in the field.

Curriculum Influences and Substitutes

The contents of school curricula are often influenced by circumstances and conditions external to the curricula. In some cases, they actually are substituted for the curriculum. The latter is particularly true with the case of textbooks for students in the various school subjects. In many schools and school districts in the United States, the cluster of adopted student textbooks is the closest thing to a curriculum available in those schools. The subjects are chosen, the subject matters are already organized, and the schools thereby have an educational program without further effort.

From time to time, state and federal governments pass laws that either influence or prescribe curriculum content, and curriculum content may be influenced by decisions made in our courts. Since education is a function of the states, more influence ensues from state governments than from the federal government. In any case, when laws prescribe curriculum content, curriculum planners have no option other than to include the content in the curriculum being planned. This constitutes the most direct and demanding influence upon curriculum content that originates outside the system.

Federal acts and titles have had a great influence in recent years upon curriculum content and organization. The National Defense Education Act of 1958 (NDEA) is an outstanding illustration. Under funding provided by that act, a plethora of projects were launched, most of which were designed to improve the character of the contents of various school subjects. Familiar examples were the Elementary School Science Project (ESSP), the Science Curriculum Improvement Study (SCIS), and the School Mathematics Study Group (SMSG). It is interesting to note that most science and mathematics projects were concerned more with the syntactics (skills and processes) of these disciplines than with fixed bodies of content. Bilingual education is another example of curriculum content added in most states because of federal funding. These are simply a few examples of another way in which the content and organization of school curricula may be influenced by federal acts and titles. Despite the fact that education is a function of the state and despite the fact that individual school systems do involve their personnel in curriculum planning activities, the federal government has exerted considerable influence upon the content and organization of school curricula in recent years.

Administrative and Conceptual Levels of Curriculum Development

Curriculum development is often thought of at two different levels. One level may be termed an administrative level; the other is more a conceptual level. I use curriculum development and curriculum planning as one and the same notion. I see no real distinction between the two.

Administrative Levels

By administrative level of curriculum development, I mean simply those political or organizational groups or agencies that may influence directly or indirectly the curricula of our schools. The influences of the federal government have already been discussed. Since education is a function of the state, however, State Departments of Education may issue curriculum materials in the form of guides. Usually those are suggested rather than mandatory guidelines, but the states have the legal right to make them mandatory if they choose to do so. States may require that certain subjects and/or topics be taught in the schools and occasionally they specify the amount of time that must be allocated to that subject or topic. In a few states, county education offices act similarly except they may also add supervisory services.

Most curriculum planning (that is, most efforts that produce curriculum documents intended to be used in the schools) is done at the school district or individual school level. If one were to look through the curriculum documents displayed at the annual ASCD conference, it would become clear that the sources of virtually all of those documents were schools or school districts. In fact, the history of curriculum planning is really a recounting of the efforts of people in schools and school districts to develop their own curricula.

The fact that ideas appropriate for school curricula are generated by various social, political, and professional groups contributes to the confusion within the curriculum field. Writers often speak of the different levels at which curriculum decisions are made, which raises the question of when an idea for curriculum content actually becomes a part of a curriculum. This brings the discussion back to the problem of defining a curriculum. In other words, when in the course of events of selecting from our total culture are those portions of our culture chosen to be included in a curriculum for specific schools? Normally, that selection is made by people working for a board of education and subject to the policy acceptance of that board. These people may be teachers, supervisors, principals, or curriculum directors. If this can be a criterion for determining the production of a curriculum then the decisions or suggestions of other groups or agencies can only be considered influences upon the decisions of those actually engaged in curriculum planning.

Conceptual Levels

At least four conceptual levels of curriculum planning are easily identifiable. They are in order of increasing complexity: textbook adoption, simple curriculum modification, broader curriculum review and overhaul, and a complete curriculum analysis.

Textbook adoption has become an almost universal task confronting schools and school districts. To the extent that the culture content to be taught in schools is a major consideration in textbook adoption and to the extent that the subjects are chosen in the process, it may be said that many curriculum-type decisions are made by those selecting textbooks. But to the extent that no document that may be called a curriculum is produced, textbook selection cannot legitimately be referred to as a process of curriculum planning.

A second level of curriculum planning may be termed a simple curriculum modification. This level of curriculum work can occur only if a curriculum (a document, that is) exists. The process of change is usually simple, involving minor changes in language, or changes in sequence due to past experience with the curriculum, or the addition of new ideas that have emerged from the teachers. This level of curriculum change frequently takes place when the existing curriculum is relatively new, and the planning group deems that substantial modifications are not warranted.

A third level may be termed a broader curriculum overhaul. Here again the assumption is that a curriculum exists, but it has been used for a sufficient length of time that the time has come to systematically revise the entire curriculum. Most of the action here is to update the curriculum content in light of new developments resulting from research and other sources, and/or to change the curriculum format in light of the experience of teachers. This level may involve such actions as review of curriculum materials from other school areas, use of consultants on problem areas, review of curriculum literature on contemporary curriculum concerns, and so forth. The most probable activity would be the mustering of and discussion of problems raised by teachers as a result of their experience in using the "old" curriculum.

The fourth level may be termed a complete curriculum analysis and development. Normally, this level is undertaken in a situation in which no policy document called a curriculum exists, or in situations where a curriculum is very old and not currently in use. The total process may take place in a series of phases or steps. First, a leadership group or a curriculum council may be needed to organize the work phases and to coordinate various subgroup efforts. A second step might be to conduct a listing and appraisal of the current curriculum practices in the school(s) as a focus for further deliberation. A third phase may be termed a study phase. Here, the curriculum planners investigate curriculum ideas and practices not present in the analysis of their own practices. This phase is essential for bringing in new curriculum ideas and is the most time consuming of all of the phases. A fourth phase may be the formulation of criteria for the selection of curriculum ideas to be included in the new curriculum. A fifth phase is the actual writing of the new curriculum. A sixth step is sometimes recommended, and that is to follow the writing phase with a testing period before the curriculum is officially implemented. Not all of these phases are recommended by all curriculum writers, and different labels may be used.

The Language of Explanation and Persuasion

In curriculum writing several terms are used to explain or persuade. These terms often are used interchangeably and occasionally inappropriately. I refer here to such terms as philosophy, ideology, theory, model, scheme, and rationale. The following discussion of these concepts is not an attempt to establish definitions for these terms, but rather is an attempt to clarify some of their more appropriate uses in the field of curriculum.

Philosophy

From a dictionary perspective, the term *philosophy* refers to the study or science of the search for truth and principles underlying knowledge and human nature and conduct. Thus, the philosopher is free to study the whole gamut of human affairs. It is extremely doubtful that anyone should propose a philosophy of curriculum even though the study of philosophy of education has been around for a long while. Theory and philosophy are often confused because a full-blown philosophy may be undergirded by related but specific theories. For example, philosophers are concerned with epistemology which is referred to as the theory of knowledge. John Dewey (1916) stated: "If we are willing to conceive education as the process of forming fundamental dispositions, intellectual and emotional, toward nature and fellow men, philosophy may even be defined *as the general theory of education*" (p. 383). If one accepts Dewey's conclusion, it becomes obvious that many theories are possible within the general area of philosophy to account for the dimensions of education and, within the sphere of education, there are possible theories to explain the specific dimensions of education such as theory of instruction, curriculum theory, administrative theory, and so forth. This does not mean, however, that the processes used by philosophers may not be used in theory development. Theorists must use logic and critical analysis, for example, in their theoretical endeavors.

Ideology

Closely related to the usage of the word philosophy is the term *ideology*. In general, ideology refers to a system of ideas derived from sensation and composed of a body of doctrine, myth, and symbols of a social movement, institution, class, or large group. Eastman (1967) exemplified the notion of ideology in relation to philosophy when he developed the idea that Dewey's educational theory (philosophy) remained in a reasonably stable state, but that it was gradually ideologized by the progressive education movement. In writing about ideology and the curriculum, Apple (1979) spoke of the hidden curriculum as an avenue through which ideological configurations of dominant interests in society are tacitly taught to students in schools.

Theory

The term *theory* frequently is used mistakenly for such notions as a point of view, an attitude, a hypothesis, or an opinion. Theory, however, is a much more vigorous concept, especially in terms of the modes of theory building. In general, theory is an explanation for an identified set of events. Variation in definition of theory hinges on interpretation of the word *explanation*.

Two definitions of theory will illustrate sufficiently. Rose (1953) defined theory as "an integrated body of definitions, assumptions, and general propositions covering a given subject matter from which a comprehensive set of specific and testable hypotheses can be deduced logically" (p. 52). Kerlinger (1973) defined theory as "a set of interrelated constructs (concepts), definitions, and propositions that present a systematic view of phenomena by specifying relations among variables, with the purpose of explaining and predicting the phenomena" (p. 10). Theory may be classed into two types: scientific and nonscientific. Theories are developed by the techniques of science, or they are developed by careful use of logic, or both, utilizing fairly stringent rules. Theories are essential to the development of knowledge.

A great deal of attention has been given in recent years to the idea of developing theory in the curriculum field. If we translate the spirit of the definitions of theory identified in the paragraph above, a curriculum theory may be defined as "a set of related statements that give meaning to a school's curriculum by pointing up the relationships among its elements and by directing its development, its use, and its evaluation" (Beauchamp, 1981, p. 60). It is interesting to note that, within the total group of curriculum writers who have addressed themselves to theory, people can be identified who advocate and use a major scientific approach to theory as well as people who are committed to a more philosophic approach. It is sad to say that, despite the hundreds of pages that have been written on the subject, there appears to be no well-developed curriculum theory. Development of curriculum theory appears to be shackled by problems of concept and definition, lack of recognized knowledge in the field, and by the paucity of theory-oriented research.

Model

Model is a term that is frequently used interchangeably with theory. A model is an analogy. The construction of a model is a way of representing given phenomena and their relationships, but the model is not the phenomena. A model of an airplane is not the airplane. A set of blueprints is not a building. Models may be used to represent events and event interactions in a compact and illustrative manner. Models are useful tools, and theorists use them extensively. But a model is not a theory, and theorists should use them as means to ends.

Scheme

The word *scheme* is properly used to refer to a systematic plan or program for something to be done. The word is not used frequently in curriculum discourse, but it does fit certain categories of curriculum proposal. Two examples will illustrate my meaning. Earlier in the chapter, I outlined five phases or steps that might be used in the process of complex curriculum planning. Those suggested phases are a scheme for that kind of undertaking. English (1980) proposed curriculum mapping as a technique in curriculum development. The procedure involves having teachers note what they have been teaching in terms of concepts, skills, and attitudes under a general subject heading such as geography or mathematics plus the amount of time spent on each subject. Both of these illustrations are schemes or systematic plans for a specific practice.

Rationale

A *rationale* is a reasoned exposition intended to give an underlying or rational foundation for some phenomena. Sometimes the word is used as an alternative for theory, but theory is the more complicated of the two conceptually. We hear the term used in curriculum, but mostly in terms of reasons for performing certain curriculum activities. The most frequently cited rationale in curriculum literature is the Tyler rationale (Tyler, 1950, pp. 1–2).

Implications for Curriculum Developers

The purpose in discussing the language concepts in the preceding pages is to help potential curriculum planners in the process of ordering their own language and behavior as they launch and carry out their projects. Where choices in language interpretation confront them, curriculum planning groups will simply have to make their own choices in meaning or interpretation. Only in this way can communication be facilitated among the members of the planning group. But in order to discuss the consequences of the foregoing problems in communication for curriculum developers, certain assumptions will have to be made. It is assumed that: (1) most curriculum developers will be people who are involved in a school or a school district, (2) people who intend to plan curricula will be concerned principally with responding to the question of what shall be taught in their schools, (3) curriculum developers are serious about their business to the extent that the results of their deliberations ultimately will become the official policy of their board of education.

One can set aside most of the considerations discussed in this chapter under curriculum inputs and substitutes with the admonition that these will be considered by the curriculum planners. One can also set aside the problems inherent in theory building because that is not the work of the curriculum developer. Some of the schemes, rationales, and conceptual systems may, however, be of help as advice to curriculum developers on procedural matters.

Clearly, the first decision that must be made by potential curriculum developers is at the administrative level. This is a simple decision for school people because they only have to choose between the planning arena of the school district and the individual school. Most will choose the district in all probability. In large urban areas, the region or subdistrict may be the choice. The second decision will have to be a choice in conceptual level of curriculum development and the choice here is conditioned by the curriculum status within the district. The most sophisticated of the choices is the complete curriculum analysis. These two decisions will probably be tentatively reached by leadership personnel in the district, but the decisions must be tentative until the next cluster of decisions is made.

The next cluster of decisions consists of the choice of personnel to be involved, their organization for work, and their tasks. Most curriculum writers who address themselves to the techniques of curriculum planning come close to agreeing that the personnel who perform the tasks of curriculum planning ought to be involved in making decisions about what to do, why it should be done, and how to do it (See Loucks and Lieberman, Chapter 10 in this Yearbook). Generally, it is perceived that teachers will constitute the majority of those involved, but it is not generally agreed that all teachers should be involved. Decisions about involvement of personnel really are part of the planning for the planning activity.

The procedures or steps to be followed are really a free choice. Most all of the schemes offered by curriculum writers would be helpful, but curriculum developers should feel very comfortable if they develop their own scheme of work.

Before launching a curriculum development project, it is most important that administrative personnel ensure time and resources for the proposed project. Curriculum literature is not helpful on this point. The history of curriculum development projects in school districts is that they are either done piecemeal periodically, such as during paid work in summer vacations, or they are carried out after school hours without additional compensation for those involved. Curriculum development is important enough to deserve better consideration.

In addition to time, other resources must be available to those expected to do the planning. Curriculum literature, curriculum plans from other school districts, and consultants are among the possible sources to be needed by planners. Serious curriculum development can be expensive for boards of education to undertake; therefore, time and resource considerations are most important at the outset of a project. Furthermore, the magnitude of the project should be guided by the resources available.

Finally, a word should be said about the design of the curriculum to be planned. Basically, the design of most curricula will be subject-centered. Curriculum literature contains accounts or descriptions of proposals for other types of design, but in most schools, such proposals have had little effect. Therefore, it is predictable that the culture content portion of new curricula will be organized around the recognized school subjects. For help with that organization, curriculum developers may wish to turn to people who specialize in the individual school subjects for guidance.

Within the organization of the subjects there are three curriculum concepts that warrant attention by the curriculum developers. Those concepts are: scope, sequence, and articulation. Scope refers to the breadth or total amount of subject content that may be planned for any group of students at any grade level or for the total school. Sequence is a matter of intentionally ordering topics or subjects. Articulation refers to intended relationships among the subjects. Articulation is particularly important in a subject-centered design.

Other concerns about curriculum design depend upon the desires of the planners. It is commonly suggested that a curriculum should contain a set of intended goals and/or objectives to be followed by the culture content referred to in the paragraph above (See also Brandt and Tyler, Chapter 4 in this Yearbook). To the extent that the curriculum planners wish to influence the planning for instruction, they may wish to include suggested activities for students to perform. Curriculum planners may wish to ensure the proper implementation of their curriculum; if so, a set of such intentions may be included in the curriculum. The same may be said for intentions for evaluation and re-planning. The total format decision really rests upon the shoulders of the curriculum developers. It is to be their curriculum, and they are the ones who must live with it once the job is completed.

References

Apple, Michael W. *Ideology and Curriculum*. Boston: Routledge & Kegan Paul, 1979.

Beauchamp, George A. *Curriculum Theory*. 4th ed. Itasca, Ill: Peacock, 1981.

Dewey, John. *Democracy and Education*. New York: Macmillan, 1916.

Eastman, George. "The Ideologizing of Theories: John Dewey's Educational Theory, A Case in Point." *Educational Theory* 17 (April 1967): 103–119.

English, Fenwick W. "Curriculum Mapping." *Educational Leadership* 37 (April 1980): 558–560.

Goodlad, John I., and associates. *Curriculum Inquiry*. New York: McGraw-Hill, 1979.

Johnson, Mauritz. *Intentionality in Education*. Albany, N.Y.: Center for Curriculum Research and Services, 1977.

Kerlinger, Fred N. *Foundations of Behavioral Research* 2nd ed. New York: Holt, Rinehart, and Winston, 1973.

Ragan, William B., and Shepherd, Gene D. *Modern Elementary Curriculum* 5th ed. New York: Holt, Rinehart and Winston, 1977.

Rose, Arnold M. "Generalizations in the Social Sciences." *American Journal of Sociology* 59 (August 1953): 49–58.

Saylor, J. Galen, and Alexander, William M. *Planning Curriculum for Schools*. New York: Holt, Rinehart, and Winston, 1974.

Smith, B. Othanel; Stanley, William O.; and Shores, J. Harlan. *Fundamentals of Curriculum Development* 2nd ed. New York: World Book Company, 1957.

Taba, Hilda. *Curriculum Development: Theory and Practice*. New York: Harcourt, Brace & World, 1962.

Tanner, Daniel T. *Secondary Curriculum*. New York: Macmillan, 1971.

Tyler, Ralph W. *Basic Principles of Curriculum and Instruction*. Chicago: University of Chicago Press, 1950.

Unruh, Glenys G. *Responsive Curriculum Development*. Berkeley, Calif.: McCutchan, 1975.

Zais, Robert S. *Curriculum: Foundations and Principles*. New York: Crowell, 1976.

Chapter 3

Curriculum Content

B. Othanel Smith

The creation and storage of information and the retrieval of it for instructing the young and for use in daily life is a persistent, if not a unique, activity of humankind. While it reaches back to the earliest human forms, the activity has become ever more productive with each new phase of biological and cultural evolution. This is an old theme, but recent discoveries and speculations in genetics and physiology and advances in electronic technology are creating new insights into the how of accumulation and conservation of information. We now recognize four epochs in this development:[1]

• The emergence of genetic information; that is, information stored in the genetic structure and which directs the infant's earliest reactions to the environment, and, for all we know, influences the infant's orientation to the world.

• The emergence of extra genetic information, acquired by experience and stored in the brain.

• The creation of symbols—line and form, writing, mathematical notation, musical notation—in which information is stored outside the brain, making possible the accumulation of knowledge beyond what can be conserved by the brain alone.

• The development of information-storage technology (that is, printing and electronic memory banks) that not only increases storage capacity but accelerates the rate of retrieval.

For aeons, we know not how long, the residue of human experience was stored in the human brain. It was passed on from generation to generation by observation of what others do, imitation of their performance, and by word of mouth. The accumulation of knowledge was limited to what could be recalled and used in daily living or passed on by rituals and legends. Learning was largely incidental and took place at a leisurely pace, differences among individuals as to

---

[1]Carl Sagan, *The Dragons of Eden* (New York: Ballantine, 1977), pp. 21–83.

their accumulated knowledge being largely determined by their range of experience and the chemistry and physiology of their neural systems.

As long as non-genetic information was stored only in the human brain, its acquisition was more likely to be through concrete experience and daily activities; study as we think of it today being nonexistent. When it became possible, through writing and other forms of symbolic expression, to store information outside of the nervous system, knowledge accumulation was not only accelerated but the amount of information one could acquire in a lifetime was multiplied manyfold. Furthermore, those who learned to use the media were able to raise their intellectual attainment far beyond the level of those who lacked the tools to tap the reservoirs of information.

The storage of information in symbolic systems not only accelerated its accumulation but also made it possible to devise ways of accelerating the rate at which one could retrieve and use information. Mass education became feasible.

Today it has become possible to store knowledge in electronic brains, further accelerating knowledge accumulation. As accumulation increases by leaps and bounds it becomes imperative that we also discover ways of increasing the learning rate. The processes of learning have perhaps not changed in thousands of years, but research on teaching and the development of educational technology from writing and printing to memory banks is enabling the teaching profession to step-up the learning pace.

Unpacking Information for Learning: Two Classic Views

One of the persistent problems of pedagogy is how to unpack stored knowledge and to handle it in such a way as to facilitate optimum learning. This problem has given rise to a recurring issue: the child versus the curriculum. The classic positions belong to Dewey and to Morrison. In Dewey's view there were two conceptions of information. There was the stored information of human-kind, selected elements of which were found in the studies that made up the school program.[2] Dewey called these the teacher's resources or available capital. This information, however, is not content for the learner except potentially. It became content for the learner as it entered into and gave meaning to some purposeful activity in which the learner was engaged.[3] Thus, for Dewey, there were not only two conceptions of content but also two conceptions of curriculum. First of all, the curriculum consisted of studies at different levels of the learner's development. This curriculum represented the instructional resources of the teacher. Then, there was the curriculum of experiences in which the student's purposeful activities appropriated content and organized it with the residue of past experiences.

These two curriculums were not identical. For one thing, the subject matter potentially present for the learner never entered in its entirety into the

---

[2]John Dewey, *Democracy and Education* (New York: Macmillan, 1916), pp. 214–15.
[3]Ibid., p. 216ff.

learner's experience. Always there was something left over. For another thing, while some of the content would enter into the learner's experience, there would be unexpected concomitant meanings that emerged in the course of the activities.

Morrison, like Dewey, recognized stored information as instructional capital. But they differed about how the capital was acquired by the student. For Dewey, the way to enter the storage room was to become involved in inquiry where capital was used in the search. To Morrison, the entry was through study, by which he meant the use of language and other symbolic skills to decode and assimilate the information.[4] This required the student to have a motive, tools of learning, and materials. If students applied themselves and teachers provided them with proper instruction—testing, diagnosing, and providing corrective instruction—to the point of mastery, the student would learn. Students learned to think as they took on knowledge. The school subject—mathematics, the sciences, linguistics, history, and so on—are primarily ways of thinking, and the student who thoroughly studies a discipline, say history, also learns to think as a historian thinks.[5]

Each of these conceptions of content, and how one appropriates content, is supported by practical experience as well as research, but the whole truth may not be the lot of either. The last word on how to stimulate, sustain, and guide the learning process is not in. The plausibility of each view is dependent partly upon the level of schooling. Morrison was concerned primarily with secondary education, defined as that which follows mastery of the fundamental tools of learning. His approach thus enjoys favor at the secondary level. While Dewey's emphasis on learning through doing and experiencing has made his approach more acceptable in the elementary schools. However, neither gives much consideration to the dimensions of information selected for curriculum content—its forms, structure, biases, and utility—and hence they neglect what the teacher needs to know about the content of instruction.

How the Teacher's Knowledge of Content is Different

Most analyses of teaching reduce it to student-teacher interaction. In some classroom situations this description is adequate. When a teacher tries to influence a student's conduct the relationship approximates a person-to-person interaction, somewhat as in animal play. There may be little information involved. The teacher may simply suggest a substitute behavior, ignore the conduct, have the student face up to the reality of what he is doing, or simply tell the student to desist. These are cases of person-to-person interaction where content is almost at the vanishing point. But in all instruction information is central. The teacher and the student interact in and through the content.

[4]Henry C. Morrison, *The Practice of Teaching in the Secondary School* (Chicago: University of Chicago Press, 1931), pp. 218ff.
[5]Ibid., p. 34.

The teacher's knowledge of the content of instruction is, or ought to be, different from that of others. The learnings students acquire from science, mathematics, or any other subject are not likely to be used directly in their occupational activities. Engineers who study history or English will not likely use what they learn in the direct pursuit of professional work. While they may use physics and mathematics directly, they are concerned with its application to particular problems rather than to its induction into the experience of another individual. The same thing can be said of students who pursue subjects for the purpose of general education. In short, the knowledge gained in undergraduate courses is seldom a specific means to a particular end. To teachers, however, content is the lifeblood of their occupation, for where there is no knowledge to be taught there is little to be learned. To teach is not only to know the content, but also to analyze it, to take it apart and put it together in new relationships, to understand and analyze its types, structure, utility, biases, and the pitfalls the learner is likely to encounter in the course of learning.

Content as Concepts

Generally students acquire the content of courses with little or no recognition of the different types of knowledge or of their structure. While this is a distinct loss to general students, for the student of pedagogy it can be critical. Teachers who acquire information from academic courses without recognizing and understanding the different forms of knowledge are handicapped in the delivery of instruction, for the forms of knowledge—concepts, causes, effects, procedures, values, rules, and facts—are precisely the objects of instruction and each form requires its own mode of teaching.

Teachers, who teach these forms of knowledge effectively, know the elements of each form and how they are related and uses of the forms in various situations. Consider *concept*, as a form of knowledge: What is it? What are its elements? How is it taught? We do not see our world as a whole; we divide it into groups. Waiving the question of whether grouping is attributable to innate mental structures or to experience, we do distinguish one thing from another and as we note differences we also note likenesses. Out of this discriminatory behavior we group the objects of our environment. Psychologically speaking, these groups or sets are concepts, cognitive baskets into which we put things that belong together and exclude those things that do not belong with them.

When concepts are rendered verbally they are definitions. In its classic form a definition designates a class (group or set) and the characteristics by which instances of the class can be identified. The nature of these characteristics will vary from one definition to another, depending upon how the teacher handles the definition. Sometimes the characteristics are simply qualities or attributes, in other cases they are what the set of objects are used for or what they do. Sometimes, especially in scientific studies, they are couched in operational terms, stated as ratios, and so on.

In the final analysis, we interpret our world with concepts. If we see something puzzling or disturbing, we understand it if we can identify it as one of a kind, as belonging in one of our cognitive baskets. Furthermore, concepts are the building blocks of our thought. With them we construct arguments, laws, rules, or whatever. Definitions, expressions of concepts, are therefore fundamental elements of content.

Teachers are concerned with how concepts, either abstract or concrete, can be taught effectively. Psychologists tell us that the way to teach a concept is to give a rule for deciding whether or not a given something belongs in the cognitive basket. We can teach the concept by helping the student learn to use the rule in deciding whether this thing or that belongs in the set. This can be done by giving positive and negative instances, or by asking students to give such instances until the student has mastered the concept; that is to say, can apply the rule accurately to case after case.

This is a simple formula and for many concepts is doubtlessly effective. However, its usefulness is limited and no successful teacher adheres to it from concept to concept. It is of course true that when students have mastered a concept they are able to tell whether a particular thing is one of a kind or not. But there is more to learning a concept than simply knowing the necessary characteristics. So, how is a concept taught? It is done in a number of ways.[6] In addition to giving characteristics of the set and instances and noninstances, we also do the following:

—discuss the function of the set

—identify a condition that produces or causes the set

—discuss the way in which the set grows, develops, changes

—discuss some procedure involving the set

—note alternative ways in which the name of the set may be used

—note the difference between one use or meaning of the name for the set and some other use or meaning it may have

—note the way the set compares with a similar but different set.

The foregoing represent some of the kinds of information that from time to time are used in the teaching of concepts.

Meta-Content and Concepts

While students learn a vast number of concepts in various disciplines and from reading and daily experience, it is equally important that they learn not just specific concepts but also what a concept is.[7] This means, among other things, that they be taught that a concept is a set, that a set has necessary characteristics by which to decide whether something is a member of it, that a set has a name, and that the name is not the concept any more than a person's name is the person.

[6]B. Othanel Smith and others, A *Study of the Strategies of Teaching* (Urbana: Bureau of Educational Research, University of Illinois, 1967), pp. 58–95.

[7]Harry S. Broudy and others, *Democracy and Excellence in American Secondary Education* (Huntington, N.Y.: Krieger, 1978), pp. 121–138.

To know what a concept is in part is to be able to distinguish a concept from other forms of knowledge. Concepts are often mistaken for facts. Consider, for example, the following statements:

1. Hanna was instrumental in getting McKinley elected governor of Ohio.
2. An adverb is a word that modifies verbs, adjectives, other adverbs, and prepositions.

At first glance each of these statements appears to be factual, but on further observation it can be seen that the first statement is quite different from the second. It is like the statement: Dogs bark at cats. That dogs act that way can be confirmed by observation; so, in a sense, can Hanna's activities in connection with the election of McKinley. We can confirm them by examining the records. The second statement simply says that an adverb is the same thing as a word that modifies verbs, adjectives, other adverbs, and prepositions; that is to say, wherever the expression "a word that modifies verbs, adjectives, other adverbs, and prepositions" appears, the word "adverb" can be substituted without loss of meaning. Definitions are thus tautologies whereas statements of fact tell us something about the world of our senses.

When we do not understand the difference between fact and definition, we easily tumble into the pitfall of arguing about words. This can happen in the classroom no less than in professional discussions. It should be noted, however, that there are standard uses of terms and that we use words as we please at the risk of being misunderstood or of confusing participants in discussion.

Causes as Content

Another type of knowledge teachers are concerned with is cause-effect. We constantly use such expressions as "results in," "contributes to," "determines," "leads to," "produces," and "is responsible for." These are synonyms for "cause." Cause-effect relationships are often difficult to identify and unravel. Ordinarily causal content is introduced when an event is to be explained or accounted for. In some cases, the teacher may begin with a description of an effect and then guide students in an exploration of its cause or causes. In other cases, the point of departure may be a cause followed by an effort to identify its effect. In the cause-effect relationship, however, the most significant element for consideration is the evidence that a cause results in a particular effect or that a given effect is attributable to a particular cause or causes.

To deal with causal relationships requires, among other things, that the teacher understand the different kinds of causal relations. There are at least four, as follows[8]:

—the relationship in which x is necessary and sufficient to produce y. Example: the polio virus is necessary and sufficient for an individual to become ill with polio; without the virus, polio will not occur, and nothing else is necessary for the disease to occur.

[8]Smith and others, *A Study of the Strategies*, pp. 96–124.

—a relationship in which x is necessary to produce y. Example: an individual will not learn to judge weights if there is no feedback; feedback is necessary for an individual to learn to judge weights but it is not sufficient. In addition, the individual must have experience in lifting weights of varying magnitudes under specified conditions.

—a relationship in which x is sufficient to produce y. Example: when cost of labor increases, the price of what is produced rises. Labor cost is sufficient to bring about price increase, but increase can occur even when labor costs do not rise. In other words, rise in labor costs is not necessary for price increases.

—a relationship in which x contributes to the production of y. Example: competition among nations for natural resources helps to induce war, but such competition is neither necessary nor sufficient to bring it about.

There is now little opportunity in programs of pedagogical preparation for teachers to learn these various relationships, to say nothing of learning them in situations where they can have experience analyzing evidence for and against causal claims. For this reason, analysis of causal relationships is too often neglected not only in social sciences but also in the more quantitative disciplines such as physics and chemistry.

Moreover, the mere teaching of causal relationships is insufficient. The student must also learn the different types of causal relationships, that causal relations are always empirical, and that beliefs, feelings, private experience, and appeals to so-called occult events do not constitute evidence.

It is an anomaly that in a culture where rigorous logic and precise procedures have pushed back the frontiers of knowledge about ourselves, about elementary particles, about the nature of the cosmos and its beginning, about the origins of life and homo sapiens that we are witnessing the rise and growth of all sorts of cults, superstitions, and fears. Could it be that the human brain is overcome by the mind-blowing concepts of time, space, velocity, and the density and relativity of events that daily float before our eyes on the screen? Or could it be that we have not yet learned how to build mental structures to support them? Or maybe we have not learned to think like scientists about ourselves and the world out there.

Values as Content

The final type of content consists of value knowledge. This type of knowledge is often confused with attitudes. To have an attitude is to be for or against something—an event, object, or whatever. Value knowledge is a particular kind of concept, a concept whose instances are determined by preferential criteria which are usually vaguely recognized, if at all, and typically controversial.

Value knowledge consists of some set of objects that are rated by criteria. To value something is to rate it. When we say that an orange, for example, is good we have implicitly rated it by some criteria. If we are asked why we say it is good, our reply might be that it is juicy, seedless, and sweet. We might add that it ships well and that the peeling's texture and color are attractive. In this case there is an object to be evaluated; namely, an orange. In addition there is a value word—"good"—and a set of criteria by which the orange is judged to be good. Whether the evaluation is about such things as conduct, beauty, truth, or whatever evaluation will consist of rating something by criteria, recognized or not.[9]

Controversies about matters of value may arise from a number of sources. There may be disagreement about whether the object has the particular qualities ascribed to it by the criteria. The disagreement is then about facts. Controversy may also arise from disagreement about criteria. In this event, the differences among individuals about the worth of the object may be more difficult to resolve. In a history class, the question arose as to whether or not John Quincy Adams was a strong president. Some students maintained that he was strong while others held the contrary view. As the discussion proceeded it became evident that there were differences about criteria. The teacher was quick to see this and made the following observation:

You know, there is a difference in the definitions of terms here, don't you? You define 'strong presidents' as self-willed and usually defiant. But Jack has defined it as the president is strong in his ability to get his own program across.

Now, these criteria—"self-willed and defiant" and "ability to get his own program across"—can be analyzed and discussed and if agreement can be reached about them, consensus can be obtained as to the rating of Adams as president. Otherwise, there will be different ratings.

The handling of value knowledge is difficult and the operations far more complex than this brief analysis suggests. Suffice it to say that value knowledge extends into and through all school subjects and into a neglected area of education—moral conduct.

Content in Relation to Goals and Objectives

In curriculum development it is important not only to understand the nature of content but also to consider its relation to educational goals. It is sometimes claimed that there is a direct connection between content and the goals of the school. But this is not necessarily so, and in many cases the connection between content and goals is very tenuous and indirect if it exists at all. Consider, for example, these goals. To develop

1. Good character and self-respect
2. Feelings of self-worth and pride in one's work
3. Good citizens
4. Good family members.

As we survey the content of the curriculum, it is indeed difficult, if not impossible, to identify the content whose mastery would result in any of the

[9]Laurence E. Metcalf, ed., *Values Education*. 41st Yearbook of the National Council for the Social Studies. (Washington, D.C.: NCSS 1971), *passim*.

foregoing goals. By means of facts, definitions, principles, and values, we comprehend our environment, solve problems, and through synthesis and insight contribute to the advancement of knowledge. They enable us to create new technologies, increase work efficiency, and facilitate the management and direction of complex social institutions. But such knowledge does not make us better marriage companions, better citizens, more humane, more self-respecting, or more likable, no matter how well it is mastered. In short, the connection between curriculum content and these goals is indirect and tenuous at best.

Not so instructional objectives. These are derived from the content and how it is handled cognitively, as when it is memorized, comprehended, interpreted, applied, analyzed, and synthesized. If properly formulated, these objectives tell us what the student is expected to learn and the sort of behavior that will be taken as indicators of learning. But dependability of inferences we make about the future behavior of the individual in relation to other individuals, or indeed what he or she will do with the knowledge thus gained, is at best uncertain. In fact, if teachers were not only to teach the content but also to control the use in out-of-school life of what their students learn, they would thereby become managers of human behavior, a role which no society is likely to tolerate.

Granted that the intangibles referred to above are important and that the school is mandated to influence the character of its students, the question naturally arises as to how and under what conditions such influence is exercised. If it does not come about through the study of facts, definitions, principles, and value concepts, how does it occur? The answer to this question is by no means certain. We do not know just how much effect the school has in these regards nor how such effects are created. On conceptual grounds, it would appear that these intangibles are induced partly by the school's informal environment, partly by the classroom atmosphere, and partly by the behavior of the teacher and the student's peers. The school's influence is broader than instruction in the content of the curriculum.[10] It is well to point out, however, that while we honor the goals of education, the attention given to them in formal curriculum planning and in the conduct of instruction is more verbal than real.

What the teacher knows, or should know, about the content of instruction is different from that of laypersons no matter how well educated they may be. The teacher should know the different ways of sequencing content, how to judge its difficulty, how to relate it to the experience of learners, how to assess its utility, how to take it apart and put it back together in new relationships, and how to recognize and analyze its different forms.

Although there is little empirical evidence to support the view that the teacher's understanding of the various forms of knowledge and how to handle them makes a difference in student learning, there are good reasons to look forward to an improvement in the rate of learning with an increase in the ability of teachers to handle forms of knowledge. To say the least, the contribution of

---

[10]B. Othanel Smith and Donald S. Orlosky, *Socialization and Schooling* (Bloomington: Phi Delta Kappa, 1975), pp. 59–85.

curriculum practitioners and scholars to the effectiveness of instruction may be related directly to exploring the forms of curriculum content in both research and practice.

Chapter 4

Goals and Objectives

**Ronald S. Brandt and
Ralph W. Tyler**

Whether planning for one classroom or many, curriculum developers must have a clear idea of what they expect students to learn. Establishing goals is an important and necessary step because there are many desirable things students could learn—more than schools have time to teach them—so schools should spend valuable instructional time only on high priority learnings.

Another reason for clarifying goals is that schools must be able to resist pressures from various sources. Some of the things schools are asked to teach are untrue, would hinder students' development, or would help make them narrow, bigoted persons. Some would focus students' learning so narrowly it would reduce, rather than increase, their life options.

Forms of Goals and Objectives

Statements of intent appear in different forms, and words such as goals, objectives, aims, ends, outcomes, and purposes are often used interchangeably. Some people find it useful to think of goals as long-term aims to be achieved eventually and objectives as specific learning students are to acquire as a result of current instruction.

Planners in the Portland, Oregon, area schools say these distinctions are not clear enough to meet organizational planning requirements. They use "goal" to mean any desired outcome of a program, regardless of its specificity, and "objective" only in connection with *program change objectives*, which are defined as statements of intent to change program elements in specified ways. Doherty and Peters (1981) say this distinction avoids confusion and is consistent with the philosophy of "management by objectives."

They refer to three types of goals: instructional, support, and management. Educational goals are defined as learnings to be acquired; support goals as services to be rendered; and management goals as functions of management, such as planning, operating, and evaluating. Such a goal structure permits evaluation to focus on measures of learning acquired (educational outcomes), measures of quantity and quality of service delivery (support outcomes), and measures of quality and effectiveness of management functions (management outcomes).

The Tri-County Goal Development Project, which has published 14 volumes containing over 25,000 goal statements,[1] is concerned only with *educational goals*. For these collections, the following distinctions are made within the general category of "goals":

System level goals (set for the school district by the board of education)

Program level goals (set by curriculum personnel in each subject field)

Course level goals (set by groups of teachers for each subject or unit of instruction)

Instructional level goals (set by individual teachers for daily planning)

Examples of this outcome hierarchy are shown in Figure 1.

What distinguishes this system of terminology from others is its recognition that a learning outcome has the same essential character at all levels of planning (hence the appropriateness of a single term, goal, to describe it); and that the level of generality used to represent learning varies with the planning requirements at each level of school organization. The degree of generality chosen for planning at each level is, of course, a matter of judgment; there is no "correct" level but only a sense of appropriateness to purpose.

Teachers, curriculum specialists, and university consultants who write and review course goals use the following guidelines (Doherty and Peters, 1980, pp. 26–27):

1. Is the stated educational outcome potentially significant?

2. Does the goal begin with "The student knows . . ." if it is a knowledge goal and "The student is able to . . ." if it is a process goal?

Figure 1: Examples of Goals at Each Level of Planning

System Goal: The student knows and is able to apply basic scientific and technological processes.

Program Goal: The student is able to use the conventional language, instruments, and operations of science.

Course Goal: The student is able to classify organisms according to their conventional taxonomic categories.

Instructional Goal: The student is able to correctly classify cuttings from the following trees as needleleaf, hemlock, pine, spruce, fir, larch, cypress, redwood, and cedar.

[1]Available from Commercial-Educational Distributing Service, P.O. Box 4791, Portland, OR 97208.

3. Is the goal stated in language that is sufficiently clear, concise, and appropriate? (Can it be stated in simpler language and/or fewer words?)

4. Can learning experiences be thought of that would lead to the goal's achievement?

5. Do curricular options exist for the goal's achievement? (Methodology should not be a part of the learning outcome statement.)

6. Does the goal clearly contribute to the attainment of one or more of the program goals in its subject area?

7. Can the goal be identified with the approximate level of student development?

8. Can criteria for evaluating the goal be identified?

Curriculum developers need to decide the types and definitions of goals most useful to them and to users of their materials. Some authors advise avoiding vagueness by using highly specific language.[2] Mager (1962) and other writers insist that words denoting observable behaviors, such as "construct" and "identify" should be used in place of words like "understand" and "appreciate." Others reject this approach, claiming that behavioral objectives "are in no way adequate for conceptualizing most of our most cherished educational aspirations" (Eisner, 1979, p. 101). Unfortunately this dispute has developed into a debate about behavioral objectives rather than dialogue over the kinds of behavior appropriate for a humane and civilized person.

The debate is partly semantic and partly conceptual. To some persons the word "behavior" carries the meaning of an observable act, like the movement of the fingers in typing. To them, behavioral objectives refer only to overt behavior. Others use the term "behavior" to emphasize the active nature of the learner. They want to emphasize that learners are not passive receptacles but living, reasoning persons. In this sense behavior refers to all kinds of human reactions.

For example, a detailed set of "behavioral goals" was prepared by French and associates (1957). Organized under the major headings of "self-realization," "face-to-face relationships," and "membership in large organizations," *Behavioral Goals of General Education in High School* includes aims such as "Shows growing ability to appreciate and apply good standards of performance and artistic principles." These are expanded by illustrative behaviors such as "Appreciates good workmanship and design in commercial products."

The other aspect of the debate over behavioral objectives arises from focusing on limited kinds of learning, such as training factory workers to perform specific tasks. The term "conditioning" is commonly used for the learning of behaviors initiated by clear stimuli and calling for automatic, fixed responses. Most driving behavior, for example, consists of conditioned responses to traffic lights, to the approach of other cars and pedestrians, and to the sensations a driver receives from the car's movements. Conditioning is a necessary and important type of learning.

[2]Collections of "measurable objectives" may be purchased from Instructional Objectives Exchange, Box 24095-M, Los Angeles, CA 90024-0095.

In some situations, though, an automatic response is inappropriate. A more complex model of learning compatible with development of responsible persons in a changing society conceives of the learner as actively seeking meaning. This implies understanding and conscious pursuit of one's goals. The rewards of such learning include the satisfaction of coping with problems successfully.

Planning curriculum for self-directed learning requires goals that are not directly observable: ways of thinking, understanding of concepts and principles, broadening and deepening of interests, changing of attitudes, developing satisfying emotional responses to aesthetic experiences, and the like.

Even these goals, however, should use terms with clearly defined meanings. Saying that a student should "understand the concept of freedom" is far too broad and ambiguous, both because the meaning of the term "concept" is not sufficiently agreed on among educators, and because concept words such as "freedom" have too great a range of possible informational loadings to ensure similar interpretation from teacher to teacher. If used at all, such a statement would be at the program level, and would require increasingly specific elaboration at the course and lesson plan levels.

Some educators find it useful to refer to a particular type of goal as a *competency*. Used in the early 1970s in connection with Oregon's effort to relate high school instruction to daily life (Oregon State Board, 1972), the term "minimum competency" has become identified with state and district testing programs designed to ensure that students have a minimum level of basic skills before being promoted or graduated. Spady (1978) and other advocates of performance-based education point out that competency involves more than "capacities" such as the ability to read and calculate; it should refer to *application* of school-learned skills in situations outside of school.

One definition of competency is the ability to perform a set of related tasks with a high degree of skill. The concept is especially useful in vocational education, where a particular competency can be broken down through task analysis into its component skills so that teachers and curriculum planners have both a broad statement of expected performance and an array of skills specific enough to be taught and measured (Chalupsky and others, 1981).

Considerations in Choosing Goals

Educational goals should reflect three important factors: the nature of organized knowledge, the nature of society, and the nature of learners (Tyler, 1949). An obvious source is the nature of organized fields of study. Schools teach music, chemistry, and algebra because these fields have been developed through centuries of painstaking inquiry. Each academic discipline has its own concepts, principles, and processes. It would be unthinkable to neglect passing on to future generations this priceless heritage and these tools for continued learning.

Another factor affecting school goals is the nature of society. For example, the goals of education in the United States are quite different from those in the Soviet Union. In the United States we stress individuality, competition, creativity, and freedom to choose government officials. Soviet schools teach loyalty to the state and subordination of one's individuality to the welfare of the collective. One result is that most American schools offer a great many electives, while the curriculum in Soviet schools consists mostly of required subjects. For example, all students in the U.S.S.R. must study advanced mathematics and science to serve their technologically advanced nation (Wirszup, 1981).

U.S. schools have assumed, explicitly or implicitly, many goals related to the nature of society. For example, schools offer drug education, sex education, driver education, and other programs because of concerns about the values and behavior of youth and adults. Schools teach visual literacy because of the influence of television, consumer education because our economic system offers so many choices, and energy education because of the shortage of natural resources.

A goal statement by Ehrenberg and Ehrenberg (1978) specifically recognizes the expectations of society. Their model for curriculum development begins with a statement of "ends sought": "It is intended that as a result of participating in the K–12 educational program students will consistently and effectively take *intelligent, ethical action:* (1) to accomplish the tasks society legitimately expects of all its members, and (2) to establish and pursue worthwhile goals of their own choosing."

The curriculum development process outlined by the Ehrenbergs involves preparing a complete rationale for the ends-sought statement and then defining, for example, areas of societal expectations. The work of the curriculum developer consists of defining a framework of "criterion tasks," all derived either from expectations of society or necessary to pursue individual goals. These tasks, at various levels of pupil development, become the focus of day-to-day instruction. In this way, all curriculum is directly related to school system goals.

A third consideration in choosing goals, sometimes overlooked, is the nature of learners. For example, because Lawrence Kohlberg (1980) has found that children pass through a series of stages in their moral development, he believes schools should adopt the goal of raising students' levels of moral reasoning. Sternberg (1981) and other "information processing" psychologists believe that intelligence is, partly at least, a set of strategies and skills that can be learned. Their research suggests, according to Sternberg, that schools can and should set a goal of improving students' intellectual performance.

Recognizing that students often have little interest in knowledge for its own sake or in adult applications of that knowledge, some educators believe goals should not only be based on what we know about students, but should come from students themselves. Many alternative schools emphasize this source of goals more than conventional schools typically do (Raywid, 1981).

While knowledge, society, and learners are all legitimate considerations, the three are sometimes in conflict. For example, many of the products of the curriculum reform movement of the 1960s had goals based almost exclusively on the nature of knowledge. The emphasis of curriculum developers was on the "structure of the disciplines" (Bruner, 1960). Goals of some curriculums failed to fully reflect the nature of society and students, so teachers either refused to use them or gave up after trying them for a year or two (Stake and Easley, 1978).

In the 1970s educators and the general public reacted against this discipline-centered emphasis by stressing practical activities drawn from daily life. Schools were urged to teach students how to balance a checkbook, how to choose economical purchases, how to complete a job application, and how to read a traffic ticket. Career education enthusiasts, not content with the reasonable idea that education should help prepare students for satisfying careers, claimed that *all* education should be career-related in some way.

Conflicts of this sort between the academic and the practical are persistent and unavoidable, but curriculum developers err if they emphasize only one source of goals and ignore the others. If noneducators are preoccupied with only one factor, educational leaders have a responsibility to stress the importance of the others and to insist on balance.

Scope of the School's Responsibility

There have been many attempts to define the general aims of schools and school programs, including the well-known Cardinal Principles listed by a national commission in 1918. The seven goals in that report—health, fundamental processes, worthy home membership, vocation, civic education, worthy use of leisure, and ethical character—encompass nearly every aspect of human existence, and most goal statements written since that time have been equally comprehensive.

Some authors contend that schools are mistaken to assume such broad aims. Martin (1980) argued that intellectual development and citizenship are the only goals for which schools should have primary responsibility and that other institutions should be mainly responsible for such goals as worthy home membership. He proposed that schools undertake a new role of coordinating educational efforts of all community agencies.

Paul (1982) reported that in three different communities large numbers of teachers, students, and parents agreed on a limited set of goals confined mostly to basic skills. Paul contended that schools often confuse the issue when involving citizens in setting goals because they ask what students should learn rather than what schools should teach. Goal surveys conducted by her organization showed, she said, that adults want young people to develop many qualities for which they do not expect schools to be responsible.

Undeniably, the aims and activities of U.S. schools are multiple and diverse. They not only teach toothbrushing, crafts, religion, care of animals, advertising, cooking, automobile repair, philosophy, hunting, and chess; they also provide health and food services to children, conduct parent education classes, and offer a variety of programs for the elderly. Periodic review of these obligations is clearly in order. However, in trying to delimit their mission schools must not minimize concern for qualities that, though hard to define and develop, distinguish educated persons from the less educated.

A carefully refined statement of goals of schooling in the United States was developed by Goodlad (1979) and his colleagues in connection with their Study of Schooling. Deliberately derived from an analysis of hundreds of goal statements adopted by school districts and state departments of education so as to reflect accurately the currently declared aims of American education, the list comprises 65 goals in 12 categories, including "intellectual development," "self-concept," and "moral and ethical character."

An equally broad set of goals is used in Pennsylvania's Educational Quality Assessment, which includes questions intended to measure such elusive aims as "understanding others" and "self-esteem." School districts must give the tests at least once every five years as part of a plan to make schools accountable for the 12 state-adopted goals (Seiverling, 1980). An adaptation of the Pennsylvania goals was used by the ASCD Committee on Research and Theory (1980) in connection with their plan for *Measuring and Attaining the Goals of Education*.

In many cases schools contribute modestly or not at all to helping students become loving parents and considerate neighbors. In other cases, school experiences may have lasting effects on values, attitudes, and behavior. We believe school goals should include such aims as "interpersonal relations" and "autonomy," as well as "intellectual development" and "basic skills" (Goodlad, 1979), although the goal statement should specifically recognize that most goals are not the exclusive domain of schools but are a shared responsibility with other institutions.

Establishing Local Goals

It is usually helpful to begin identification of goals by listing all the promising possibilities from various sources. Consider contemporary *society*. What things could one's students learn that would help them meet current demands and take advantage of future opportunities? General data about modern society may be found in studies of economic, political, and social conditions. Data directly relevant to the lives of one's students will usually require local studies, which can be made by older students, parents, and other local people.

Consider the *background of the students*: their previous experiences, things they have already learned, their interests and needs; that is, the gaps between desired ways of thinking, feeling, and acting and their present ways. This information should be specific to one's own students, although generalized studies of the development of children and youth in our culture will suggest what to look for.

Consider the potential of the various *subject fields*. What things could one's students learn about their world and themselves from the sciences, history, literature, and so on? What can mathematics provide as a resource for their lives? Visual arts? Music? Each new generation is likely to find new possibilities in these growing fields of knowledge and human expression.

In the effort to identify possible goals don't be unduly concerned about the form in which you state these "things to be learned." For example, you may find a possibility in "learn new ways of expressing emotions through various experiences provided in literature," and another in "understanding how animal ecologies are disturbed and the consequences of the disturbance." These are in different forms and at different levels of generality, but at this stage the purpose is only to consider carefully all the promising possibilities. Later on, those selected as most important and appropriate for one's students can be refined and restated in common form so as to guide curriculum developers in designing learning experiences. At that point, it will probably be helpful to standardize terms and definitions. At early stages, however, curriculum developers should use terminology familiar and understandable to teachers, principals, parents, and citizens rather than insisting on distinctions that others may have difficulty remembering and using.

The comprehensive list of possible outcomes should be carefully scrutinized to sift out those that appear to be of minor importance or in conflict with the school's educational philosophy. The list should also be examined in the light of the apparent prospects for one's students being able to learn these things in school. For example, we know that things once learned are usually forgotten unless there are continuing opportunities to use them. So one criterion for retaining a goal is that students will have opportunities in and out of school to think, feel, and act as expected. We also know that learning of habits requires continuous practice with few errors, so work and study habits should be selected as goals only if they are to be emphasized consistently in school work.

This procedure for identifying what students are to be helped to learn is designed to prevent a common weakness in curriculum development: selection of goals that are obsolete or irrelevant, inappropriate for students' current level of development, not in keeping with sound scholarship, not in harmony with America's democratic philosophy, or for which the school cannot provide the necessary learning conditions.

A common practice when planning curriculum is to refer to published taxonomies (Bloom and others, 1956; Krathwohl and others, 1964). Taxonomies can be useful for their original purpose—classifying goals already formulated—but they do not resolve the issue of the relevance of any particular goal to contemporary society or to one's own students. The Bloom and Krathwohl taxonomies are organized in terms of what the authors conceive to be higher or lower levels, but higher ones are not always more important or even necessary. In typewriting, for example, so-called "higher mental processes" interfere with the speed and accuracy of typing.

A similar caution applies to uncritically taking goals from curriculum materials of other school systems. The fact that educators in Scarsdale or some other district chose certain goals is not in itself evidence that they are appropriate for your students.

Development of general goals for a school system should be a lengthy process with opportunities for students, parents, and others to participate. This can be done, for example, by sponsoring "town meetings," publishing draft statements of goals in local newspapers with an invitation to respond, and by holding and publicizing hearings on goals sponsored by the board of education.

A factor that complicates the matter is that some sources of goals are simply not subject to a majority vote. Knowledge—whether about physics, poetry, or welding—is the province of specialists. Educators sometimes know more about the nature of children and the learning process than many other adults in the community. Nevertheless, in a democracy there is no higher authority than the people, so the people must be involved in deciding what public schools are to teach.

Most general goals, because they are so broad and because they deal with major categories of human experience, are acceptable to most people. Few will quarrel with a goal such as "Know about human beings, their environments and their achievements, past and present." The problem in developing a general goal statement is usually not to decide which goals are proper and which are not, but to select among many possibilities those which are most important, are at the proper level of generality, and are at least partially the responsibility of schools.

While general goals are not usually controversial, more specific ones can be. For example, parents might not quarrel with "Understand and follow practices associated with good health," but some would reject "Describe two effective and two ineffective methods of birth control." Thus, parents and other citizens should be involved in formulating course and program goals as well as general system goals.

Using Goals to Plan Learning Activities

To some extent, well-stated goals imply the kinds of learning activities that would be appropriate for achieving them. For example, if an instructional goal is "Solve word problems requiring estimation involving use of simple fractions such as ½, ¼, ⅔," students would have to practice estimating solutions to practical problems as well as learning to calculate using fractions. In many instances, however, knowing the goal does not automatically help an educator know how to teach it. For example, to enable students to "understand and appreciate significant human achievements," one teacher might have students read about outstanding scientists of the 19th century, supplement the readings with several lectures, and give a multiple choice examination. Another teacher might decide to divide students into groups and have each group prepare a presentation to the class about a great scientist using demonstrations, dramatic skits, and so on. Forging the link between goals and other steps in curriculum development requires professional knowledge, experience, and imagination.

A factor that distorts what might appear to be a straightforward relationship between goals and activities is that every instructional activity has multiple goals. The goal-setting process is sometimes seen as a one-to-one relationship between various levels of goals and levels of school activity. For example, the mission of a local school system might be to "Offer all students equitable opportunities for a basic education plus some opportunities to develop individual talents and interests." "Basic education" would be defined to include "Communicate effectively by reading, writing, speaking, observing, and listening." A middle school in that district might have a goal such as "Read and understand non-fiction at a level of the average article in *Reader's Digest*," or more specifically, "Students will be able to distinguish between expressions of fact and opinion in writing."

While similar chains of related goals are basic to sound curriculum planning, developers should never assume that such simplicity fully represents the reality of schools. When a teacher is engaged in teaching reading he or she must also be conscious of and teach toward other goals: thinking ability, knowledge of human achievements, relationships with others, positive self-concept, and so on.

Not only must teachers address several officially adopted "outside" goals all at once; they must cope with "inside" goals as well. Although Goodlad (1979) uses declared goals to remind educators and the public what schools are said to be for, he cautions that the ends-means model doesn't do justice to the educational process and offers, as an alternative, an ecological perspective. Insisting that school activities should "be viewed for their intrinsic value, quite apart from their linkage or lack of linkage to stated ends" (p. 76), he points out that in addition to "goals that have been set outside of the system for the system" there are also goals inside the system—"students' goals, teachers' goals, principals' goals, and so on—and . . . these goals are not necessarily compatible" (p. 77).

The message to curriculum developers is that although "outside" goals and objectives are fundamental to educational planning, the relationship between purposes and practices is more complex than it may seem.

Using Goals in Curriculum Evaluation

Some writers argue that specific objectives are essential in order to design suitable evaluation plans and write valid test items. The work of the National Assessment of Educational Progress shows, however, that even evaluators may not require objectives written in highly technical language.[3] National Assessment objectives do not contain stipulations of conditions or performance standards; in fact they are expected to meet just two criteria: clarity and importance. The educators, citizens, and subject matter experts who review the objectives are asked, "Do you understand what this objective means? How important is it that students learn this in school?" Objectives are often considered clear and important even though they are stated briefly and simply. When the objectives have been identified, National Assessment staff members or consul-

---

[3]National Assessment has developed objectives for a number of subject areas, including art, citizenship, career and occupational development, literature, mathematics, music, reading, science, social studies, and writing. Because they have been carefully written and thoroughly reviewed, the objectives and accompanying exercises are a helpful resource for local curriculum developers, although they are designed only for assessment, not for curriculum planning.

tants develop exercises designed to be operational definitions of the intended outcomes. Conditions, standards of performance, and so on are specified for the exercises, not for the objectives.

Summary

Setting goals is difficult because it requires assembling and weighing all the factors to be considered in selecting the relatively few but important goals that can be attained with the limited time and resources available to schools. The demands and opportunities of society, the needs of students, the resources of scholarship, the values of democracy, and the conditions needed for effective learning must all be considered.

A common error is the failure to distinguish purposes appropriate for the school from those attainable largely through experiences in the home and community. The school can reinforce the family in helping children develop punctuality, dependability, self-discipline, and other important habits. The school can be and usually is a community in which children and adults respect each other, treat each other fairly, and cooperate. But the primary task for which public schools were established is to enlarge students' vision and experience by helping them learn to draw upon the resources of scholarship, thus overcoming the limitations of direct experience and the narrow confines of a local environment. Students can learn to use sources of knowledge that are more accurate and reliable than folklore and superstition. They can participate vicariously through literature and the arts with peoples whose lives are both similar and different from those they have known. The school is the only institution whose primary purpose is enabling students to explore these scholarly fields and to learn to use them as resources in their own lives. Great emphasis should be given to goals of this sort.

Goals are frequently not stated at the appropriate degree of generality-specificity for each level of educational responsibility. Goals promulgated by state education authorities should not be too specific because of the wide variation in conditions among districts in the state. State goals should furnish general guidance for the kinds and areas of learning for which schools are responsible in that state. The school district should furnish more detailed guidance by identifying goals that fall between the general aims listed by the state and those appropriate to the local school. School goals should be adapted to the background of students and the needs and resources of the neighborhood, especially the educational role the parents can assume. The goals of each teacher should be designed to attain the goals of the school. The test of whether a goal is stated at the appropriate degree of generality-specificity is its clarity and helpfulness in guiding the educational activities necessary at that level of responsibility.

When states list specific skills as goals and develop statewide testing programs to measure them, they may overlook a significant part of what schools should teach: understanding, analysis, and problem solving. If students are taught only to follow prescribed rules, they will be unable to deal with varied situations. Another common limitation of such lists is their neglect of affective components, such as finding satisfaction in reading and developing the habit of reading to learn.

The form and wording of goals and objectives should be appropriate for the way they are to be used. For clarity, we have generally used the term "goal" for all statements of intended learning outcomes regardless of their degree of specificity, but we recognize that no one formula is best for all situations. The criterion for judging goals and objectives is their usefulness in communicating educational purposes and their helpfulness to teachers in the planning of educational activities.

References

ASCD Committee on Research and Theory, Wilbur B. Brookover, Chairman. *Measuring and Attaining the Goals of Education.* Alexandria, Va.: Association for Supervision and Curriculum Development, 1980.

Bloom, Benjamin S., ed. *Taxonomy of Educational Objectives: The Classification of Educational Goals. Handbook 1: Cognitive Domain.* New York: David McKay Co., Inc., 1956.

Bruner, Jerome. *The Process of Education.* Cambridge: Belknap Press, 1960.

Chalupsky, Albert B.; Phillips-Jones, Linda; and Danoff, Malcolm N. "Competency Measurement in Vocational Education: A Review of the State of the Art." Prepared by American Institute for Research. Washington, D.C.: Office of Vocational and Adult Education, U.S. Department of Education, 1981.

Commission on the Reorganization of Secondary Education, U.S. Office of Education. *Cardinal Principles of Secondary Education.* Washington, D.C.: Government Printing Office, 1918.

Doherty, Victor W., and Peters, Linda B. "Introduction to K–12 Course Goals for Educational Planning and Evaluation." 3rd ed. Portland, Oregon: Commercial-Educational Distributing Services, 1980.

Doherty, Victor W., and Peters, Linda B. "Goals and Objectives in Educational Planning and Evaluation." *Educational Leadership* 38 (May 1981): 606.

Ehrenberg, Sydelle D.; and Ehrenberg, Lyle, M. *A Strategy for Curriculum Design—The ICI Model.* Miami, Florida: Institute for Curriculum and Instruction, 1978.

Eisner, Eliot W. *The Educational Imagination.* New York: Macmillan Publishing Co., Inc., 1979.

French, Will. *Behavioral Goals of General Education in High School.* New York: Russell Sage Foundation, 1957.

Goodlad, John I. *What Schools Are For?* Bloomington, Indiana: Phi Delta Kappa, 1979.

Kohlberg, Lawrence. "Moral Education: A Response to Thomas Sobol." *Educational Leadership* 38 (October 1980): 19–23.

Krathwohl, David R., and others. *Taxonomy of Educational Objectives: The Classification of Educational Goals, Handbook II: Affective Domain.* New York: David McKay Company, Inc., 1964.

Lindvall, C. M., ed. *Defining Educational Objectives.* Pittsburgh: University of Pittsburgh Press, 1964.

Mager, R. F. *Preparing Instructional Objectives.* Palo Alto: Fearon Publishers, 1962.

Martin, John Henry. "Reconsidering the Goals of High School Education." *Educational Leadership* 37 (January 1980): 278–285.

Mathematics Objectives, Second Assessment. Denver: National Assessment of Educational Programs, 1978.

Oregon State Board of Education. "Minimum State Requirements Standards for Graduation from High School." Salem, Oregon, 1972.

Paul, Regina. "Are You Out On a Limb?" *Educational Leadership* 39 (January 1982): 260–264.

Raywid, Mary Anne. "The First Decade of Public School Alternatives." *Phi Delta Kappan* 62 (April 1981): 551–554.

Saylor, J. Galen; Alexander, William M.; and Lewis, Arthur J. *Curriculum Planning for Better Teaching and Learning.* 4th ed. New York: Holt, Rinehart and Winston, 1981.

Seiverling, Richard F., ed. *Educational Quality Assessment: Getting Out The EQA Results.* Harrisburg, Pa.: Pennsylvania Department of Education, 1980.

Spady, William G. "The Concept and Implications of Competency-Based Education." *Educational Leadership* 36 (October 1978): 16–22.

Stake, R. E., and Easley, J. A., Jr. *Case Studies in Science Education.* 2 vols. Washington, D.C.: U.S. Government Printing Office, 1978.

Sternberg, Robert J. "Intelligence as Thinking and Learning Skills." *Educational Leadership* 39 (October 1981): 18–20.

Tyler, Ralph W. *Basic Principles of Curriculum and Instruction.* 1974 ed. Chicago: University of Chicago Press, 1949.

Ward, Barbara. "The National Assessment Approach to Objectives and Exercise Development." Report No. 12-IP-55. Denver, Colo.: Education Commission of the States, September 1980.

Wirszup, Izaak. "The Soviet Challenge." *Educational Leadership* 38 (February 1981): 358–360.

Chapter 5

Needs Assessment

Roger A. Kaufman

A good idea may fail for the wrong reasons. Recognition of this fact has propelled "needs assessment" into an integral part of curriculum development in recent years. But with this new status, a cloud hangs over the field: A cloud that often leads to semantic and real problems for those who want to identify and justify needs and want these needs to form the basis of useful curriculum development. First, let's look at semantics.

In the English language, "need" is used in many confusing ways: as a verb, a noun, and as a verb used as a noun. Few words are asked to carry as many different meanings. The net result of this imprecision in usage has been confusion about the word itself, as well as a growing ambiguity regarding means and ends in education. Can a "need" be both a means and an end?

This chapter is about "need" as a gap in results and "needs assessment" as a process for identifying gaps in results, about placing "needs" in priority order and selecting the "needs" of highest priority, and about why using "needs assessment" correctly can improve the usefulness of curriculum. Although we have many varied perceptions of "need" and "needs assessment" approaches, there is as yet no consensus on operational definitions for use in curriculum development. This chapter intends to provide such useful and practical definitions.

While not specifically designed to be popular, just precise, a rigorous concept of "need" and "needs assessment" might make it possible to enjoy all of the richness of current (and less than appropriate) uses and intentions of "need" while specifying useful distinctions between means and ends. And since a functional "needs assessment" should provide a valid rationale for relating means to validated ends, separating means and ends in our language and professional work is essential.

This chapter will (1) review the major "needs assessment" models that have been used, (2) define "need" and "quasi-need," (3) identify and justify an overarching frame of reference in which most "needs assessment" models and procedures may be fit and successfully related, (4) provide an analytical framework for determining the scope and potential usefulness of existing (and

future) models and procedures, and (5) suggest some trends and recommendations for a future useful definition and use of "needs assessment" in curriculum
development.

For some time, Kaufman (see 1972, 1982 and Kaufman and English, 1979)
has proposed a limiting definition of "need" as a gap between current results and
required results: a delineation of gaps in results, not in processes and resources.
This is often contrary to folk language (I "need" money; we "need" fewer
teachers; we "need" more accountability) and requires a shift to a more precise,
limited definition—the word "need" should be used only to relate to gaps in
results.

Thus, "need" when used only as a noun will allow us to select "means" or
interventions (such as schools, curriculum, vocational education, liberal arts
education) based upon closing *important* gaps in result. A more useful linking
between "means" and "ends"—solutions related to gaps in results—is possible.
With this perspective, we will witness a reduction in selecting educational means
that do not close the gaps in ends.

If one were to use the word "need" only as a gap in results, then one would
be free to choose, among possible alternatives, the best ways and means for
closing the gaps between "what is" and "what should be" in results. The first
forerunners of needs assessment, emerging with Ralph Tyler's writing on
objectives and needs, allowed, however, for a type of need that would be better
called a "quasi-need": a gap in processes and/or in resources (Kaufman and
Thomas, 1980; Kaufman and others, 1981). A "need" is therefore a gap in *results*
between "what is" and "what should be." A "quasi-need" is a gap in inputs,
resources, ingredients, and/or processes and means; a gap in anything *other* than
a result.

A "needs assessment" is a process that consists of the determination of gaps
in results between "what is" and "what should be," placing the gaps in priority
order for closure ("meeting the needs"), and selecting the gaps in results of the
highest priority for closure. Some would criticize this approach as too narrow
(Scriven and Roth, 1978), but it is believed that only when "need" is viewed as a
gap in results will the process of curriculum development make the kind of
impact that improves learner performance in valid and desirable ways.

Curriculum is a means to an end. It should be judged as a means and
changed accordingly. If our initial approach precludes analyzing curriculum as a
"means," the curriculum developer may be misled into believing that he or she
had the right (and only possible) solution, which ended up not being responsive
to the actual problem. Perhaps this curriculum-is-the-end-not-the-means thinking is best captured in the phrase, "The operation was a success, but the patient
died."

Education in Context: The Organizational Elements Model

Building upon the distinction between "means" and "ends," the following
is a formulation for relating organizational efforts, organizational results, and

Figure 1.

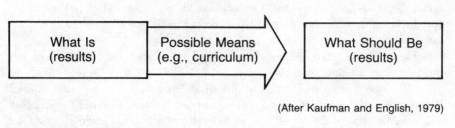

(After Kaufman and English, 1979)

societal impact and usefulness. This is called "The Organizational Elements Model" (Kaufman, 1982; Kaufman and English, 1979; Kaufman and Thomas, 1980). Let's take a closer look at the basic parts of this model.

Organizational Efforts

In getting things accomplished, any organization—be it a school, a school district, or even a business—uses ingredients and resources, and orchestrates these to achieve results. There are two types of organizational efforts: "inputs" and "processes."

Inputs: the existing ingredients, raw materials, resources, laws, "needs," rules, objectives, regulations, and people that exist, who are available, or are required to be used by an organization.

Inputs may include currently such things as personnel, laws, rules, regulations, goals, objectives, and "needs" statements. Buildings, equipment, and facilities that are in the current inventory are also "inputs," as are current and available budget. And the most important "input" of all is learners, including their unique values and characteristics.

Processes: the how-to-do-its, "means," and procedures used to convert the inputs into results.

Processes are the ways and means by which one is the steward of the resources, orchestrates them, and puts them to work. Processes are the methods-means, the how-to-do-its, for achieving results, including curriculum, courses, teaching-learning methods (such as team teaching, differentiated staffing, computer-based instruction, teaching of basic skills, planning, competency-based education), testing (but not the test results), and teaching itself. Processes take most of our educational time, effort, and energies—they are the *how* of education. It is critical that processes be the correct ones in order for educators to wisely use resources and achieve useful results. But inputs and processes alone only *intend* to achieve results.

Organizational and External Results

There are three varieties of results that are of concern to education: "products," "outputs," and "outcomes." Unfortunately, the literature and common language usage intermix these three words. A unique word usage for each of these three kinds of results is useful, practical, precise—but nonconventional. In the context of the Organizational Elements Model (Figure 2), "products" and "outputs" are two types of organizational results; outcomes are external results.

Products: the en route results a school or educational system achieves utilizing "inputs" and "processes."

"Products" are usually the results of greatest concern to teachers and learners alike: the completion of a course, or passing a test. Another "product" is a validated course of study that has been developed and is available for others to use (as an "input" after it is completed and proven), or a self-instructional module that has been proven and validated.

"Products" include the most commonly observed learner accomplishments and teacher accomplishments such as the completion of a course in history, the completed painting of a landscape, the passing of a tenth-grade competency test. "Products" are the results achieved by learners, teachers, or both.

Outputs: the results delivered or deliverable by the educational organization to society.

Examples of "outputs" include graduates of high school or persons with certified job-entry skills. When an organization gathers all of its "products" and has them delivered or deliverable to society, they are "outputs." "Outputs" mark the transition point between what an organization uses and produces, what it achieves, and the impact and effects the organizational results have in and for society.

Outcomes: are the effects or impact the "outputs" have in and for society. These are the external or outside-of-school results (or indicators of results) that determine the utility of organizational efforts and organizational results in and for society.

The emphasis upon and inclusion of external, societal results allow the Organizational Elements Model to be holistic and not just concerned with the organization or parts of the organization. It requires the additional concern for education as a means to societal ends (Kaufman, 1972, 1982).

By considering "outcomes" in educational "needs assessment" and planning and resulting efforts, one looks to the ultimate contribution of learners in society, and the ways in which education may help learners help themselves to be successful in today's and tomorrow's world and legally change that which should be changed. It counts on and builds toward a constructive, participative, changing society and world. The use of *all* of the Organizational Elements is considered to be a "holistic" approach (Kaufman and Stakenas, 1981).

The relationships among the Organizational Elements are shown in Figure 2.

This formulation is useful in allowing one to relate the factors of success (or nonsuccess) and to note that most organizational efforts (curriculum, teaching methods, course content, and so on) are most useful when related to both internal results ("products" and "outputs") *and* external results ("outcomes").

There are two reasons for doing a "needs assessment": you have to or you

Figure 2. The Organizational Elements Model (OEM) Including Some Educational Examples of Each and the Relationship Between the Elements and the Internal and External Frames of Reference

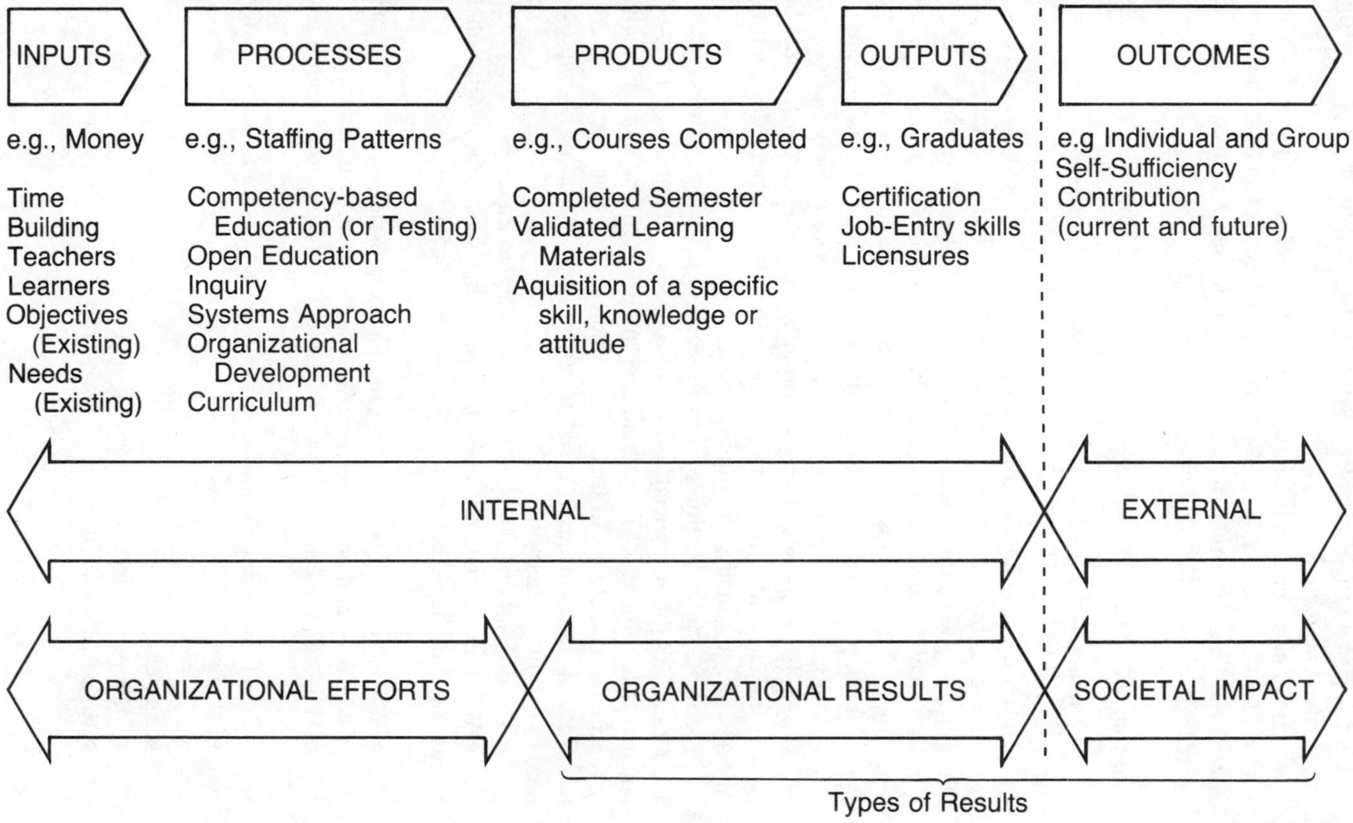

INPUTS | PROCESSES | PRODUCTS | OUTPUTS | OUTCOMES

e.g., Money

Time
Building
Teachers
Learners
Objectives (Existing)
Needs (Existing)

e.g., Staffing Patterns

Competency-based Education (or Testing)
Open Education
Inquiry
Systems Approach
Organizational Development
Curriculum

e.g., Courses Completed

Completed Semester
Validated Learning Materials
Aquisition of a specific skill, knowledge or attitude

e.g., Graduates

Certification
Job-Entry skills
Licensures

e.g Individual and Group Self-Sufficiency
Contribution
(current and future)

INTERNAL

EXTERNAL

ORGANIZATIONAL EFFORTS | ORGANIZATIONAL RESULTS | SOCIETAL IMPACT

Types of Results

(After Kaufman, 1982)

want to. The have-to's usually find interesting ways to look at gaps and usually find nothing requiring substantive change. The want-to's have a more difficult and challenging regime.

Many well-intentioned efforts in education seem to fail or do not reach expected levels of success. This is often explained by the fact that "organizational efforts" and "organizational results" were not formally derived from justified, societally useful results (Kaufman and English, 1979).

Applying the Organizational Elements Model (OEM)*

We noted earlier that a "need" is a gap in results between "what is" and "what should be."

Thus, for each element in the Organizational Elements Model (OEM) we determine gaps between "what is" and "what should be." Figure 3 shows the OEM and the two dimensions of "what is" and "what should be."

One may proceed through the Organizational Elements Model, moving from "inputs" to "processes" to "products" to "outputs" and finally to "outcomes" for the "what is" row. Then, after determining "what is" for each of the Organizational Elements and *specifying each in measurable performance terms* (see Mager, 1975) one may turn the corner and determine "what should be" for each of the elements, moving from "outcomes" to "outputs" to "products" to "processes" and, finally, to "inputs."

Based on this collection of data for each of the Organizational Elements, and for each of the two "need" dimensions of "what is" and "what should be," one may determine gaps. But not all gaps are really "needs"! The possible types of gap analyses are shown in Figure 5 and indicate the three types of "needs" and two types of "quasi-needs." Based upon the gaps (both "needs" and "quasi-needs") one may determine:

● What should be changed to be responsive to the "needs"

● What should be continued to ensure that successful efforts and useful results currently being achieved do not get eliminated

Then

● What alternative ways and means may be considered to close the gaps that should be closed and continue efforts that are currently successful

● What are the currently successful methods-means to be continued

Then

● Select the best ways and means to achieve the results, both changes and continuations

Then

● Implement

● Determine effectiveness and efficiency

● Revise as required.

*This section is based on Kaufman and Thomas, 1980; Kaufman and others, 1981; and Kaufman, 1982.

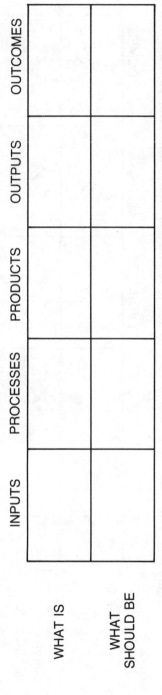

Figure 3: The "What Is" and "What Should Be" Dimensions of the Organizational Elements Model

INPUTS   PROCESSES   PRODUCTS   OUTPUTS   OUTCOMES

WHAT IS

WHAT
SHOULD BE

(From Kaufman, 1982; Kaufman and Thomas, 1980)

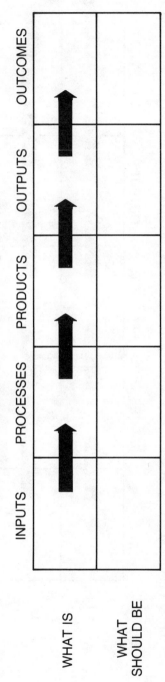

Figure 4. A Sequence for Determining "What Is"

INPUTS   PROCESSES   PRODUCTS   OUTPUTS   OUTCOMES

WHAT IS

WHAT
SHOULD BE

Figure 5. Designing Needs Assessments and Evaluations Based on the Organizational Elements Model

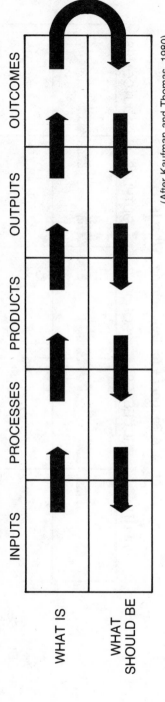

(After Kaufman and Thomas, 1980)

Figure 6. Possible Gap Analyses: Three Related to Needs and Two to Quasi-Needs

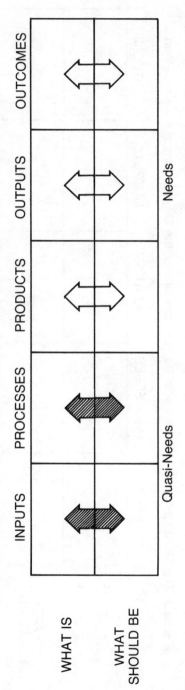

(After Kaufman and Thomas, 1980)

Needs Assessment and Evaluation

"Needs assessment" and evaluation are not the same, nor is one a subset of the other. They are related, however.

"Needs assessments" are concerned with gaps between "what is" and "what should be"—with the emphasis on *should be*.

Evaluations are concerned with gaps between "what is" and what was intended—and thus can only be concerned with a system in current operation (Kaufman and Thomas, 1980).

If one is willing to change the current goals and objectives, then "needs assessment," with its concern with "what should be," is the technique of choice. If one wishes only to look at the gaps between accomplishments and intentions, then only evaluation is required.

"Needs assessments" may be accomplished for "products," "outputs," and "outcomes." Evaluations may be accomplished for each of the Organizational Elements, but cannot be used to generate new requirements for the "what should be's." Thus, the linking between "needs assessment" and evaluation may come *after* implementation, when a new "what is" has been created by the implementation of the methods-means selected to close the gaps initially identified and selected for closure. First comes "needs assessment" then, later, evaluation identifies how well we did in closing the gaps.

Needs Assessments Are Not Deficit Analyses

While some authors (for example, Scriven and Roth, 1978) have perceived "needs assessments" that deal with discrepancy analyses as deficit studies, this can be an unwarranted assumption.

Gaps in results are *not necessarily* deficits: a gap may show an abundance of something over and above the minimal required levels.

Some efforts called "needs assessments" are really "quasi-needs assessments," and often are merely surveys of perceived desires or attempts to justify one set of solutions over others ("processes"). Thus, many efforts that are not "needs assessments" as defined here are merely "wish lists"—statements of desired resources or processes.

Seventeen models of "needs assessments" are shown briefly in the following chart. Some observations may be made assuming that the description is reasonably accurate:

● Except for one model—developed quite recently—most models, techniques, and procedures deal with *internal* elements. Thus, they will tend not to challenge directly or indirectly the status quo of the results and societal impact (and payoffs) of education.

● Most models tend to shy away from hard empirical data, but rely more on people's perceptions. Thus, there is a tendency to gravitate toward considerations of methods, curriculum content, and courses, not to learner performance, school performance, or societal payoffs.

● Most models deal with middle-level concerns; that is, they are concerned at the classroom level with learner characteristics, teaching methods and techniques, and scores on tests or course grades. They usually (with three exceptions noted in this current review) confine themselves to the teaching/ learning process and most do not examine what the schools deliver to society and how well learners do (or should do) when they become citizens.

• Many so-called "needs assessment" models and techniques (and these were not included in this review) are really status surveys, and these usually are most concerned with "what is."

• Only one model covered all of the Organizational Elements and required a formal focus on societal "needs."

• Future "needs assessment" should be holistic and include all of the Organizational Elements for two dimensions: "what is" and "what should be."

• Curriculum as means to useful ends should be derived only after a holistic "needs assessment."

While it is conceptually easier to conceive all discrepancy analyses as relating only to deficits, it is not necessarily true or useful.

While it is tempting for a needs assessor to ask for the maximum or the ideal in a statement of "what should be," (see Scriven and Roth, 1978), such unwarranted or unsupportable idealism will be isolated and eliminated if the "what is" criteria are derived from gaps in "outcomes," *then* gaps in "outputs," *then* gaps in "products" *before* determining gaps in "processes" and "inputs." By using all of the Organizational Elements, one better ensures that premature wish lists for "inputs" and "processes" will not be generated.

It also may be noted that blue-sky wish lists are almost always "inputs" or "process"-oriented, and thus additionally represent the possible selection of means that are *not* rigorously related to useful and justifiable ends.

Currently Available Models and Procedures

Good intentions are not the same as useful results. There are no existing "needs assessment" models and procedures that knowingly preselect favored methods and means, and none overtly intend to mask more important considerations than the ones under study. Rather most are employed to find out the current status of things, and then move to determine what should be changed.

Virtually all educational planning efforts ("needs assessment" models, kits, and procedures) may be related to one or more of the Organizational Elements. By classifying each model in terms of the Element with which it is concerned, one may get clues as to its results and limitations.

Chart of Needs Assessment Models*

MODEL	PURPOSE	METHODS USED	DATE EMPLOYED	MAJOR FOCUS
1. Alameda County Needs Assessment Model (ACNAM)	For school level program planning	Predetermined goals are rated on a five point scale according to perceived importance	1974	Student needs relative to program components
2. Atlanta Assessment Project (AAP)	For system planning	Delphi studies used to validate and rank order goals	1977	Student needs based on goal rankings for life in 1985
3. Battelle Needs Assessment Survey (BNAS)	For school district program planning	Participants rate perceived program status on two five-point scales	1972	Program conditions
4. Bucks County Model Quality Education Program Study (QEPS)	For school or district planning	Goals are rated on a five-point rating scale	1971	Pupil learning goals
5. CSE Elementary School Evaluation Kit (UCLA)	For school planning	106 possible goals are rated by respondent groups on a five-point rating scale	1972	School goal areas
6. Dallas Model for Shared Decision Making (DMSDM)	For budget development	Program conditions are ranked on perceived importance	1973	Program focused

7. Phi Delta Kappa (PDK)	For school program planning	Goals are rated and high priority ones are translated into performance objectives	1974	School centered from goals to programs
8. Houston Needs Assessment System (HNAS)	For school or a school system	Program priorities are identified based on discrepancies between perceived needs and current status assessments	1972	School programs and inservice training programs for professional educators
9. Institutional Goals Inventory (IGI)	Developed by ETS to help colleges and universities define goals and priorities	90 goal statements are rated on a five-point scale	unknown	Both student goals and support or process goals are enclosed
10. Needs Assessment-Social Studies Curriculum (NAIBSSCG)	Local schools districts use to improve social studies programs	Respondents indicate if statement is a high priority or not very important	1979	Program-oriented, reflects local priorities and current status of local program
11. Ohio Dept. of Education Needs Assessment (ODENA)	To help local school districts conduct a needs assessment	Respondents indicate discrepancy between actual and desired student achievement levels by ranking a need on two scales: importance and achievement	unknown	Both student goals and support or process goals are included
12. Operation SNAP (School Needs Assessment Project)	School-based focus	Opinion surveys are used with student achievement data and concerns are rated on a five point scale	1971	Program oriented

13. Sensing Educational Needs in the Far West Region (SENFR)	School- and program-based approach to prioritizing	Needs "sensing" includes four functions: sensing, analysis of resources, setting priorities, and program planning	1980	Program oriented
14. Skyline West Education Plan (SWEP)	To examine secondary school facilities and programs	Two futuristic 92 item questtionnaires are used employing a five point scale. Delphi, scenario writing, and cross impact analysis are used	unknown	Program and facilities
15. Targeting Resources for Educational Needs of the Disadvantaged (TREND)	Identifies child-oriented needs with attention to financial aspects of program planning	Child-centered concerns are identified and prioritized according to locally developed goals	1971	used to generate application for state or federal funds
16. Westinghouse Learning Corporation Educational Needs Assessment (WLCENA)	To establish a focal point to develop school district goals	Participants rate 50 goals for importance, present degree of attainment, and school responsibility	unknown	School district planning
17. Needs Assessment for Vocational Educators (VENAP)	To establish the basis for a training program for vocational educators	Uses a comprehension model to engage in a series of self-assessment inventories for vocational teachers and administrators	1980	Program level or vocational/technical school faculty

(*Hanna Mayer of the Center for Needs Assessment and Planning, Florida State University, assisted in reviewing and abstracting the Needs Assessment Models.)

Figure 7.*

	INPUTS	PROCESSES	PRODUCTS	OUTPUTS	OUTCOMES
WHAT IS	0	6	7	2	1
WHAT SHOULD BE	0	5	8	2	1

*A classification of 17 needs assessment models into the various organizational elements. Only frequencies are shown in order to reduce possible bias introduced by the analyst. Other reviewers might arrive at different classifications.

Because not all models actually dealt with "what is" and "what should be," there are some unequal numbers in "processes" and "products."

Note: There were 17 so-called needs assessments selected for study and used in arm-chair classification. There are totals of 16 for each row of this figure since one model did not have both what is and what should be dimensions.

References

Beals, R. L. "Resistance and Adaptations to Technological Change: Some Anthropological Views." *Human Factors*, December 1968, pp. 579–588.

Houston, W. R., and associates. *Assessing School/College/Community Needs*. Omaha, Nebr.: Center for Urban Education, The University of Nebraska, 1978.

Kaufman, R. *Educational System Planning*. Englewood Cliffs, N.J.: Prentice-Hall, 1972.

Kaufman, R. "Determining and Diagnosing Organizational Studies." *Group and Organizational Studies* 6 (September 1981): 312–322.

Kaufman, R. *Identifying and Solving Problems: A System Approach*. 3rd ed. La Jolla: University Associates, 1982.

Kaufman, R., and Carron, A. S. "Utility and Self-Sufficiency in the Selection of Educational Alternatives." *Journal of Instructional Development* (September 1980).

Kaufman, R., and English, F. W. *Needs Assessment: Concept and Application*. Englewood Cliffs, N.J.: Educational Technology Publishers, 1979.

Kaufman, R., and Mayer, H. "Educating for Beyond Performance and Instruction: A Pragmatic Appraisal." *Performance and Instruction* 20 (February 1981): 8–9; 12.

Kaufman, R., and Mayer, H. "Needs Assessment: A Holistic Perspective." Accepted for publication in *Revista de Technologia Educativa*.

Kaufman, R., and Stakenas, R. "Needs Assessment and Holistic Planning: An Arriving Trend." *Educational Leadership* 38 (May 1981): 612–616.

Kaufman, R., and others. "Relating Needs Assessment, Program Development, Implementation, and Evaluation." *Journal of Instructional Development* 4 (Summer 1981): 17–26.

Kaufman, R., and Thomas, S. *Evaluation Without Fear*. New York: New Viewpoints Division of Franklin Watts, 1980.

Mager, R. I. *Preparing Instructional Objectives*. 2nd ed. Belmont, Calif.: Fearon, 1975.

Maslow, A. H. *Toward a Psychology of Being*. 2nd ed. New York: Van Nostrand, 1968.

Ruesch, J. *Knowledge in Action: Communication, Social Operations, and Management*. New York: Aronson, 1975.

Roth, J. E. "Theory and Practice of Needs Assessment with Special Application to Institutions of Higher Learning." Unpublished doctoral dissertation, University of California, 1978.

Scriven, M., and Roth, J. "Needs Assessment: Concept and Practice." *New Directions for Program Evaluation* 1, 1 (Spring 1978).

Trimby, M. "Needs Assessment Models: A Comparison." *Educational Technology* (December 1979).

Witkin, B. "Needs Assessment Kits, Models, and Tools." *Educational Technology* 17, 11 (November 1977).

Chapter 6

Curriculum Planning

Arthur W. Steller

E ducators have come to recognize that very little happens by itself in an organization, other than disorder and friction. Success in education is almost never the result of sheer luck. It is, instead, the outcome of careful planning.

Realistically, educators have to develop better methods of managing instruction and resources to allow for maximum efficiency, while curriculum programs to meet the needs of all students are maintained or instituted. Tax-weary citizens and anxious parents expect schools to account for all aspects of the educational program. Curriculum planning is needed to ensure the best allocation of human and material resources toward high priority needs.[1]

School boards and lay citizens are growing in their understanding of curriculum matters and the need for improved curriculum planning. Robert Shutes demystified the topic when he wrote:

Curriculum: one of education's most misunderstood concepts. The public hears the word bandied about so much that it naturally assumes "the curriculum" is a tangible, official document (no doubt locked away in some school board office) that embodies the entire structure of the school program. I'm guessing that eight times out of ten the public is wrong in its assumption. That's because administrators and board members often *talk* as if they have a clear-cut, written curriculum when all they *really* have is a set of vague assumptions about what is being taught in their schools.[2]

Curriculum planning may be defined in various ways. This issue is complicated further because there is no single accepted definition of curriculum among educators (see following section titled First Things First). Planning is the operation that ties relations among the following factors: identification of "what is," comparison with "what should be," agreement upon needs, establishment of

[1]Arthur Steller, "Changing Conditions Necessitate Resetting of Priorities and Policies for Schools," in *Updating School Board Policies*, vol. 11, no. 3, March, 1980.

[2]Robert Shutes, "How to Control Your Curriculum," *The American School Board Journal* 168, 8 (August 1981), p. 21.

goals and objectives, setting of priorities, development of programs, and allocation of resources. Figure 1 describes this relationship.

A working definition of curriculum planning might state that it is the clarification of the current status of the prescribed educational program, deciding what that program should be, and then determining how to get there. At another level, curriculum planning should specify the opportunities for children as they

---

Figure 1. Curriculum Planning

Current Status	**Need**	**Goal**
"What is"	Gap between "what is" and "what should be"	Ideal state of "what should be"
	Program	**Objective**
	Treatment to move from current status toward goal	Acceptable state of "what should be"
	Resources	
	What is required for a program to function	

The planning relationship using a reading example would be:

Planning for a specific reading need

Current Status	**Need**	**Goal**
Fifteen percent of third graders are reading below grade level. (This is an example of needs assessment data)	The number of third graders reading below grade level should be reduced.	One hundred percent of third graders should be reading at or above grade level.
	Program	**Objective**
	The XYZ Instructional System for Reading will be implemented	Ninety percent of third graders should be reading at or above grade level as shown on next year's testing results.
	Resources	
	List of Performance Objectives; Instructional Guides; 60 minute per day study allocation per child; and so on	

advance through school. Fortunately, practicing educators are less in need of a rigorous definition than they are of good planning systems and techniques.

This chapter attempts to highlight the main elements of curriculum planning beginning with the mind set of the curriculum planner and going through the presentation of a generic curriculum planning model.

Plan to Plan

Like virtually everything else, curriculum planning ought to be very carefully introduced into an educational organization. School administrators, curriculum coordinators, teachers, and parents should have a clear understanding of what curriculum planning can and cannot do for them and the organization. Curriculum planners must decide what they wish to obtain as a result of planning; such as, improve student achievement, provide public accountability, change directions, introduce new technology and/or pedagogy, weed out poor staff performers. This thinking is called the "plan to plan." It can be extremely comprehensive and may include a formalized planning manual that has come on the heels of a rigorous analysis of organizational characteristics. William Rothschild, has delineated three guidelines for planning to plan: (a) know yourself, (b) appraise your planning resources, and (c) assess your own and your stakeholders' desires.[3]

There are advantages to written planning manuals, but informal notes based upon brainstorming sessions can serve a similar purpose. The crucial element in any plan to plan is a commitment to effective planning. In most educational organizations, curriculum planning is likely to be most successful if planning to plan proceeds quickly, informally, and with the involvement of key actors, such as the school superintendent. Thoughtful efforts at planning the plan increase the chances of developing a good curriculum plan.

Preparing the Curriculum Planner(s)

Right away, the heading of this section raises a seemingly innocent question: who are the curriculum planners? Surely teachers are curriculum planners. The assistant superintendent for curriculum and instruction obviously is a curriculum planner. And, of course, that's within the job description of the superintendent, principals, coordinators, and so on. Children and parents plan the curriculum in a way; are they curriculum planners? A case can be made that everyone could carry that title. For purposes of this discussion, the term "curriculum planner" indicates the working head of a team engaged in a defined curriculum planning project. This project could be the refinement of an existing physics course, a complete revision of a school system's curriculum, or the statewide establishment of reading standards. A curriculum planner could be an

[3]William Rothschild, *Putting It All Together* (New York: AMACOM, 1976), pp. 22–23.

elementary teacher, a general supervisor, a mathematics specialist, an assistant superintendent.

Regardless of his or her regular organizational role, a curriculum planner has undeniable obligations to this function. Foremost is being knowledgeable about the field of curriculum in general and the project under development in particular. An understanding of how to implement planning strategies in educational settings is a valuable asset to a curriculum planner, although a rare commodity.

Few persons who find themselves fulfilling curriculum planning assignments are equipped in all respects for such a formidable job. The textbook description of such an individual is awesome. Even for the well educated curriculum planner, there's the matter of staying current. It is virtually impossible to know everything that ought to be known. There is some solace in the fact that others have been in the same spot.

The available vicarious experiences of others are sufficiently rich so that a curriculum planner does not have to be a know-it-all. One does, however, have to formulate his or her own opinions of what constitutes the curriculum and how it should be organized. A good educational background and an awareness of the professional literature and research provide enough data for a curriculum planner to form a set of assumptions. These assumptions are the foundation for curriculum planning. If ratified and reinforced by those engaged on a planning team, this common ground enhances the implementation of curriculum planning.

First Things First

Curriculum is a term educators and laypersons alike often bandy about without a clearly agreed upon definition. Historically, this concept has undergone a discernible transformation throughout the last century and a half. The classical definition equated curriculum with a course of study. This view has been captured and only slightly refined by conservative educational philosophers. Arthur Bestor's position was rather representative of the latter when he stated:

> The curriculum must consist essentially of disciplined study in five great areas: (1) command of mother tongue and the systematic study of grammar, literature, and writing, (2) mathematics, (3) sciences, (4) history, (5) foreign languages.[4]

The significant departure from this traditional curriculum thinking occurred in the mid 1930s when Hollis Caswell and Doak Campbell proposed that the curriculum is "to be composed of all the experiences children have under the guidance of teachers."[5] For the next 30 years, most educational scholars utilized various derivatives of either the "curriculum as experiences" or classical

[4]Arthur Bestor, *The Restoration of Learning* (New York: Alfred A. Knopf, 1956), pp. 48–49.
[5]Caswell Hollis and Doak Campbell, *Curriculum Development* (New York: American Book Company, 1935), p. 69.

interpretations. Notable exceptions to this mainstream were the "progressives" or "open educators." Paul Goodman and John Bremer, writing in a special theme issue of the *Principal* journal, offered these two "progressive" definitions of curriculum:

> If the young, as they mature, can follow their bent and choose their topics, times, and teachers, and if teachers teach what they themselves consider important—which is all they can skillfully teach anyway—the needs of society will be adequately met; there will be more lively, independent, and inventive people; and in fairly short run there will be a more sensible and efficient society.[6]

> The alternative before us, as educators, is to create the curriculum anew in such a way that it provides the opportunity for students to learn the arts, the skills by which they can take control of their own lives. In the long run, this means that every student's curriculum is to learn how to create his own curriculum.[7]

Such a philosophy was carried further by Allen Graubard in *Free the Children* with the statement that "Obviously, there is no school subject that is essential to individual survival.[8] Not all those sympathetic to progressive educational ventures agreed with such a stance. Charles Silverman wrote "Knowing one thing is not the same as knowing another, and some things are more worth knowing than others."[9] The value of curriculum was expressed by Robert Hutchins in this manner: "A curriculum is simply a way of saving lost motion. It is an attempt to profit by the most obvious mistakes of the past and to make it unnecessary for the child to commit every last one of them all over again."[10] The formal specified curriculum cannot encompass everything that can be said to be educationally vital. Each day unanticipated classroom events give life to the concept of "the teachable moment."

> The so-called "incidental" interests of children cannot be ignored, for if they are, we miss some excellent learning opportunities. Neither can they form the chief basis for our courses. If they do, we leave out valuable material and have a hodgepodge curriculum.[11]

Nevertheless, most scholars side with Fenwick English's position that:

> A curriculum exists to enhance the probability that what is desired to occur will reoccur with the same or less effort in successive applications than when initially applied. In this sense a curriculum is a symbol of economics of scale of time, energy, and resource utilization in the schools. It is an improvement upon random occurrence or chance.[12]

Such an emphasis upon the planned nature of curriculum manifested itself through numerous definitions surfacing first in the 1950s and continuing today.

[6]Paul Goodman, "Freedom and Learning: The Need for Choice," *Principal* 7, 6 (April 1973): 39.

[7]John Bremer, "On Socializing Schools," *Principal* 7, 6 (April 1973): 59.

[8]Allen Graubard, *Free the Children* (New York: Random House, 1972), p. 228.

[9]Charles E. Silberman, *Crisis in the Classroom* (New York: Random House, 1970), p. 333.

[10]Robert M. Hutchins, "Why The Schools Must Stay," *Principal* 7, 6 (April 1973): 68–69.

[11]G. O. Blough and J. Schwartz, *Elementary School Science and How to Teach It* (New York: Holt, Rinehart and Winston, 1964), p. 41.

[12]Fenwick W. English, *Quality Control in Curriculum Development* (Arlington: American Association of School Administrators, 1978), p. 18.

The curriculum is all of the learning of students which is planned by and directed by the school to attain its educational goals.[13]

A curriculum is a plan for learning.[14]

Specifically, we define curriculum as a plan for providing sets of learning opportunities to achieve broad goals and related specific objectives for an identifiable population served by a single school center.[15]

Curriculum is a plan that describes the necessary and insufficient "means" for achieving particular learning "ends."[16]

Curriculum is . . . the planned and guided learning experiences and intended outcomes, formulated through systematic reconstruction of knowledge and experience, under the auspices of the school, for the learners' continuous and willfull growth in person-social competence.[17]

The public appetite for accountability for results through the 1970s and early 1980s has maintained and strengthened the definition of curriculum as a plan.[18] Moreover, this pressure has also affected the constantly evolving field of curriculum development.

Curriculum development . . . it is basically a plan of structuring the environment to coordinate in an orderly manner the elements of time, space, materials, equipment and personnel.[19]

In spite of all the national and local curriculum projects that have attempted to foster order out of the "patchwork curriculum," educators have only scratched the surface with respect to what should be done. The maturity of curriculum theory, let alone practice, has experienced periodic forges ahead with occasional backslides. The net gain, however, has been relatively modest, particularly when compared with the advances in other parts of society. Curriculum as a field of study or an activity of professionals can regretfully still be described as one writer did in the early 1960s:

Organizing the curriculum properly means, among other things, selecting those concepts which are vital in life, and leaving the others out. This we have not done yet. The whole system is too haphazard and indefinite.[20]

[13]Ralph Tyler, "The Curriculum Then and Now," in proceedings of the 1956 Conference on Testing Problems, (Princeton, N.J.: Educational Testing Service, 1957), p. 79.

[14]Hilda Taba, Curriculum Development: Theory and Practice (New York: Harcourt, Brace, Jovanovich, Inc., 1962), p. 11.

[15]Galen Saylor and William Alexander, Planning Curriculum for Schools (New York: Holt, Rinehart and Winston, Inc., 1974), p. 6.

[16]Daniel Tanner and Laurel Tanner, Curriculum Development: Theory Into Practice (New York: Macmillan Publishing Co., 1975), p. 45.

[17]Sydelle Ehrenberg, "The Case for Structure," Educational Leadership 34, 1 (October 1976): 48.

[18]Henry Dyer, How to Achieve Accountability in the Public Schools (Bloomington, Ind.: Phi Delta Kappa Educational Foundation, 1973).

[19]Kathryn Feyereisen, A. John Fiorino, and Alene Nowak, Supervision and Curriculum Renewal: A System Approach (New York: Appleton-Century-Crofts, 1970), p. 204.

[20]Asahel Woodruff, Basic Concepts of Teaching (San Francisco: Chandler Publishing Co., 1961), p. 102.

The degree to which curriculum should be organized and what is defined as being curriculum are thorny judgments. Yet, these are fundamental issues that must be addressed at the outset of a curriculum development effort. This is not to say that formal and precise statements of circumscription have to be hammered out and committed to paper. While such behavior may be warranted, it is only essential that as a project is begun, there be a generalized understanding by the curriculum planners. Exacting definitions can be left to the curriculum theorists,[21] at least for the time being. Children simply cannot wait until curriculum is more systematic. Curriculum planners have to wade into an inexact science.

Curricular Assumptions and Beliefs

Assumptions are part of the armor curriculum planners wear to protect themselves from the uncertainties of their profession. By taking some things for granted, planners are able to proceed without the necessity of verifying the absolute correctness of every step in curriculum development. Assumptions are vital prerequisites in the process of curriculum planning. Some assumptions may be based, if not confirmed, via educational research, while others may represent opinions or values.

Serious scholars usually prefer to use terms like "curriculum theory," "curriculum generalizations," or "curriculum principles" which imply more refinement than "assumptions." Curriculum planners often do not make such distinctions, perhaps because of the close association among terms as illustrated by this frequently quoted definition of theory: "I propose to define a 'theory' as a set of assumptions from which can be derived by purely logico-mathematical procedures, a larger set of empirical laws."[22] Experienced curriculum planners nevertheless recognize that: "The principles that exist in the field of curriculum have evolved primarily from practice rather than deductive logic. This unusual condition results from the philosophical nature of curriculum thinking."[23]

It is certainly more impressive to speak of "curriculum theory" than "curricular assumptions or beliefs," but the latter classification has more utility in curriculum planning. Curriculum theory building is in its infancy.

George Beauchamp has written: "Theory building in the field of curriculum is in somewhat of a shambles. Despite the amount of writing and talk about curriculum theory that has been put forth in the last two decades, there are no extant curriculum theories to which we can look for models."[24]

---

[21]Elizabeth Vallance, "The Practical Uses of Curriculum Theory," *Theory Into Practice* 21, 1 (Winter 1982): 4.

[22]Herbert Feigl, "Principles and Problems of Theory Construction in Psychology," in *Current Trends in Psychological Theory* (Pittsburgh: University of Pittsburgh Press, 1951).

[23]Jon Wiles and Joseph Bondi, *Curriculum Development: A Guide to Practice* (Columbus, Ohio: Charles Merrill Publishing Co., 1980), p. 7.

[24]George Beauchamp, "Curriculum Theory: Meaning, Development, and Use," *Theory Into Practice* 21, 1 (Winter 1982): 24.

Likewise, in summarizing curriculum research, Gail McCutcheon has stated: ". . . we have not synthesized it into theories. Perhaps we're getting closer, although it still appears to be piecemeal."[25]

The proliferation and complexity of educational research has made it difficult for educational planners to rely upon *agreed upon* curricular principles or generalizations. Theories are even harder to come by. Therefore, curriculum planners draw from all available sources what they believe to be true about curriculum. Such beliefs are expressed as planning assumptions.

Curriculum planners typically have used society, learners, pedagogy, subject matter, and instructional organizations as points of origin for these assumptions. Morton Alpren compiled a lengthy list of what he labeled "curriculum determiners,"[26] which includes additional influences or possibilities from which to draw assumptions. Al Schuster and Milt Ploghoft, in recognizing "The Emerging Elementary Curriculum," presented philosophies, economic conditions, sociological factors, political situations, technological developments, and psychological factors as the sources of curriculum.[27] Such areas have been the standard fare for stated assumptions.

How one believes the curriculum should be organized is also a basic assumption. The "scope and sequence" chart is the most common format, but examples of other patterns follow.

Jerome Bruner is famous for his original statement, since refined, that ". . . the foundations of any subject may be taught to anybody at any age in some form."[28] Some refer to this idea as the rationale for the "spiral curriculum."

Four kinds of curricular sequencing are offered by Charles Faber and Gilbert Shearron: simple to complex, prerequisites, whole to part, and chronological.[29]

Some educators have objected to the whole notion of curriculum sequencing. Neil Postman and Charles Weingartner wrote ". . . the sequential curriculum is inadequate because students are not sequential."[30] Lillian Stephens expressed her belief that "Not all children follow the same pattern of skill development. In fact no single sequence of instruction has been agreed upon."[31] James Moffett took this criticism further with his claim that "One error of traditional curriculum planning has been to assume that specific sequences can

[25]Gail McCutcheon, "What in the World is Curriculum Theory?" *Theory Into Practice* 21, 1 (Winter 1982): 22.

[26]Morton Alpren, *The Subject Curriculum: Grades K-12* (Columbus, Ohio: Charles Merrill Books, Inc., 1967), pp. 68–73.

[27]Albert Shuster and Milton Ploghoft, *The Emerging Elementary Curriculum* (Columbus, Ohio: Charles E. Merrill Books, Inc., 1963), p. 16.

[28]Jerome Bruner, *The Process of Education* (Cambridge, Mass.: Harvard University Press, 1961), p. 12.

[29]Charles Faber and Gilbert Shearron, *Elementary School Administration* (New York: Holt, Rinehart and Winston, Inc., 1970), p. 192.

[30]Neil Postman and Charles Weingartner, *Teaching As a Subversive Activity* (New York: Dell Publishing Co. Inc., 1969), p. 30.

[31]Lillian Stephens, *The Teacher's Guide to Open Education* (New York: Holt, Rinehart, and Winston, Inc., 1974), p. 174.

apply to all students. . . . It is stages, not ages, that are important for sequence. . . . What holds for different people is the *order*, regardless of the timing."[32]

In an attempt to address the match of curriculum materials and sequencing, Jack Frymier wrote:

If curriculum materials are smaller in size, larger in number and variable in sequence, then teachers will be able to search the system and create new and different patterns of materials for each learner. In actual practice this will mean that teachers will regularly and continuously be confronting themselves with new and unique sequences and arrangements of information and materials. They will not be bored. In fact, they will be stimulated intellectually. Curriculum materials will remain fresh and interesting to teachers as well as relevant and appropriate to learners.[33]

Curriculum Planning Should Also Include Assumptions About the Future and Curricular Politics

Over the last 15 or so years, the future has become a powerful attraction for educators and curriculum planners. Futurist Alvin Toffler contributed to educational literature and sparked interest with *Learning for Tomorrow: The Role of the Future in Education*.[34] Harold Shane has recently proposed "the derived curriculum" based upon interviewing 132 international scholars about their views of the future.[35] Until an infallible crystal ball hits the market, curriculum planners will have to invent assumptions about the future, if education is to keep up with the changing global picture.

As if there are not enough other issues, educational planners must also take into account the political conditions of the larger society. While there are more sophisticated means of monitoring political events, as a minimum, curriculum planners should produce some relevant assumptions about anticipated impacts. Glenys Unruh in another chapter of this Yearbook describes the effects of political activity upon the educational program.. Arthur Wise in his landmark work, *Legislated Learning*,[36] details the often disruptive laws that have been passed with the designated purpose of altering instructional practices. Political influences can easily push the management of instructional processes beyond the grasp of educators, as John Goodlad notes:

In periods of unusual political, economic, or social stress, curriculum change is likely to be more counter-cyclical in relation to the past, to occur rapidly, and to be led by

[32]James Moffett and Betty Jane Wagner, *Student-Centered Language Arts and Reading K-12* (Boston: Houghton Mifflin Co., 1976), p. 28.

[33]Jack Frymier, *Annehurst Curriculum Classification System* (West Lafayette, Ind.: Kappa Delta Pi Press, 1977), p. 34.

[34]Alvin Toffler, ed., *Learning for Tomorrow: The Role of the Future in Education* (New York: Random House, 1974).

[35]Harold Shane with M. Bernadine Tabler, *Educating for a New Millennium* (Bloomington, Ind.: Phi Delta Kappa Educational Foundation, 1981).

[36]Arthur Wise, *Legislated Learning*.

persons not identified with earlier curriculum change, or, for that matter, with the schools.[37]

Local school districts are not immune to politics when it comes to curriculum planning. "In a politically active community it's like treading water in a hurricane while wearing concrete boots. External pressure groups toss anchors rather than life preservers."[38] This author utilized a carefully designed plan in such a community to capitalize upon prevailing political winds to institute constructive educational change.[39] Curriculum planners should provide dynamic political leadership instead of the traditional passive role as Bruce Joyce argues:

> In the past, educational planners have been technically weak (unable often to clarify ends or engineer means) and morally or technically unable to bring about a humanistic revolution in education. . . . curriculum workers have defined themselves as helpers, not leaders, letting the community and teachers make decisions and then assisting in the implementation of those decisions.[40]

Politics has manifested itself on the school scene quite dramatically in some cases. In recent years an unprecedented number of critics have protested parts of the school curriculum and called for the censor of certain books and materials. School yards have been converted to political battlegrounds in some communities. Censorship is clearly a political issue that should be taken into consideration in curriculum planning.[41]

Obviously, developing total and sweeping assumptions for each of the areas given herein is a monstrous job. Each curriculum planner must come to grips with what he or she believes will affect the curriculum area under study and pick and choose those areas to draw from in forming assumptions. The basic question for which the curriculum planner must have some tentative answers or assumptions is given in Figure 2 with a smorgasbord of basic sources from which to invent other planning assumptions. Curriculum planners share this responsibility with the curriculum planning team as represented in the scheme depicted in Figure 3.

Selection of the Curriculum Planning Team

Many school districts, when faced with the need for a revision in a part of the curriculum, simply appoint a committee and chairperson. Then off they go

[37]John Goodlad, *The Changing American School*, 65th Yearbook of the National Society for the Study of Education (Chicago: University of Chicago Press, 1966), p. 32.

[38]Arthur Steller, "Curriculum Development as Politics," *Educational Leadership* 38, 2 (November 1980): 161.

[39]Ibid.

[40]Bruce Joyce, "The Curriculum Worker of the Future," *The Curriculum: Retrospect and Prospect*, 71st Yearbook of the National Society for the Study of Education (Chicago: University of Chicago Press, 1971), p. 307.

[41]Jack Taylor and Arthur Steller, "Curriculum Development and Censorship," *Ohio Media Spectrum* (Fall & Winter 1981): 27.

with instructions to report back in six months or so with a new curriculum guide or a recommendation for a textbook adoption or both. This approach may work. A more organized method of curriculum planning, starting with the selection of a planning team, multiplies the potentiality of a positive outcome.

Figure 2. Curriculum Planning: Basic Sources for Planning Assumptions

Basic question: In general, how should curriculum be defined, structured, designed, and sequenced?

Basic Sources for Planning Assumptions

Accreditation Standards	Principles of Learning
Administrative Structures	Professional Literature
Commercial Materials	Psychological Factors
Economic Conditions	Public Opinion
Educational Theories	Research
Expectations of Colleges	School Codes
Instructional Organization	Societal Influences
National and World Events	Sociological Factors
Nature of Learners	Standardized Tests
Pedagogy	Subject Matter
Philosophies	Teacher Competence
Political Situations	Technological Developments

Figure 3. Curriculum Planning Prerequisites

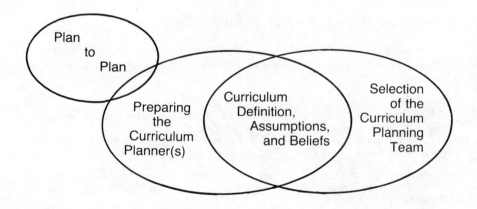

Someone must operate as the leader for a curricular planning team. For practical reasons, it seldom works well to have more than two formal leaders. Few groups accomplish much with more co-leaders. This chapter will stick to the singular and refer to this individual as the curriculum planner. Earlier it was stated that the curriculum planner may occupy an established position, such as a math coordinator, and may then be heading up this development effort for the math program. Bearing such a title is not necessary, as long as the powers-that-be have endowed the curriculum planner with the responsibility and authority.

The curriculum planner's preliminary obligations have been previously identified with a possible exception. The curriculum planner may be expected to think through and, perhaps, even prepare a written "plan to plan." The reader is reminded that the critical element here is a commitment to the curriculum planning under study. The expressed endorsement of the superintendent or another high ranking official should be secured. This promotes the idea that the organization supports the particular instructional project and builds the concept of team.

Obtaining this recognition is natural, since the vast majority of superintendents have an instructional orientation as one commented in an American Association of School Administrators' book titled, *Profiles of the Administrative Team:*

Leadership in the development of the curriculum is the prime responsibility of the superintendent. Operation of a school system without strong leadership in curriculum is potentially a detriment to the quality of education each child receives.[42]

Besides including a statement from top management, the rest of the organization will be watching for clues regarding the influence of the curriculum planner in the way the planning team is assembled. Organizational norms may be followed or broken. Either way people watch and form judgments that affect the eventual implementation. Terrence Deal and Allan Kennedy, authors of *Corporate Cultures: The Rites and Rituals of Corporate Life,* have noted that:

Every business—in fact every organization—has a culture. . . . Whether strong or weak, culture has a powerful influence throughout an organization; it affects practically everything. . . . Because of this impact, we think that culture also has a major effect on the success of the business.[43]

At times the curriculum planner has a preordained curriculum planning team. For example, in the Shaker Heights (Ohio) City School District every elementary classroom teacher volunteers for a curriculum committee, which plans the program for a particular discipline. Every school has several delegates on each committee and all grade levels are also represented. This structure ensures cross fertilization of ideas since everyone participates. It is based on

---

[42]American Association of School Administrators, *Profiles of the Administrative Team* (Arlington, Va: AASA, 1971), p. 70.

[43]Terrence Deal and Allan Kennedy, *Corporate Cultures: The Rites and Rituals of Corporate Life* (Reading, Mass.: Addison-Wesley Pub. Co., 1982), p. 4.

Rensis Likert's "linking pin" theory.[44] Each Shaker Heights elementary principal leads a committee as its curriculum planner.

If there is a choice, it is suggested the curriculum planner include on the planning team as wide a representation as can be effectively managed. The curriculum planner might select some members of his or her immediate organizational unit, of units supervised, of other units with whom he or she interacts, and, perhaps, of the community. For instance, a social studies planning team could consist of a social studies supervisor, some classroom social studies teachers, a nearby college professor or other consultant, a librarian, the student council advisor, a parent, another citizen, and a student or two. Anyone with a direct stake in the social studies program should be considered for membership on the planning team. Since every stakeholder or client cannot be accommodated, feedback could be obtained through a liaison system or survey.

In fact, some curriculum writers would prefer such indirect participation as they believe extensive involvement cannot be well managed. In their opinion massive involvement leads to frustration. William Walker puts it this way:

> The effort to involve teachers in curriculum development began in earnest about 50 years ago. Great faith was put in the idea of teachers as professionals who could and would redirect and rebuild education. Little else but faith, however, was ever really given to them. No real consistent, substantive help in their monumental task was provided by institutions of teacher preparation or school administrators at any level. Countless thousands of teachers have eventually become discouraged, angry, and depleted by having to stand alone and try to fulfill an unrealistic role as a developer of curriculum.[45]

Lorraine Sullivan feels the same way:

> Teachers at the local school level, in many cases, are not ready to accept responsibility for all instructional decisions. They have had little experience with decision making in curriculum development for which they will be held accountable. They vary in the quality of their preparation and experience for writing curriculum. It has been traditional for teachers to let others make instructional decisions about what will be taught.[46]

Perhaps this last thought has dismayed some writers, like David Selden who believes teachers should behave and be treated as professionals capable of contributing to curriculum planning.

> . . . teachers must be involved in curriculum development and revision as a professional right and obligation. . . . Teachers are professionals, or aspiring professionals, at least. . . .[47]

[44]Rensis Likert and Jane Likert, *New Ways of Managing Conflict* (New York: McGraw-Hill Book Co., 1976), p. 190.

[45]William Walker, "Education's New Movement-Privatism," *Educational Leadership* 35, 6 (March 1978): 472.

[46]Lorraine Sullivan, "Urban School Decentralization and Curriculum Development: Views and Implications," in *Impact of Decentralization on Curriculum: Selected Viewpoints* (Washington, D.C.: ASCD, 1975), p. 15.

[47]David Selden, "How Fares Curriculum in Collective Bargaining," *Educational Leadership* 33, 1 (October 1975): 28.

Likewise, the inclusion of students on a curriculum planning team is generally, but not unanimously, accepted. Harold Webb, currently an educational consultant, has written: "The decision to involve students in curriculum planning is generally advocated in the literature. However, I have yet to see a model that effectively incorporates student input into this process."[48]

Another group to consider is citizens. Adding citizens to curriculum planning teams or curriculum councils may reap substantial benefits. Delmo Della-Dora believes, "Parents and other community people can be effective and active participants in planning curriculum, carrying it out, and evaluating its effectiveness."[49]

Involving citizens, of course, also creates positive relations between the educational professionals and the community. The National School Public Relations Association has noted the practicality of such inclusion: ". . . the way to achieve the backing of parents and others in the community for the new system, experts agree, is to involve them as much as possible in the planning and implementation stages."[50]

The selection of the curriculum planning team, whether the process is open or predetermined, and the composition of the membership will send off signals to the organization and the larger environment. This delicate matter deserves a measured decision calculated to capitalize upon local culture and customs.

The overriding responsibilities of the curriculum planning team are to help define curriculum and related assumptions and beliefs, to coordinate the planning process, to make deliberate decisions, and to communicate progress. The ultimate success of many a curriculum project is determined by these factors, as well as the adherence to a curriculum planning model.

A Generic Model for Curriculum Planning

Generic planning models are inherently limited. Practitioners and theoretical planners can take cheap potshots at such models for their flaws. Generic planning models are imperfect, even when apparently explaining all phenomena. Locally designed or adapted planning models can be superior, but they, too, are never quite complete.

Generic planning models are like suits-off-the-rack. Occasionally, one can be worn without alterations. Normally, it takes a tuck here and some "letting out" there for a well proportioned fit.

Russell Ackoff, a firm believer in planning models, acknowledges their boundaries.

[48]Harold Webb, "School Boards and the Curriculum: A Case of Accountability," *Educational Leadership* 35, 3 (December 1977): 181.

[49]Delmo Della-Dora, "Parents and Other Citizens in Curriculum Development," in *Partners: Parents and Schools*, ed. Ron Brandt (Alexandria, Va.: ASCD, 1979).

[50]National School Public Relations Association Editors, "Managing Informal Schools," in *Informal Education* (Arlington, Va: NSPRA, 1972).

Ideally, the scientific planner would like to have one model that represents and explains the entire system and its environment. However, he is not yet able to construct such comprehensive models. At best, he can only construct models of parts or aspects of the system and sometimes link these together in a way that approximates an overall model.[51]

The generic model for curriculum planning presented herein has eight major stages: (1) formulation and/or review of ongoing guiding statements; (2) assessment of progress; (3) setting priorities; (4) developing goals and objectives; (5) selecting from alternatives; (6) action planning; (7) implementation; and (8) monitoring, evaluating, and recycling. These stages are pictured in Figure 4 and described in the remainder of this chapter.

It should be noted that curriculum planning includes all eight stages. When it comes to the quality or sophistication of the procedures, techniques, or tools which can be incorporated within any stage, there are no restrictions. However, *every* state must be addressed by the curriculum planning team.

Various educational planning models exist, both in theory and practice.[52] Most contain similar elements and follow somewhat similar stages, if not steps. Some planning models are rather linear, others include numerous feedback loops, and a few are even circular with multiple points of entry. What follows is a generic model for curriculum planning. As such, it has nearly universal application, but would not have the same degree of success when implemented by two or more curriculum planners. Besides differences in personal competence, each planning situation is unique. Therefore, it is suggested that

---

Figure 4. A Generic Curriculum Planning Model

Stage One: Formulation and/or Review of Ongoing Guiding Statements ←
              ↓
Stage Two: Assessment of Progress   ←
              ↓
Stage Three: Setting Priorities   ←
              ↓
Stage Four: Developing Goals and Objectives   ←
              ↓
Stage Five: Selecting from Alternatives   ←
              ↓
Stage Six: Action Planning   ←
              ↓
Stage Seven: Implementation   ←
              ↓
Stage Eight: Monitoring, Evaluating, and Recycling

---

[51]Russell Ackoff, A *Concept of Corporate Planning* (New York: Wiley-Interscience, 1970), p. 46.

[52]Arthur Steller, *Educational Planning for Education Success* (Bloomington, Ind.: Phi Delta Kappa Educational Foundation, 1980), pp. 13–20.

appropriate modifications be made to tailor this model to the nuances of particular organizations. One notable omission is the lack of an apparatus for decision making or gaining approval for proceeding to the next step. Such wide variations in these matters exist that little can be said here that would be meaningful. Some superiors require all decisions of their subordinates to be cleared along the way, while others wait for the final product.

Stage One: Formulation and/or Review of Ongoing Guiding Statements

Any organization to survive and prosper must have a clear sense of mission or purpose. Most boards of education are required to have a stated educational philosophy. These often are buried in a file cabinet and may need to be revised. Curriculum planners should push for the recognition that this formal philosophy should be used as the foundation for the instructional program. Every curriculum guide or major instructional project should make reference to the school district's philosophy and/or formulate a philosophy specific to the curriculum area being developed.

In addition to a philosophy, there are a variety of other ongoing guiding statements that should be reviewed or, in some cases, formulated, if they do not already exist. It is the function of boards of education to develop formal expressions of purpose. Writing such statements forces a board to spell out specifically what the school's job is and guides the organizational unit along intended lines. Policies, administrative guidelines, other courses of study, and goals and objectives previously approved constitute ongoing guiding statements or "what should be." The curriculum planning team needs to examine and review these "givens."

Curriculum planning occurs within the overall context defined by the society at large and the total community of the organizational unit. Federal, state, and local requirements, guidelines, and procedures provide ongoing guidance and, at times, outright encumbrances which, nonetheless, have to receive attention. Relevant documents should be collected and analyzed for their conceivable impact.

The formulation and/or review of ongoing guiding statements can become an exceedingly time consuming and psychologically draining activity, if the team attempts an exhaustive review. Therefore, it is suggested that only major items like a philosophy, significantly related laws, and required minimum standards be acquired. Of course, the process can be speeded up more if the curriculum planning team assumes it possesses sufficient knowledge of the existing ongoing guiding statements. Then, the team can concentrate upon identifying any recent major changes that might affect its planning.

Stage Two: Assessment of Progress

The present program ("what is") is the foundation upon which curriculum planning and future actions are built. Current curriculum and instructional materials should be inspected and the relationship with other programs clarified.

Where possible, progress is measured in terms of some established objective or goal. The curriculum team should evaluate the accomplishments (or lack thereof) relative to prior goals and objectives and other pertinent evaluation information. It must be noted that not all worthwhile goals are capable of precise measurement given realistic levels of resources. Evaluation of progress based upon professional judgment and on subjective factors must, therefore, be permitted in any plan of progress evaluation. The curriculum planning team should harvest an assortment of data, including opinions, appropriate to the clients (usually students) of the organizational unit doing the study.

An element often omitted from this stage of assessing progress is the identification of noteworthy programs. This may be due to the tendency of educators to engage in elaborate rites of self-flagellation. Weaknesses are usually reported by most educational institutions with more frequency than successes. By identifying any outstanding results and sharing this information, the curriculum planning team can jump off to a good start. The subsequent rising esprit de corps will lend credence to the principle that organizations improve themselves by building upon strengths.

Another source of invigoration for curriculum planning is the admission of new knowledge from beyond the immediate realm of the school district or other organizational unit. Research and promising theories should be given their due. Exemplary or novel programs or practices in the curriculum area being studied should be researched and, perhaps, visited.

Promising commerical materials should also be examined by the curriculum planning team. Educators are oftentimes loath to admit it, but commercial publishers are powerful forces when it comes to the real curriculum. Textbooks in essence can become the curriculum. Curriculum planners should concede that teachers for the most part rely heavily upon textbooks as the mainstay in their classrooms. Michael Kirst and Decker Walker have defended teachers in this regard, but acknowledge the influence of the major instructional publishers:

> The bold fact is that most teaching in our schools is and must be from a textbook or other curriculum package. We do not trust teachers to write their own materials, we do not give them the time or money, and we insist on standardization. So long as this is true, the suppliers of teaching materials will have a potentially powerful effect on the curriculum. [53]

A major problem faced by curriculum planners nowadays is deciding what not to do. All needs cannot be met. More may be presently being done than ought to be done. In such instances, the particular curriculum can be reduced or even eliminated. Determining what can be modified in this fashion can be part of a needs assessment process.

A needs assessment, broadly conceived, is a collection of information on needs which is subsequently analyzed. A wealth of literature is available on needs assessment procedures (see chapter on Needs Assessment by Roger

---

[53]Michael Kirst and Decker Walker, "An Analysis of Curriculum Policy-Making," *Review of Educational Research* (December 1971).

Kaufman). Previously compiled data should be examined as a first step in verifying needs. It is conceivable that sufficient information is already on hand to substantiate or refute a particular need without further assessment. Consequently, it is unnecessary to harvest additional data to reconfirm a need. For each need being assessed, all of the available sources of relevant documentation should be collected and reviewed.

Assessment of progress depends on an identification of unsatisfied needs. One function of a needs assessment is to strip away false perceptions and deal with reality. This is a value-laden process since it involves both "what is" and "what should be." Each statement of need must be formally assessed in order to confirm its validity. Without such an assessment, needs are merely unsubstantiated personal preferences. Then priorities must be set as to which needs will become the basis for immediate action.

Stage Three: Setting Priorities

The manner in which priorities are established is crucial to effective curriculum planning. Analyzing the collected data and determining the order of priority in relation to the overall mission is the most important aspect of doing a needs assessment. When completed by the curriculum planning team, it brings to bear the judgment of what needs are most critical to resolve. The setting of priorities should not necessarily be interpreted as ordering needs according to "the greatest good for the greatest number." For example, a need for minority or handicapped students may have a higher priority than a need relative to a larger portion of the student body. The values and insights of the members of the curriculum planning team are crystallized as they wrestle with settling upon a rank ordered listing of needs.

Resources in an organization are limited. Therefore, all of the needs identified and verified cannot likely be addressed. By focusing efforts on a few of the most prevalent and significant needs, it is expected that they can be satisfactorily resolved. Selecting some needs as targets upon which to concentrate eases the pressure of "trying to do everything and accomplishing little" or "spreading oneself too thin."

Stage Four: Developing Goals and Objectives

Following the setting of priorities, the planning team is ready to define the goals and objectives to be pursued within the given curriculum area. The definition of a need implies some means of measurement or determining what level of achievement will be necessary for resolving the need. Such standards should make it possible to know how well the gap is being closed relative to the targeted needs. The curriculum planners are well advised to have the broadest manageable involvement in gaining commitment toward the goals and objectives.

Comprehensive curriculum planning includes both long-range and short-range goals and objectives. These should be clearly related to the philosophy of the organization. Educational goals and objectives can be established at all levels of school organization and for various purposes. They are the basic building blocks for curriculum planning (see chapter entitled "Goals and Objectives"). Goals and objectives must be stated in terms of concrete and observable outcomes to address the high priority needs. Objectives stating the desired results at the end of a given length of time may be extended over a period of years by forming a progressively higher standard of achievement.

Stage Five: Selecting from Alternatives

The curriculum planning team has the arduous task of deliberating over alternative ways of reaching the agreed upon objectives. The extent and detail of the alternatives will depend on the nature of the objectives and the corresponding needs. Minor modifications in existing curricular programs may satisfy a high priority need or it may require a new program, additional staffing, etc. Slight adjustments in existing curricular programs may be sufficient to reap desired aims. Curriculum planners should adhere to the tempered adage: "If it ain't broke, don't fix it—or just fix the broke part."

The thrust of selecting from alternatives is to choose a preferred approach that appears to be best able to achieve the goals and objectives in a cost-effective way. The universe of all probable alternatives cannot be thoroughly investigated. In this stage it behooves the planning team to quickly discard unpromising alternatives. Much time can be wasted by going down dead ends and over detours. Only a few alternatives can be fully scrutinized and compared point-by-point.

As selected alternative curricular approaches are contrasted via their advantages and disadvantages, some of the factors to consider are: potential of goal achievement; cost; organizational patterns required; staffing requirements; possible outside funding; commitment of stakeholders; relationship to present programs; equipment, supplies, and materials; instructional strategies; inservice; and so on.

The curricular alternative that ought to be selected is the method deemed capable of accomplishing the desired goals in a cost-effective fashion. Making such a decision is not as easy as this abstraction makes it seem. Mistakes abound. The most vocal and aggressive member of the planning team may be able to manipulate the decision. Even after the best alternative is found, politics may infringe upon an otherwise rational process. Still the above generalized criteria are the ideal rule for this decision making.

The effort expended researching and calling out the most logical curriculum alternative pays handsome dividends. This is true even if the selected alternative cannot be realized for some reason. Good curriculum planning identifies alternative plans from which to choose. Sometimes the labors put into analyzing an alternative result in a plan superior to the original. Contingency planning has helped many a planner deal with unexpected diversions.

Stage Six: Action Planning

Action planning is the process of preparing the selected curricular alternative for implementation. Effective curriculum planning anticipates what it will take for successful implementation. Thus, the planning team accounts for key concepts in implementing curriculum projects (see chapter on Curriculum Implementation). Furthermore, at this stage the learning activities (see chapter on Learning Activities) for students or other clients are elaborated.

A consummate action plan restates the need(s), provides a plan overview, predicts the expected results, and shows the impact of the plan upon students, staff, and the community. The job title of each person designated to carry out certain objectives is designated. The costs and time frame for each goal are broken down in terms of personnel, equipment, supplies, and other factors. Possibilities for other than local funding, where such exist, are mentioned. In addition to staff salaries and supporting services, needs for supplies, materials, and contractual services (consultants, advertising, and rental costs) are specified in detail. Provisions are also made for giving travel, utility, and other fixed charges. Furniture, equipment, transportation, food services, maintenance, and facilities can be accounted for as necessary. The action planning format should provide space for listing the milestone events for each objective within a specified time frame. Responsibility for each milestone can be indicated by the job title of the person accountable for that function.

The alternative selected by the curriculum planning team will dictate the unique curriculum design to be utilized. However, later stages of curriculum planning call for evaluative feedback, which implies inclusion of student assessment procedures, a record-keeping system, and a means of reporting progress to parents and/or the public.

Stage Seven: Implementation

As stated earlier, the formal decision-making structure has not been covered in this short piece because of the great diversity of such arrangements. The perfect curriculum plan is for naught if it cannot be approved for implementation by the appropriate bodies or individuals. The curriculum planning team should be prepared for this indispensable rung on the way to implementation. The planning team has the duty to organize the actual plan for appeal to its constituents, be they teachers, parents, students, board members, or others.

Of prime concern for implementation is the issue of funding. Without money for textbooks, supplies, inservice, and so on, a curriculum plan may never really be implemented. In other words, students will not be helped by the planning team's labors unless the curriculum is related to funding requests. Curriculum plans should state how program execution can be paced to meet educational and financial requirements.

One of the first concepts that comes to mind when curriculum implementation is mentioned is inservice. Certainly the training of staff in the skills required of the new curriculum is important. But this is hardly the salient key regarding real curriculum change that is manifested in classroom performances.

If teachers participate in the determination of goals and objectives, policy-making, the appraisal of effectiveness, and inservice growth activities, they have gone a long way towards curriculum planning and change. The important principle to keep in mind here is that curriculum change is dependent upon the changes that take place in people.[54]

Dianne Common has studied the last two decades of curriculum innovation in Canada and concluded that: "Before a school begins to implement a new curriculum, it must adopt that curriculum. Adoption is not implementation. Adoption is the decision to begin to use, to implement, the curriculum."[55]

Curriculum planning incorporates this adoption phase, but goes beyond this initial aspect of implementation. Dianne Common has written: "The major function of implementation, or implementation planning, is to provide or construct a set of conditions within a school so that the instructional practices implied or prescribed by the curriculum can then occur."[56]

Stage Eight: Monitoring, Evaluating, and Recycling

Implementation of curriculum plans cannot proceed effectively without monitoring and evaluation. Tasks and responsibilities should be assigned specifically to individuals who are held responsible for the resulting outcomes. Supervisory strategies are directed at reaching the organization's goals within the confines of human relationships.

School principals and other instructional supervisors cannot ignore the perspectives of the classroom as they monitor the implementation of the curriculum plan.

Teaching is not easily separated from teaching arrangements or from the curriculum. Teaching and structural arrangements and teaching and curriculum interact and modify each other. The *curriculum in use* is a hybrid born of the stated curriculum on the one hand and the inclinations, biases, and beliefs of teachers on the other.[57]

Educational goals involve many intangibles such as character and values. In sharp contrast to business products, not all school "products" are measurable. Indeed, some of the most valuable services a school performs are not measurable at all in the scientific sense of the word. An overemphasis upon measuring *all* educational outcomes can result in what John Goodlad has labeled "The Reductionist Approach to Curriculum."[58] Attempting to measure *all* education-

[54]Roald Campbell, Edwin Bridges, John Corbally, Raphael Nystrand, and John Ramseyer, *Introduction to Educational Administration* (Boston: Allyn & Bacon, Inc., 1971). pp. 290–291.

[55]Dianne Common, "Two Decades of Curriculum Innovation and So Little Change," *Education Canada* (Fall/Autumn 1981): 43.

[56]Ibid.

[57]Thomas Sergiovanni, "Introduction," in *Supervision of Teaching* (Alexandria, Va.: ASCD, 1982), p. vii.

[58]John Goodlad, *The Dynamics of Educational Change: Toward Responsive Schools* (New York: McGraw-Hill Book Co., 1975), pp. xii–xiii.

al competencies carries with it the danger of producing an unbalanced curriculum, as Elliot Eisner warns:

> I believe the current emphasis on the production of measurable competencies in the three R's is creating an unbalanced curriculum that will, in the long run, weaken rather than strengthen the quality of children's education.[59]

Nevertheless, it is imperative that schools conduct performance evaluations if they are to be held accountable for a preponderance of their mandated objectives. Evaluation must be based on explicitly stated goals and objectives that are consistent with the philosophy of the organization. A well-monitored and evaluated curriculum plan will detect mistakes and successes which can lead to decisions to recycle the plan or terminate it. The curriculum planning team should construct an evaluation model (see chapter on Curriculum Research and Evaluation) to ensure that the curriculum is upgraded past initial implementation. Curriculum planning should be a continuous, ongoing process embracing all spheres of educational interests. A curriculum plan, therefore, is not a final report, but an interim report.

Concluding Remarks

Curriculum planners are encouraged to use the generic planning model just presented as a springboard for creating their own planning process. There is no single curriculum planning model suited to all situations. Planning is an art, due to the fact that people defy being confined to boxes on a chart. Curriculum planning models must be designed to fit unique characteristics. Ultimately, all curriculum planners must rely on their personal experiences as a guide to the assumptions they make about curriculum planning.

Curriculum planning must proceed at the same time that students are being taught, teachers are being evaluated, and buildings are being cleaned. Unlike the ideal textbook case on curriculum planning, educators must plan in an extremely complex environment. Ron Brandt describes the plight rather well.

> *Comprehensive* curriculum planning takes time and money. It cannot be undertaken by individual teachers or schools. Even most school districts lack resources to do the whole job. Agencies with sufficient resources to attempt it may include states, intermediate agencies, voluntary consortia, or regional laboratories. At these levels, the involvement of people in appropriate ways does not happen naturally; it must be provided for.[60]

While I believe local school districts can pursue productive curriculum planning, it definitely does not transpire by itself. What is needed is planning based on good judgment, open communication, and proper timing. Furthermore, curriculum planning cannot afford to stray too far from the practical needs of users. Curriculum planning, regardless of how brilliantly structured the model, is a failure if it does not result in improved learning opportunities for students.

[59]Elliot Eisner, "The Impoverished Mind," *Educational Leadership* 35, 8 (May 1978): 615.
[60]Ron Brandt, "Who Should Be Involved In Curriculum Development," *Educational Leadership* 34, 1 (October 1976): 11.

Chapter 7

Curriculum Design

George A. Beauchamp

People cannot intelligently discuss and communicate with others about curriculum without first making very clear what their interpretation of a curriculum is. In this chapter, we will be thinking of a curriculum as a written plan for the educational program of a school or schools. Curriculum design then will consist of those considerations having to do with the contents, the form, and the arrangement of the various elements of a curriculum. We distinguish between curriculum planning and instructional planning with curriculum planning being the antecedent task.

Curriculum planners are forced to make design decisions almost from the outset of their work. The design decisions revolve around three important considerations: (1) the range of school levels and schools to be covered by the curriculum, (2) the number of elements to be included in the curriculum, and (3) the nature and scope of each of those elements. Each of these requires additional explanations.

Decisions about the range of school levels and schools to be covered by the curriculum normally are not very complicated, and the range usually coincides with the sphere of authority of the board of education. Districts may elect to plan a curriculum from kindergarten through grade 12; they may elect to plan one curriculum for the elementary schools and one for the secondary schools; or they may elect to direct each school unit to plan its own curriculum.

Planning groups will have to decide about the number of elements to be included in the curriculum. Among the options for inclusion are: (1) a statement of goals or purposes, (2) a statement of document intent and use, (3) an evaluation scheme, and (4) a body of culture content selected and organized with the expectancy that if the culture content is judiciously implemented in classrooms through the instructional program, the goals or purposes for the schools will be achieved. To this list, some would add suggested pupil activities, instructional materials, and so forth, but these matters belong more rightfully in the domain of instructional planning and we will not consider them here. A few comments about each of these four elements will be helpful to the reader in understanding their import for curriculum decisions.

Most curriculum writers would agree that it is desirable to include a statement of goals or purposes to be achieved by schools through the implementation of the planned curriculum. They may disagree as to what the goals ought to be, or they may disagree about the degree of specificity of the statements to be included. The most famous statement of goals or purposes for schools became known as the Seven Cardinal Principles of Education as formulated by the Commission on the Reorganization of Secondary Schools in 1918. They were: health, command of the fundamental processes, worthy home membership, vocation, civic education, worthy use of leisure, and ethical character.

There is less consistency among curriculum writers in terms of their insistence upon including a statement of document intent and use in a curriculum, and in practice many curricula do not contain such statements. Curricula have, in the past, contained statements intended to reveal the philosophy or point of view of the planners, but this is not what we mean by a statement of document intent and use. A statement of document intent and use should be forthright and direct about such matters as: (1) how teachers are expected to use the curriculum as a point of departure for developing their teaching strategies, (2) the fact that the curriculum is the official educational policy of the board of education, (3) the degree of universality in expectancy with regard to the discretion of teachers in implementing the curriculum, and (4) the degree to which teachers are to be held accountable for the implementation of the curriculum. These are illustrative of the kind of statement that may be formulated, but each planning group will have to decide on the number and character of such statements.

With the amount of emphasis put upon curriculum evaluation in recent years, some mandate with respect to the curriculum evaluation is a very reasonable option for inclusion in a curriculum. The most common method of pupil evaluation used in the past has been the standardized (norm referenced) achievement test. In most cases, there were no deliberate attempts to relate published curricula and the test batteries. Therefore, any leap in assumption about the directness of the relationship between curriculum content and whatever was measured by the tests was likely to be untenable. All the more reason for formalizing an evaluation scheme by including it in the curriculum.

In one form or another, a curriculum must include a body of culture content that has been deemed by the planners and directing authorities to be important for schools to use in fulfilling their roles as transmitters of culture to the oncoming generations of young people. The basic curriculum question is, and always has been, that of what shall be taught in schools, and a major function of a curriculum is to translate the answer to that question into such forms that schools can fulfill their commitment and demonstrate that they have done so. Most of the remainder of this chapter is devoted to discussion of this element of a curriculum; so we will leave it at this point. But it should be made clear that from these options as potential elements of a curriculum, there emerge two dimensions of curriculum design. One is the choice of and the arrangement of the elements to be included in the curriculum. The other is the form and arrangement of the contents of each of the elements internally. The design problem is greatest in the case of the form and arrangement of the culture content, and it is the one most frequently discussed under the heading of curriculum design by curriculum writers past and present.

Culture Content—Knowledge—Curriculum Content

A curriculum is an expression of the choice of content selected from our total culture content and, as such, it is an expression of the role of the school in the society for which the school has been established to serve. A word needs to be said here about the meaning associated with the expression "culture content." Ralph Linton provided us with a classical and very useful definition of "culture." He stated: "A culture is the configuration of learned behavior and results of behavior whose component elements are shared and transmitted by the members of a particular society" (1945, p. 32). The term "society" is ordinarily used to refer to a group of individuals who live together with common norms and shared frames of reference. Societies tend to generate their own culture and to transmit that culture to oncoming generations within that society. So long as societies and their cultures remained in a primitive state, their cultures were simple and could be transmitted to oncoming generations by direct contact between the young and the older members of the society. But as societies became more complex and the scope of their culture content increased so that the transmission of the culture content to the young could no longer be accomplished by direct contact in daily living, societies were forced to create institutions to take on the responsibility for all or part of the cultural transmission task. The school is one of those institutions. The church is another. Both of these institutions have unique roles to play in society, and they tend to transmit different culture content to the young. Parochial schools tend to do both.

As Smith indicated in Chapter 3 of this Yearbook, the culture content selected to be included in the curriculum of the school may be thought of as equivalent to the knowledge to which school students are to be exposed. In any case, it is critically important to be aware that not all culture content, or knowledge, accumulated by society comes under the purview of the school; curriculum planning is a process of selecting and organizing culture content for transmission to students by the school. The process is very complex, involving input from many sources, but the organized end-result of the process is the design of the curriculum.

The most sophisticated mode of organization of culture content for purposes of teaching is reflected by the various disciplines such as history, chemistry, or mathematics. In addition to the established and recognized disciplines, school subjects have been created out of conventional wisdom or the applications of selected portions of the disciplines to applied areas of our culture such as vocational subjects, social studies, or reading and handwriting. In general, the separate subject organization of culture content has predominated in curriculum design.

Another way of speaking about curriculum content is to refer to cognitive content, skill content, and value or attitudinal content. As Smith discussed more fully in Chapter 3, all three types of content represent knowledge in some form, either in the form of direct knowledge or a knowledge base. The three forms have been used as a classification scheme or a taxonomy for curriculum content formulation.

Historic Curriculum Design Conflicts

One must realize that the basic curriculum question is, and always has been, one of what shall be taught in the schools. An immediate corollary to that question has been that of how shall what has been chosen to be taught in the school be organized so as to best facilitate the subsequent decisions about teaching and learning. Those two questions are the primary curriculum questions, and the organized decisions made in response to them culminate in a curriculum design. A few reflections about our curriculum past will illustrate some of the conflicts in curriculum design that have taken place.

In her study, Sequel observed that curriculum as we use the term today was not a subject of professional discussion until after 1890 (1966, p. 1). Rugg contended that decisions about curriculum content prior to the 20th century were decided primarily by textbook writers and textbook publishers (1926, pp. 10–11). It was not until 1918 that Bobbitt wrote the first definitive work on curriculum, and since that time curriculum writers have directed their attention to the substance and organization of curriculum content (curriculum design) and to the processes of curriculum planning, implementing, and evaluating.

By the early 1900s, the stage had been set for the separate subjects organization of the culture content to be used in schools. In our very early elementary or primary schools, for example, pupils were taught to read, to write, and to compute; the subjects were called reading, writing, and arithmetic. Much later such subjects as geography, history, and civics were added to the curriculum. In our early secondary schools, pupils were taught a selection of subjects (disciplines) that were directly associated with the disciplines taught in the college or university. Even though the separate subjects organization of culture content was used before curriculum became an area of professional study, it is still with us. True, subjects have been added and others altered, but it remains the dominant approach to curriculum design.

The separate subjects mode of curriculum design has been significantly challenged only once in our history. That challenge came with the advent of the Progressive Education movement. A principal feature of the Progressive Education movement was its dramatic emphasis on the learner in school settings. A substantial portion of the Progressive emphasis on the learner was stimulated by John Dewey's (1916) call for more active and less passive learning in schools. This focus on the learner when applied to the organization of curriculum content led to endeavors to move away from the separate subjects organization of the curriculum content. The movement away form the separate subjects organization (sometimes called subject-centered) was toward the integration, or fusion, of subjects under the assumption that such integration would not only facilitate learning on the part of pupils but would additionally make the knowledge, skills, and attitudes more easily available to the pupils in post-school life (the transfer problem).

The basic process involved here was the fusion of the contents of two or more of the separate subjects into another organization in which the individual subjects lost their separate identities. As one might expect, names were associated with the various integration or fusion attempts. Figure 1 adapted from Hopkins (1941, p. 18) illustrates the variety of names associated with curricula resulting from integrative or fusion processes. Hopkins here polarized the subject curriculum and the experience curriculum. The broad fields curriculum was placed in the center so as to show that it had a reasonable number of the characteristics of the two extremes. Others are indicated on either side depending on emphasis.

Figure 1. A Scale of Types of Curriculums

Subject Curriculum	Integrated Correlated Fused Coordinated Core	Broad Fields (1) Subject Type (2) Experience Type	Coordinated Core Integrated Unit of Work Functions of Social Life	*Experience Curriculum*

Source: L. Thomas Hopkins, *Interaction: The Democratic Process* (Boston: D. C. Heath and Company, 1941), p. 18.

Space in this volume will not permit extensive description of curricula developed as part of the efforts to move away from separate subjects organization. The best we can do here is to identify some of them and cite sources for further investigation on the part of the reader. For example, in their book *The Child-Centered School*, Rugg and Shumaker (1928) presented brief descriptions of the curricula of the Lincoln School, The Frances Parker School, and others of that time. In most cases, the curricula were built around child-centered units of work, but attention was focused as needed on such basic subjects as reading, mathematics, history, geography, and so forth.

One of the most extreme departures from separate subjects organization was proposed by Stratemeyer and others (1957). The authors proposed the "persistent life situations" concept as a basis for dealing with the curriculum building issues of scope, sequence, continuity, balance, and depth.

At the junior and senior high school levels, special mention should be made of the core curriculum. The core curriculum idea was to get away from nothing but the discipline-centered curriculum. Most core programs were organized around larger and more flexible blocks of time, and the content was generally centered on personal and social problems and problems of living. In many respects the core curriculum idea was an attempt to solve the general education problem in our upper schools.

It is important to note that in practice in schools, curriculum design failed to get very far away from the subject- or discipline-centered design. The most lasting effect of the movement was the broad fields idea as represented by social studies, language arts, and general science, and they have persisted mostly in curricula for elementary and junior high schools.

Contemporary Arguments About Curriculum Design

Probably the most persistent movement in curriculum design in recent years has been the proposed use of specific behavioral objectives as a basis for curriculum organization. Curriculum writers have long proposed that curricula ought to contain statements of goals or objectives, but not as the only content of a curriculum. Some contemporary writers have proposed that curricula should be thought of in terms of the anticipated consequences of instruction, or intended learning outcomes. (For example, see Popham and Baker, 1970; Johnson, 1977). The culture content in such cases would either be implied in the objectives or be considered as an insructional decision. A distinct advantage of this type of curriculum design is that supervision of the implementation and of the evaluation of the curriculum is simplified and facilitated.

Such proposals are in direct contrast to a proposal that a curriculum should be composed in four parts: (1) a statement of goals, (2) an outline of the culture content that has the potential for reaching the goals, (3) a statement of the intended use of the curriculum, and (4) a schema for the evaluation of the curriculum (Beauchamp, 1981, p. 136). They are in even greater contrast to those who would include instructional considerations such as suggested activities for learners and instructional materials to be used. Curriculum planners should be warned that the inclusion of all of these things produces fat and unmanageable curricula.

With respect to the culture content of curricula, two organizational concepts persist both in the literature and in the practice of writing curricula. The first is the tendency to continue with the basic framework of the subjects, or disciplines, that are to be taught. The second is to break the subject areas down into three identifiable components: (1) cognitive, (2) inquiry and skill, and (3) affective (value, moral, attitudinal).

Curriculum planners will probably wish to begin their thinking about design with the familiar, which will unquestionably be the conventional school subjects. They will consist of mathematics, social sciences (including social studies as a subject), the natural sciences, fine and applied arts, health and physical education, communications, and other languages. At the secondary school level, planners will add to these whatever vocational and technical subjects they may wish to offer. Some planners will wish to add an area that may be termed social problems, molar problems, or problems of living that may call for applications of elements learned in various conventional subjects.

Curriculum planning is an educative process. For this reason classroom teachers should be involved in the undertaking. A very important reason for their involvement is that the process of curriculum planning presents an opportunity for them to engage in analysis of the culture content so that they may be more effective in their classrooms at the level of instruction. The analytic process of breaking down the culture content into cognitive, affective, and inquiry and skill components is one way that teachers may become more knowledgeable about what they do. Also in this process of analyzing the culture content, the content is more specifically related to goals and at the same time it fosters better curriculum implementation. For these reasons, teachers' participation in curriculum deliberations has been proposed frequently as a needed dimension of continuous teacher education.

In Chapter 3, Smith raised the very important question of the utility of the culture content selected to be part of the curriculum content, and he posed several ways in which the utility of knowledge can be emphasized. In a more specific vein, Broudy, Smith, and Burnett (1964) suggested four potential uses of learnings acquired in school to be taken into consideration. They are the associative use, the replicative use, the applicative use, and the interpretive use (pp. 43–60). Very briefly, the associative use of knowledge refers to the psychological process of responding to a new situation with elements of knowledge previously acquired. The replicative use refers to situations that call for direct and familiar use of schooling such as when we read a newspaper, write a letter, or balance a checkbook. The applicative use occurs when an individual is confronted with a new problem and is able to solve the new problem by the use of knowledge acquired in the study of school subjects or through previous experience in solving problems demanding similar applications. The interpretive use of schooling refers to the orientation and perspective the individual brings to new stiuations because the individual has acquired ways of conceptualizing and classifying experience.

Much of the discussion about uses of schooling (especially use external to the school) is an elaboration of the transfer problem that has plagued educators ever since Edward L. Thorndike first set forth his theory of transfer through the existence of identical elements in 1908. The most easily explained is the replicative use as described above because of the direct similarity between the use external to the school and the mode of learning and practice in school. Take reading for example. Reading from school materials is directly similar to reading of materials outside the school. But when it comes to applying knowledge or making new interpretations or associations between knowledge acquired in school and life situations external to schools, a more complicated transfer situation exists.

Unfortunately, many of the questions raised about utility and uses of schooling have not been answered through curriculum design. Nor are they likely to be because so much is dependent upon classroom teaching technique and the design of instructional strategies. The best efforts in curriculum design have been through the generation of new courses (subjects if you please) in which the content is purportedly more like life external to the school. Reference here is made not only to specialized courses such as technical, vocational, commercial, and occupational courses but also to courses designed around molar problems, problems of living, and core programs. In many respects, the broad fields courses were designed for purposes of saving time during the school day and to facilitate the transfer of knowledge acquired. But whatever the curriculum design, if teachers are not aware of and sensitive to the kind of analyses of the content to be taught as we have been discussing it, the uses of schooling will not be maximized. All the more reason why teachers should be part of the curriculum planning effort and participate in the required dialogue.

In summary, then, what courses of action with respect to curriculum design appear to be the most appropriate for today's curriculum planners? The most important aspect of curriculum design is the display to be made of culture content once the content has been selected. The total amount of culture content is constantly growing thus making the problem of selection for curriculum content more difficult as time goes on. Unquestionably, the role of those schools (elementary and secondary) that operate under compulsory school attendance laws must constantly be examined in terms of what they should or should not offer in their curricula. The elementary school curriculum has always been designed with general education in mind. In our contemporary society, the secondary school seems to be moving in that same direction. Both, however, have seen fit to divide the content selected into realms or courses as appropriate.

Scope and sequence have long been two major problems in curriculum design. The display of course content into topical outline is one way planners can watch for discrepancies in scope and sequence. It also helps with horizontal articulation among the various subjects.

To help teachers generate greater insight into the content outline, it is desirable that the curriculum design reveal the expected cognitive, inquiry or skill, and affective outcomes. These are conventionally arranged in the design of the content in parallel with the topics in the outline. How behaviorally the outcomes are to be stated is optional to the planners. These outcomes should also be thought of in terms of any goals or purposes that may be stated in the curriculum.

What else to include in the design is optional to the planners. It has become quite conventional to think of goals or purposes first and then to select the content. Such procedure is quite arbitrary because all content is selected with some purpose in mind. Nonetheless, a statement of goals and purposes is a useful element in curriculum design.

I would add to the topic outline and the expected outcomes a directive statement about the intended use to be made of the curriculum and a statement outlining a scheme for evaluating it.

References

Beauchamp, George A. *Curriculum Theory*. 4th ed. Itasca, Ill.: Peacock, 1981.

Bobbitt, Franklin. *The Curriculum*. Boston: Houghton Mifflin, 1918.

Broudy, Harry S.; Smith, B. Othanel; and Burnett, Joe R. *Democracy and Excellence in American Secondary Education*. Chicago: Rand McNally, 1964.

Dewey, John. *Democracy and Education*. New York: Macmillan, 1916.

Hopkins, L. Thomas. *Interaction: The Democratic Process*. Boston: Heath, 1941.

Johnson, Mauritz. *Intentionality in Education*. Albany, N.Y.: Center for Curriculum Research and Services, 1977.

Linton, Ralph. *The Cultural Background of Personality*. New York: Appleton-Century-Crofts, 1945.

Popham, W. James, and Baker, Eva L. *Systematic Evaluation*. Englewood Cliffs, N.J.: Prentice-Hall, 1970, p. 48.

Rugg, Harold, Chairman. *Curriculum-Making: Past and Present*. 26th Yearbook of the National Society for the Study of Education, Part I. Bloomington, Ill.: Public School Publishing Co., 1926.

Rugg, Harold, and Shumaker, Ann. *The Child-Centered School*. New York: World Book Co., 1928.

Seguel, Mary Louise. *The Curriculum Field: Its Formative Years*. New York: Teachers College Press, Columbia University, 1966.

Stratemeyer, Florence B.; Forkner, Hamden L.; McKim, Margaret G.; and Passow, A. Harry. *Developing a Curriculum for Modern Living*. 2nd ed. New York: Bureau of Publications, Teachers College, Columbia University, 1957.

Chapter 8

Curriculum Politics

Glenys G. Unruh

Political astuteness is an indispensable qualification for curriculum leaders and developers. Naiveté about the politics of education or willful disregard of formal and informal power centers are out of place today. Curriculum decision making takes place in a complex political milieu. It requires expertness, political awareness, and a continuing dialogue among the decision makers for resolution of conflicts and agreement on major goals.*

Historically educators were thought to be apolitical and the public was encouraged to view education as a "professional" activity to be taken care of by professional educators and their local school boards. This ostrich-like posture became more and more inappropriate over the years and would now be considered a mark of incompetence and ineffectuality.

A number of years ago, Kimbrough's studies of community power (1964) recognized the significance of political influence in educational decision making. He noted that educational training programs for school administrators had not included systematic empirical knowledge about the nature of the power forces and decision making processes in local school districts. Consequently, many educational leaders had been reluctant to acknowledge that a considerable amount of political activity was going on in addition to the observable formal meetings of school boards, committees, and faculties.

Previous studies by Counts (1972), Morphet and others (1959), and Callahan (1962) had warned educators of their domination by business interests. Callahan said that he was not surprised to find business practices used in schools but was surprised to find the extent and degree of capitulation by school administrators to demands made on them; to learn how decisions were made, not on educational grounds, but as a means of appeasing their critics (Preface). Business interests have not been the only threat of "outside" influence on educational policy making.

*The politics of education refers to the influence of government, other agencies, power groups, or individuals on the process of making educational decisions based on the allocation of values in education.

Other illustrations of problems that have arisen and how school boards have reacted to them are provided by Hurlburd (1961), Masotti (1967), and Bendiner (1969), who explored in depth the positive and negative experiences of various cities and towns that have tried to meet or evade their challenges: integration, community control, academic freedom, teacher power, planned change, and location of a new high school building. A major study of the politics of education, the impact on school programs, and the sources of demands that impinge on the process of educational decision making is provided by Scribner and others (1977). Issues continue to arise, particularly in communities whose populations are diverse, and consequently educators' needs for political skills have been intensified.

Today, issues revolving around the schools are featured by the news media. Constant information is provided on the activities of special interest groups and new legislation and court decisions affecting schools. Beyond the formal board and professional sessions are informal meetings of concerned citizens and protest groups, telephone networks, and gathering of signatures on petitions. Board members and educators are required not only to be aware and sensitive to problems but to be involved in their solutions.

Each community is different; there is no exact model for explaining the power and decision-making phenomena that fits all. However, it is important that the informal power system of the local school district be recognized as functioning interactively with the formal legitimized power structure as established by law, regulation, and standard procedure. It is important that curriculum developers use problem-solving skills and that students learn problem-solving skills so they will be equipped to meet problems as they come along.

The Changing Scene

This is a time in which many individuals are supercritical, even cynical about the schools. This has come about as greater and greater hopes and expectations have been pinned on education and as more people are affected by the educational process. More people are seeking to participate in decision making. A main conclusion of a survey by the NIE Curriculum Development Task Force was that the classic curriculum questions of what shall be taught and how shall educational programs be organized were overshadowed by the desire to be involved. This desire was accompanied or perhaps motivated by a feeling of impotence and by the view that "someone else" was in control (1976).

Pressures on curriculum developers accelerated sharply during the 1950s with renewed emphasis on academic excellence and revision of subject matter. This gave way during the 1960s to pressure on schools to serve as agents for social reform. Demands for attention to disadvantaged minorities reached a crescendo in the 1970s with new attention to racial minorities, handicapped children, non-English-speaking students, and feminist interests. Accountability for results in terms of student achievement moved to the public arena. This brought about numerous federal and state laws that now impinge on if not control much of what is done in the school's curriculum.

Legislators at both the federal and state levels have concerned themselves not only with educational achievement, desegregation, affirmative action, due process standards, and equal educational opportunities but also have become involved with single interest advocacy groups.

Local school boards have frequently found themselves hemmed into narrow decision zones in some matters as a result of centralized and legalized pressures from federal and state legislatures, courts, and agencies. Governmental authority stems from multiple power centers, not from a single control point; thus, school boards often find themselves dealing simultaneously with a range of requirements and regulations. In addition, local school board meetings are frequently opportunities for indignant citizens or special interest groups to express themselves and may range from orderly forums to shouting matches that can bring a meeting to a state of pandemonium.

In addition, organized teachers groups are becoming highly expert in bargaining for their interests, especially salaries, fringe benefits, hours, and working conditions, with curriculum implications on the horizon. Advocated are proposals such as smaller class sizes, more preparation time, and additional help for children and youth with equal opportunity needs (Shanker, 1979). Caution, expressed by Lieberman (1979), emphasizes that the activities of teachers unions are generally limited to the interests of members, not public interest considerations.

However, a position paper of the National Education Association sets forth its beliefs about a strengthened future role for teachers in curriculum decisions. NEA advocates central involvement of teachers in curriculum planning and staff development programs underwritten by school districts to help teachers acquire curriculum development skills (1980, pp. 23–27).

School board members have found, in dealing with pressures from varied groups, that they must increasingly enlist expertise on their side, especially legal counsel. They must depend more and more on the superintendent and the superintendent's staff for gathering relevant information. School boards also need access to higher levels of government through lobbyists and representatives.

Nevertheless, within this complex political setting, school boards, as policy making bodies, can make it possible or impossible to open a curriculum dialogue with the professional staff, parents, other community members, and students. Boards have the power to initiate processes for formulating meaningful educational goals for the district and to set priorities supported by adequate resources. From the more general goal statements, the professional staff should formulate specific objectives and instructional plans, follow through, and report evaluative data to the board for further curriculum decisions.

What are the spheres of power of governmental levels and publics who are affecting curriculum decisions? What are some of the effects on school programs of increased political activity? What barriers or constraints must be taken into account by curriculum developers and what positive forces can be utilized?

Federal Influence

Although the U.S. Constitution has not given Congress explicit authority to control the school program, Congress has found ways to do so by taxing and spending on behalf of education and then attaching conditions to its grants to schools that must be met in order to continue to receive federal money. Congress has exercised its power to influence school programs by providing categorical grants for programs for the educationally disadvantaged, the handicapped, bilingual students with limited English-speaking ability, for the development of curriculum materials in science, math, environmental education, and ethnic studies. Funds have been provided to help schools purchase materials and equipment for selected courses. Vocational education has enjoyed support for many years. Other funds have been available to help districts plan desegregation efforts and for educational programs that are designed to reduce racial isolation of students and the consequent educational disadvantages. Money has been given to schools for improvement of the teaching of reading, for the arts, preschool education, career education, consumer education, special attention to gifted children, and for school library materials.

Although current trends are toward less federal spending for education, consolidation of dozens of programs into block grants, and toward more control by state and local governments, several federal programs have had an unusually strong impact on the curriculum of the schools (van Geel, 1979). Federal regulations that prohibit discrimination on the basis of race or sex have forced far-ranging changes in school organization and policy through regulations and guidelines for local districts that were developed by the Office of Civil Rights and the Department of Health, Education, and Welfare. Schools that failed to observe these regulations could lose financial assistance from the federal government—a loss schools could not afford.

As federal and state governments increased their regulations for public education, the courts became more and more involved in school issues. Lawyers and courts, although claiming no special expertise in professional education, were called on to resolve various school problems. Generally, these have been problems that relate to basic rights set forth in the First and Fourteenth Amendments to the U.S. Constitution and similar provisions in state constitutions. These can be roughly classified as matters pertaining to race, distribution of wealth to schools, and individual freedoms. The main interest of the courts has been to enforce minimum constitutional requirements and ensure at least a minimally adequate public school program for all students. Thus, in several ways, constitutionally required programs are emerging from the courts (see Hooker, 1978).

There is no question that federal courts have directed major efforts toward increasing the integration of minority students. Almost every school in the country with a racially heterogeneous student body has had to develop an integration plan and many school districts have been involved in litigation over racial integration, particularly when busing was required. Although the busing issue has been volatile in some localities, it has not been a failure according to a Harris Poll (1981). Findings were that 54 percent of the parents whose children were bused as part of an effort to achieve racial balance found the experience "very satisfactory," 33 percent found it "partly satisfactory," and only 11 percent found it unsatisfactory. Nineteen percent of American families have been involved in busing for racial integration.

The passage of Public Law 94-142, the federal Education for All Handicapped Children Act of 1975, has had a dramatic impact on the operation and administration of public schools. Curriculum and services must now be provided for children with severe to mild handicaps, children who until recently were almost never found in the public schools. A thorough diagnosis of each child's strengths and weaknesses is required followed by sessions involving the parent and specialists for planning the child's Individual Educational Program (IEP). Appropriate programming must follow and the child must be reevaluated periodically followed by necessary changes or advancements in the child's program (Orelove, 1978, pp. 699–702).

Implementation of bilingual education became a national issue after the Supreme Court ruled in Lau v. Nichols, a class action suit, that failure to provide non-English-speaking Chinese students with special instruction denied them a meaningful opportunity to participate in the public education programs and thus violated Section 601 of the Civil Rights Act of 1964 and its federal regulations and guidelines. (See Zirkel, 1978, for this and other Supreme Court decisions affecting education.) Disagreements at the cabinet level on the degree to which federal regulations should control the specific methods for providing bilingual education in local districts were resolved by delegating responsibility to local school boards.

The broader significance to the changed legal scene in regard to the school's program is the expansion of the concept of equal educational opportunity. Intervention by the federal government and courts came about to assist students whom local school boards had tended to neglect in the past.

The apparent preoccupation of federal and state governments with the rudiments of education should not deter curriculum leaders from also attending to the substantive content of the whole curriculum and to the development and stimulation of students' talents—intellectual, social, aesthetic—at all academic levels. Local and state governments are expected to assume more and more responsibility as federal funding decreases. While continuing to keep the pressure on for equalizing educational opportunities, curriculum developers are expected to increase their emphasis on *effective* school programs.

Over the past two decades astronomical sums of money have been poured into developmental and innovative approaches to teaching and learning. Millions of students, teachers, and supervisors have been involved in federally funded programs. Millions of reports, research studies, curriculum guides, and lesson plans have been written. Films and videotapes have been made. Sites to be visited and observed and programs to be transplanted are available. What have been the successes? The failures? It behooves curriculum decision makers to find out what works, what doesn't, and in what settings. Information is being published. An example of an analysis of successes and failures is the Rand study of the implementation of reading improvement programs (Berman and McLaughlin, 1978, and Wood and others, 1981). Stressed was the importance of job-embedded inservice in which teams engage in the study of one another's teaching and carry out the coaching element within school time and environment.

That teachers must be involved in curriculum development if the end product is to be used successfully in the classroom was one of the basic findings of a large scale study of the effect of the federally and foundation-funded curriculum reforms in science, mathematics, and social sciences of the 1960s and 1970s (National Science Foundation, 1979). Predicted changes in teaching techniques and content did not often take place when teachers were expected to bridge the gap from summer institutes and printed manuals to actual practice without further assistance. The NSF report provides ample suggestions for correcting this situation.

Efforts directed toward improvement of students' writing abilities are beginning to attract attention. The Bay Area Writing Project (Applebee, 1981), which features holistic scoring and frequent writing by students, is being adapted in numerous school districts. Also, the National Assessment of Educational Progress' Third National Writing Assessment (1981) concluded that if specific writing assignments are not included in the school curriculum, they should be and supervisors should make sure that writing techniques are taught.

Title I (compensatory education) has taught educators how to develop individual educational programs for educationally disadvantaged children, to evaluate seriously, and use the data annually for upgrading and improving their Title I programs. This has produced a management style for curriculum workers that was foreign to most schools of the past.

In the arts and aesthetics fields there are indications that creative thinking and resourcefulness have been unleashed through stimulation of federal funds that may continue to have impact on curriculum even though federal financing decreases. An illustration is a part-time enrichment program for public school students in St. Louis and St. Louis County, Missouri, which will use 11 city arts and other cultural institutions for activities designed to bring city and suburban students together. About 3,000 students from different schools are expected to meet in integrated groups about two hours a week for eight weeks at the various sites for arts and aesthetics studies. A privately financed creative venture in cable television, the Alpha Repertory Television Service (ARTS) offers schools as well as homes a range of arts-related programs that can "teach the ABCs of the arts" (Bry, 1981).

Renewed national interest in the sources and limitations of federal money and taxation, and budget processes generally, should stimulate the teaching of economics in interesting ways at all levels. Federal funds previously spent on the development of economic education materials may come to fruition. Similarly, the recent intervention and interest of the courts in education and in the rights and responsibilities of American citizens should give impetus to the introduction and expansion of law-related education into the curriculum.

Of particular significance, and an outgrowth of governmental interest in education, is a series of studies of effective schools; that is, what are the determinants of achievement. Funding has come from several sources including federal, state, and local. An early study of four instructionally effective inner-city schools (Weber, 1971) tended to disprove the Coleman (1966) and Jensen (1969) conclusions that low achievement by poor children was an inherent characteristic of the poor. Weber's major findings were confirmed later in a case study of two inner-city New York City public schools. Numerous other studies have since verified and expanded the conclusions; that is, high achievement was associated with schools that had strong leadership, high teacher expectations, good atmosphere, strong emphasis on reading, and careful monitoring of pupil progress. Missing in all four schools were factors usually thought necessary for high achievement, including: small class size, homogeneous ability grouping, superior teachers, ethnic background of teachers similar to that of the students, preschool education, and optimal physical facilities.

The search for unusually effective classrooms, programs, and schools—those whose students consistently achieve better than their peers—has extended into several states including New York, Pennsylvania, Delaware, Maryland, California, and Michigan (Edmonds, 1979). Major findings that characterized successful elementary and high schools are reported in School Learning Climate and Student Achievement (Lezotte and others, 1980).

A typical illustration of an effective school study is the Brookover and Lezotte study (1977) in Michigan. Beginning in 1970, the Michigan Department of Education annually tested all public school pupils in grades four and seven using criterion-referenced standardized measures of basic skills. Over time, these data were analyzed to identify elementary schools characterized by consistent improvement or decline in pupil performance. Eight schools (six improving, two declining) were selected for intensive analysis on site to determine differences bearing on improvement or decline. Ten factors were identified. These included emphasis on mathematics and reading objectives based on the belief that *all* children can master basic objectives, high expectations for students, acceptance of responsibility by the school (not shifting blame to parents or students), more time on task by cutting back on unnecessary interruptions and mechanical tasks, acceptance of the state's accountability model, and a strong principal role as instructional leader. (Also see Bloom, 1976, for the case for mastery learning.)

State Influence

Increasing influence on school programs by state legislatures has paralleled the growth of federal influence. The turn toward heavier state control over local school districts signified a drastic change in understanding of who is in charge. Historically, the Tenth Amendment left legal authority over the school program entirely to the state. Actually, state legislatures and state boards of education have had more authority than they have used and have not exercised their full power in the past, but have left curriculum decisions to local school boards except for the barest directives, usually only listing broad subject areas.

Legislatures have usually required that schools offer and students take certain courses in U.S. history, English, mathematics, and the U.S. and State Constitutions. Some states have added other requirements such as courses in driver education, the effects of alcoholic beverages, consumer education, career education, and the contributions of minority populations. A few states have legislated curriculum emphasis on values such as moral character, truth, justice, civic virtues, free enterprise, the evils of communism, and so on. In recent years curriculum mandates have increased drastically. The scope of legislative mandating of curriculum has been the subject of a comprehensive study sponsored by the American Bar Association, the Social Science Education Consortium, and the ERIC Clearinghouse on Educational Management (see Henning and others, 1979). A summary and analysis of state curriculum mandates was provided as well as suggestions for the future.

Interestingly, it appears that many teachers do not know what is mandated but rely on their administrators and supervisors to keep them informed. The state departments of education generally have not had fail-proof methods for reaching teachers with information on mandates. Confusion has resulted when unexpected reports are required or funding is cut off for lack of compliance. Supervisory personnel, therefore, have necessarily added regulatory and monitoring functions to their repertoire of skills.

The most spectacular efforts of state legislatures have been the development of competency-based instructional programs. An example of a comprehensive competency-based plan is the Louisiana Pupil Progression Plan which mandates tests for determining promotion from one grade to another, kindergarten through grade twelve. Many states mandate testing at one or more levels but usually not at all grade levels. An informal survey found that by 1981 38 states had enacted competency-testing legislation and others reportedly were planning some form of required competency-testing for students. In addition, several states, such as Louisiana, Florida, and Georgia, had enacted competency tests for teachers to be sure the schools will be supplied with future teachers who meet literacy standards as measured by standardized tests.

Although some critics have deplored mandatory state testing programs, most schools have followed their state's advice and requirements. Positive feedback is increasing in volume as educators find that assessment programs are leading to improvement. Pennsylvania's Educational Quality Assessment program includes broader goals (self-esteem, understanding others) as well as academic achievement. Analysis of results shows a high correlation between achievement and a positive attitude and good communication among teachers, parents, and pupils (ASCD, 1981).

Data are regularly published by several states indicating that competency tests are producing gains in achievement. Florida's competency program, for example, has survived opposition and somewhat dramatic gains are said to "prove that students can achieve when spurred by the motivation of knowing that something is expected of them" (Turlington, 1979, p. 650).

The political context that spawned competency testing and other state and federal controls on school programs was the accountability movement. Accountability means "those systems or arrangements that supply the general public, as well as educators, with accurate information about school output performance— test scores and other data that show how well groups of children are learning in school" (Wynne, 1972, p. ix).

Competency testing seemed to legislators an obvious solution to the monumental task of monitoring accountability for educational policy and practice in the local schools. The fact that results of mandated state tests are being published in newspapers serves the purpose of accountability to some extent. It has placed the spotlight on the low achieving schools and has caused teachers and administrators to intensify their efforts to bring up the test scores of the lower achieving students.

Another expression of accountability and related to objectives-based assessment programs is management by objectives (MBO) a method of checking outcomes against objectives. This may be the modern interpretation of John Dewey's emphasis on the power of purpose and his accompanying admonition that intelligent observation and judgment are necessary in developing a purpose (1938, p. 71). MBO can be mismanagement by objectives when the focus is on the trivial, not linked to pupil learning, or when professional autonomy is jeopardized. MBO works best when it reinforces the major objectives of a school district, keeps paperwork simple and reasonable, emphasizes the performance of the larger group (not stars), reinforces professional work ethics and personal growth, is developed *with* the staff, and establishes reasonable relationships between salary and performance (English, 1981).

Modification of systems of taxing and allocating resources to the schools represents another relationship to accountability. Recent court decisions declaring that property taxes unconstitutionally deny equal access have caused revisions of funding in several states. The assumption is that sufficient funding will provide quality education, a premise that has been questioned (Schaffarzick and Sykes, 1979, pp. 56–57).

Special Interests

The influence of informal or nongovernmental groups, agencies, and organizations on curriculum decisions should not be underestimated. Polarization has frequently tended to obscure reasonableness and prevent meaningful dialogue between parents and educators in regard to controversial topics and teaching materials. It behooves curriculum decision makers to be fully aware of the political climate. Although there have been surprise attacks on school programs that have caught the school's leaders unprepared, potential issues and controversies generally can be predicted by politically-aware educators. Early in the planning stages, parents and other citizens should be involved in constructive exchanges of views. Rationale, objectives, proposed teaching activities and materials, and methods of evaluation can be explored and through rational processes usually agreed-on plans can be developed.

Issues fanned by special interest groups change with time as they become resolved or obsolete, but new ones continually appear. Constant alertness on the part of curriculum deciders and developers is needed as well as competence in problem solving.

Book censoring periodically gains local and even national attention. The widely publicized 1974 textbook battle in Kanawha County, West Virginia, fanned book censoring flames in other parts of the country. More recently a zealous husband and wife team in Texas organized a school book censoring group known as "Educational Research Analysts" and by tirelessly campaigning across the state and elsewhere were able to pressure schools through their parent groups away from the purchase of certain books alleged to instill disrespect for American values and the family (Larsen, 1980; Park, 1980).

Caught in the middle of book censoring controversies are publishers of school materials, who are forced to compromise, and boards of education, both state and local, who are pressed by special interest groups to censor books. On one side are parents and other citizens who contend that certain passages in textbooks or library books are warping the traditional values that should be "inculcated" in students and on the other side are advocates of intellectual freedom who say that the school and library should provide a forum of ideas for students to question and examine.

The curriculum decision maker should be prepared to protect a school climate in which intellectual freedom can reign and at the same time recognize the parents' rights in a free society. An educational campaign may be in order.

Religion in the schools is another major issue that has come before the courts on numerous occasions. The basic principle on which various decisions have rested is that public schools may neither advance nor inhibit religion. On this basis the Supreme Court struck down school ceremonies that involve reading from the Bible and recitation of prayers, even though these may be nondenominational prayers and even though students who object may be excused from participation. But just as the courts have barred instruction in what we typically call religion, the Supreme Court has said that the school may not establish a religion of secularism; that is, atheism (van Geel, 1979, p. 29).

In regard to the issue of creationism vs. evolution, court decisions have declared it in conflict with the First Amendment of the Constitution to require science textbooks and curricula to include the Genesis account of creation (see Skoog, 1980, and Bird, 1980). Bills are constantly being presented in state legislatures to seek ways to include school prayer, creationism, and so on, in the schools and circumvent previous court rulings. The current national administration appears to favor school prayer and it seems destined for further discussion in Congress. It appears advisable, however, for curriculum developers in the public schools to note that any ideas or concepts that seem to stem from a religious point of view must be justified for inclusion in the curriculum on the basis that they advance students' knowledge of society's cultural and religious heritage in a historical framework.

Sex education courses frequently provoke controversy. Fundamentalist groups have objected to the topic being part of the curriculum based on the claim that the study of sex education would encourage teenage pregnancies, lesbian-ism, and homosexuality. Counselors and other educators have maintained that schools must fill the information gap or at least counteract teenagers' misinfor-mation about sex. Participation in sex education or other potentially controver-sial courses should be voluntary. Parents and students should be informed before the course begins of the rationale and proposed outline of the course so that they can decide whether to elect the particular course. In planning the course in the first place, parents and students should be involved.

Leadership in Curriculum Development

It can be concluded that the political context in which vital curriculum decisions will be made must be a context in which all parties concerned with school improvement are involved and working cooperatively. Curriculum leadership can be measured by the degree of competence shown in acquainting the participating groups and individuals with the best that is known from related research and employing a range of organizational skills including: identifying needs and problems by unbiased methods, defining goals and objectives at several levels of decision making, developing plans and procedures that elicit the trust and cooperation of the participants, involving people of different as well as like interests and backgrounds, finding ways to communicate and use feedback from inside the school and with external groups, and using implementation and evaluation processes that will produce continuing and constructive change and renewal.

According to several studies the principal is a key in attaining at the building level excellence in curriculum, a learning climate in the school, and growth in student achievement. (For example, see Edmunds, 1979; Austin, 1979; Good-lad, 1979; and Bentzen and others, 1980.) Principals have considerable power to influence curriculum development. In fact, in many districts where enrollment is declining the principal has become a curriculum leader while other superviso-ry resources have vanished. Thus, principals have found themselves in a role that was not uppermost in their training programs.

The effective principal needs these among other necessary competencies: skill in instructional leadership to the extent that everyone in the building is committed to instruction and learning as the main emphasis; ability to maintain an orderly, purposeful climate in which cooperation for the good of all is a priority; and success in setting and meeting high levels of expectation for students, teachers, supervisors, and the principalship.

Curriculum leaders at all levels, whether principal, superintendent, curric-ulum director, government official, or others, have unique opportunities for growth in political skills. Sharing power over curriculum development with teachers, students, experts, scholars, parents, and other citizens is difficult and involves risks. Whether the involvement of these various groups leads to success in curriculum development may depend on the ability of the leaders to view the new constituents in education not as competitors for a limited amount of power but as previously untapped sources of leadership and influence in the field of education.

References

Applebee, Arthur N. "Looking at Writing." *Educational Leadership* 38 (March 1981): 458–462.

ASCD Update 23 (March 1981): 1,6.

Austin, Gilbert R. "Exemplary Schools and the Search for Effectiveness." *Educational Leadership* 37 (October 1979): 10–12.

Bendiner, Robert. *The Politics of Schools: A Crisis in Self-Government.* New York: Harper and Row, 1969.

Bentzen, Mary M.; Williams, Richard C.; and Heckman, Paul. "A Study of Schooling: Adult Experiences in Schools." *Phi Delta Kappan* 61 (February 1980): 394–397.

Berman, Paul, and McLaughlin, Milbrey W. *Federal Programs Supporting Educational Change, Vol. VIII: Implementing and Sustaining Innovations.* Santa Monica, Calif.: Rand, 1978.

Bird, Wendell R. "Creationism and Evolution." *Educational Leadership* 38 (November 1980): 157.

Bloom, Benjamin S. *Human Characteristics and School Learning.* New York: McGraw-Hill, 1976.

Brookover, Wilbur B., and Lezotte, Lawrence W. *Changes in School Characteristics Coincident with Changes in Student Achievement.* East Lansing: College of Urban Development, Michigan State University, 1977.

Bry, Charlene. "New Cable TV Service Teaches the ABCs of the Arts." St. Louis *Globe Democrat,* April 14, 1981, p. C1,4.

Callahan, Raymond E. *Education and the Cult of Efficiency.* Chicago: University of Chicago Press, 1962.

Coleman, James S., and others. *Equality of Educational Opportunity.* Washington, D.C.: U.S. Office of Education, National Center for Education Statistics, 1966.

Counts, George S. *The Social Composition of Boards of Education.* Chicago: University of Chicago Press, 1927.

Dewey, John. *Experience and Education.* New York: Collier, 1938.

Edmonds, Ronald. "Effective Schools for the Urban Poor." *Educational Leadership* 37 (October 1979): 15–24.

English, Fenwick W. "Management or Mismanagement by Objectives." *The School Administrator* 38 (March 1981): 8–9.

Goodlad, John I.; Sirotnik, Kenneth A.; and Overman, Betty C. "An Overview of 'A Study of Schooling.' " *Phi Delta Kappan* 61 (November 1979): 174–178.

Harris, Louis. "Most Whose Children Were Bused Approved." St. Louis *Globe Democrat,* March 26, 1981, p. A11.

Henning, Joel F.; White, Charles; Sorgen, Michael; and Steizer, Leigh. *Mandate for Change: The Impact of Law on Educational Innovation.* Chicago: American Bar Association, 1979.

Hooker, Clifford P. *The Courts and Education.* 77th Yearbook of the National Society for the Study of Education. Chicago: University of Chicago Press, 1978.

Hurlburd, David. *This Happened in Pasadena.* New York: Macmillan, 1961.

Jensen, Arthur. "How Much Can We Boost IQ and Scholastic Achievement?" *Harvard Educational Review* (Winter 1969).

Kimbrough, Ralph B. *Political Power and Educational Decision Making.* Chicago: Rand McNally, 1964.

Larsen, Terry J. "The Power of the Board of Education to Censor." *Educational Leadership* 38 (November 1980): 139–142.

Lezotte, Lawrence W., and others. *School Learning Climate and Student Achievement.* Tallahassee: Teacher Education Projects, 1980.

Lieberman, Myron. "Eggs That I Have Laid: Teacher Bargaining Reconsidered." *Phi Delta Kappan* 60 (February 1979): 415–419.

Masotti, Louis H. *Education and Politics in Suburbia: The New Trier Experience.* Cleveland: The Press of Western Reserve University, 1967.

Morphet, Edgar L.; Johns, Roe L.; and Reller, Theodore L. *Educational Administration Concepts, Practices, and Issues.* Englewood Cliffs, N.J.: Prentice-Hall, 1959.

National Assessment of Educational Progress. *Third National Writing Assessment.* Denver: Education Commission of the States, January 1981.

National Education Association. *Curriculum Issues for the Eighties: Structure, Content, Context.* Washington, D.C.: NEA, 1980.

National Institute of Education, Curriculum Development Task Force. *Current Issues, Problems, and Concerns in Curriculum Development.* Washington, D.C.: NIE, 1976.

National Science Foundation. *What Are the Needs in Precollege Science, Mathematics, and Social Science Education? Views from the Field.* Washington, D.C.: NSF, 1979.

Orelove, Fred P. "Administering Education for the Severely Handicapped After P.L. 94-142." *Phi Delta Kappan* 59 (June 1978): 699–702.

Park, J. Charles. "The New Right: Threat to Democracy in Education." *Educational Leadership* 38 (November 1980): 146–149.

Schaffarzick, Jon, and Sykes, Gary. *Value Conflicts and Curriculum Issues.* Berkeley: McCutchan, 1979.

Scribner, Jay D., ed. *The Politics of Education.* 76th Yearbook of the National Society for the Study of Education. Chicago: University of Chicago Press, 1977.

Shanker, Albert. "A Reply to Myron Lieberman." *Phi Delta Kappan* 60 (May 1979): 652–654.

Skoog, Gerald. "Legal Issues Involved in Evolution vs. Creationism." *Educational Leadership* 38 (November 1980): 154–156.

Turlington, Ralph D. "Good News from Florida: Our Minimum Competency Program is Working." *Phi Delta Kappan* 60 (May 1979): 649–654.

van Geel, Tyll. "The New Law of the Curriculum." In *Value Conflicts and Curriculum Issues,* pp. 25–72. Edited by John Schaffarzick and Gary Sykes. Berkeley: McCutchan, 1979.

Weber, George. *Inner City Children Can Be Taught to Read: Four Successful Schools.* Washington, D.C.: Council for Basic Education, 1971.

Wood, Fred H.; Thompson, Steven R.; Russell, Frances. "Designing Effective Staff Development Programs." In *Staff Development/Organization Development,* pp. 37–58. Alexandria, Va.: Association for Supervision and Curriculum Development, 1981.

Wynne, Edward. *The Politics of School Accountability.* Berkeley: McCutchan, 1972.

Zirkel, Perry A., ed. *A Digest of Supreme Court Decisions Affecting Education.* Bloomington, Ind.: Phi Delta Kappa, 1978.

Chapter 9

Selecting Learning Activities

Doris T. Gow and Tommye W. Casey

L earning activities are the planned interaction of the student with the instructional environment. These activities are derived from the goals of the curriculum and student engagement in the activities is aimed at mastery of the curriculum's specific objectives. Since "all genuine education comes about through experiences" (Dewey, 1938, p. 13) and learning activities are designed to provide such experience, the identification of appropriate learning activities is one of the most critical tasks in curriculum design.

The identification of learning activities, however, is not solely the prerogative of the curriculum developer. Teachers tend to use curriculum guides flexibly. They may emphasize different portions of the course of study, put together different supplemental and remedial materials to meet the perceived needs of each class, and often select from texts, workbooks, teacher's journals, and other sources learning activities that were not a part of the curriculum. This mixing and matching of materials may result in gaps and deficiencies in student learning.

Moreover, Jackson (1968) suggests that student learning may not be the primary goal in the selection of these activities anyway.

Teachers seem to be making some kind of an educated guess about what would be a beneficial activity for a student or group of students and then doing whatever is necessary to see that participants remain involved in that activity. The teacher's goal, in other words, is student involvement rather than student learning. It is true, of course, that the teacher hopes the involvement will result in certain beneficial changes in students, but learning is in this sense a by-product rather than the thing about which the teacher is most directly concerned (p. 24).

Several solutions to the problem of discrepancies between the planned curriculum and the actual instruction have been suggested. These include teaching teachers curriculum materials design and analysis skills (Gow, 1976, 1980), learning principles (Gagné, 1965), and a repertoire of proven effective instructional strategies (Joyce and Weil, 1972). Another suggested remedy from the administrator's point of view is curriculum mapping as a means of quality control (English, 1978). The identification of learning activities that keep the

112

student involved by virtue of their careful tailoring to the specific school and student population and the communication to the teacher of the rationale for their selection may be another way to ensure the use of learning activities that are consistent with the planned curriculum.

This chapter will treat the identification or definition of learning activities as a culminating step in the systematic process of curriculum development which began with the identification of general educational goals. Pertinent topics to be covered are categories of learning activities, criteria for their selection, and procedures for their design and development.

Categories of Curriculum Learning Activities

The characteristics of a curriculum and the procedures used for its design and development may hinge on the developer's general orientation toward the curriculum field. Eisner and Vallance (1974) have identified five such conceptions of curriculum: curriculum as the development of cognitive processes, curriculum as technology, self-actualization or curriculum as consummatory experience, curriculum for social reconstruction–relevance, and curriculum as academic rationalism.

The curriculum developer may take an eclectic stance, however, and may select learning activities and employ design procedures according to the specific objectives emphasized in any given sequence of instruction rather than from a singular global orientation. This is the Tyler approach (1949, 1975). He identifies four types of learning activities: to develop skill in thinking, to acquire information, to develop social attitudes, and to develop interests. These are the source of the categories we shall use to describe and analyze learning activities in this chapter. The slightly different wording fits more precisely the research that will be cited in support of the selection of appropriate activities. The following four categories of learning activities are those that seem to demand substantially different kinds of student behavior for goal attainment:
- To acquire information and basic skills
- To develop social attitudes
- To develop self
- To develop information-processing and problem-solving skills.

Of course learning activities that fit best in any one category may contribute to attainment of other categories of goals as well. However, there appear to be fundamental differences among these four kinds of goals.

To Acquire Information and Basic Skills

Learning activities to acquire information and basic skills are those activities that are required for learning the fundamentals of reading and mathematics and the acquisition of information through low level cognitive processing (knowledge, comprehension, and perhaps application).

Studies of effective practices in basic skill acquisition provide evidence for incorporating direct instruction learning activities in basic skills curricula for both elementary and secondary schools. Bereiter and Engelmann (1966), in their work with "disadvantaged" preschool children, found that providing demonstrations, drills, exercises, practice, and feedback as well as performance criteria for the children ensured that most instructional objectives were mastered. Rosenshine's review of the research (1976, 1978, 1979) highlighted as related to achievement the same type of direct, structured, academically focused, teacher-directed activities for primary and middle grades. Goals were clear to students, coverage of content extensive, and feedback to students immediate and academically oriented. In junior and senior high school, similar findings with total group instruction were that maximum time on task, direct questions to specific students, and regular feedback were positively related to achievement (Stallings, Needels, and Staybrook, 1979).

Mastery learning is another construct that is particularly, though not exclusively, applicable to goals aimed at acquiring information and basic skills. It is based on the premise that 90 to 95 percent of all students can master school subjects given sufficient time. Mastery learning activities are characterized by careful structure, small steps, frequent monitoring of progress, and a feedback-corrective process (Bloom, 1968, 1976). Group instruction is augmented by individualized corrective procedures. A similar system, based on mastery objectives, is the Keller Personalized System of Instruction (PSI) which is individualized and uses tutors permitting continuous progress at the college and university level.

Mastery learning has been proven effective for acquisition and comprehension of subject matter content and acquisition of basic reading and math skills, although it may work for other kinds of learning as well (Burns, 1979; Hyman and Cohen, 1979).

One essential element to include in the design of learning activities to acquire information and basic skills is structure. Another critical element is time. For basic skills, time is direct instructional time. For acquiring information, it is flexible time for mastery.

Other elements that have proven to be effective and can be incorporated in the curriculum design of learning activities in this category are frequent monitoring of student progress, small steps, academic focus, and immediate feedback.

To Develop Social Attitudes

One reason for development of free universal education in this country was to provide the literate, participatory citizenship demanded by a democracy. Learning activities to develop social attitudes include: (1) those designed to produce an informed electorate, and (2) those designed to develop democratic social behaviors.

Activities that help students analyze real or hypothetical issues or situations and, more important, to work toward resolution of conflicts in values are designed to supply experience for present or future political action. The activities in Oliver and Shaver's (1966) Harvard Social Studies Project curriculum materials are an example of this category. Case studies are provided to give students the opportunity to engage in the process of analysis. The process is guided by questions that lead the student to recognize types of value conflicts and to work toward general policies to apply to value conflict situations.

Similarly, Massialas and Hurst (1978) are bent on making the entire school a laboratory for understanding issues and participating in decision making to enable the students to develop a sense of control over their environment. This, they argue, can be achieved through "knowledge, understanding, participatory activity, and the development of a set of defensible values" (p. 3).

The fostering of social attitudes that go beyond intellectual activity to action is possible through both in-school and out-of-school activities ranging from peer tutoring in classrooms to community educational activities which Bronfenbrenner (Brandt, 1979) calls "a curriculum for caring." Such activities may include volunteer work in hospitals or geriatric homes and other social action programs such as working at recycling centers or cleaning up stream beds. Massialas and Hurst (1978) have attempted to ensure the inclusion of this type of activity in the school curriculum by expanding the usual cognitive and affective domains of school learning to include a participatory domain.

The American Sociological Association was the sponsor, more than a decade ago, of Sociological Resources for the Social Studies, which include laboratory units for social inquiry. These activities teach basic social science concepts and sociological methods, but students also conduct independent investigations into social attitudes and behaviors, including their own (Lippett, Fox, and Schaible, 1969).

Group investigations, as proposed by Thelen (1960), provide group interactions as well as inquiry into social problems. The students, in groups of 10–15, identify a problem and organize to solve it, assuming the necessary roles, performing the tasks they have identified as essential, and evaluating the results. The organizing and group interaction in themselves are learning activities that are directed to the development of social attitudes and skills and to self-conscious observation by the student of his or her own group participation.

Learning experiences designed to produce students who can analyze public issues teach them to process information about public issues which is very similar to the kinds of critical thinking involved in the information processing and problem solving category of activities. However, the difference lies not only in the goal emphasis of the activities designed to produce an informed electorate, but also in the activities themselves. The social focus is always uppermost in the use of process to moderate conflict, in the emphasis on respect for alternative views, and in participatory activity in decision making and socialization.

The critical elements of the typical learning activity to develop social attitudes are use of an inquiry method; practice of social analysis, usually in a group situation; and observation of attitudes of self and others.

While social attitude is one indicator of the individual personality, the focus of social attitude learning activities is on their social aspect. The third category of learning activities, to develop self, focuses more directly on the individual person.

To Develop Self

The design of learning activities to develop or enhance student self-concept has been the focus of several clinical and developmental psychologists. They are guided by the belief that "to be effective, education must find ways of helping students discover the personal meaning of events for them" (Combs and Snygg, 1959, p. 149). The emphasis is on helping the student become a self-actualized learner (Maslow, 1954). The most effective and lasting learning according to Rogers (1969) is self-initiated or self-directed and occurs in a nonthreatening environment. Nondirective teaching (student-centered instruction) is the primary vehicle for achieving this goal.

While climate is more closely identified with instruction than with curriculum, curriculum materials themselves provide a climate for learning and the information and recommendations they supply for teachers set the stage for the creation of a desired classroom climate. Dunkin and Biddle (1974) have pointed out that climate is usually identified on the basis of frequency counts (of praise, criticism, and the like) and most communications in the classroom are neutral in terms of warmth (Flanders, 1960).

Certainly there can be no criticism of the attempt to make learning activities pleasant and enjoyable and the clinical evidence in support of a nonthreatening environment seems sufficient to suggest that curriculum materials to develop self explicitly attempt to create such an environment or urge the teacher to do so.

Not only is the climate of the classroom an important element to consider but the learning activities should offer student experiences with "practical problems, social problems, ethical and philosophical problems, personal issues and research problems" (Rogers, 1969, p. 162). The instructional designer can find experiences with ethical and philosophical questions in the work of Kohlberg (1969). He has identified stages of moral growth and development in children and has developed moral dilemmas to raise such questions. Group discussion of the dilemmas can help students move to a higher stage of moral development (Hersh, Paolitto, and Reimer, 1979).

Activities to encourage creativity also fall into this category. The self-actualized person described by Maslow (1971) has many of the same characteristics as the creative person described by Torrance (1962). Learning activities designed specifically for the creative individual should encourage imagination, divergent thinking, and discovery according to Getzels and Jackson (1962). Grouping of creative individuals homogeneously may ease their sense of isolation (Torrance, 1962).

One critical element in the development of learning activities for development of self is the nonthreatening environment. Another important element is challenge: of issues, problems, ethical and philosophical questions. The third characteristic is student-centered instruction.

To Develop Information-Processing and Problem-Solving Skills

The fourth category of learning activities is related to the educational goal of developing information-processing and problem-solving skills.

The curriculum reform movement of the 60s focused on ways to help students better process information. Teaching students the structure of the subject discipline, its fundamental methods, concepts, principles, constructs, and their interrelationships became the focus of learning activities (Bruner, 1966). The hierarchical arrangement or structure of the disciplines was studied because it offered an approach to developing instructional materials that fostered mastery of lower-level concepts before proceeding to higher level concepts (Gagné, 1965). Ausubel (1978) also proposed an instructional strategy to aid in information processing, providing the student with an advance organizer, a brief introduction to the structure of the information to be presented. Advance organizers can take a variety of forms (an entire lesson preceding other lessons, a film, and so on). However, the concepts presented are inclusive and more abstract than the information that follows and must be related to what the student already knows.

The process of concept attainment has been studied extensively (Bruner, Goodnow, and Austin, 1956; Glaser, 1968). Taba's teaching strategies (1967), in the form of "eliciting questions" that help students to process information at increasingly complex levels, offer an excellent way of using an inductive approach to develop information processing skills. Piaget's study of intellectual development (1950) indicated that young children will acquire a better understanding of concepts and relationships if they are given an opportunity to work with concrete materials—to manipulate them, touch them, feel them. The implications of Piaget's work for selecting learning activities for the preschool and early elementary school child cannot be ignored.

Most inquiry learning activities (Schwab, 1965; Suchman, 1967; Massialas and Cox, 1966) are based on the five phases of problem solving described by Dewey (1910). The stages are:

1. A stage of doubt or perplexity
2. An attempt to identify the problem and goal
3. Relating these propositions to present knowledge and formation of a hypothesis
4. Testing of hypotheses and reformulating problem as necessary
5. Understanding and applying the solution to other examples of the same problem.

Information-processing and problem-solving skills learning activities are built around the fundamental structure of a discipline and typically present problems to be solved using the methods of that discipline. The level of the student's cognitive processing for this category of activities is consistently higher (analysis and synthesis) than for the category of information acquisition (knowledge, comprehension, application), although both categories of activity may be structured on the conceptual structure of the disciplines.

These, then, are the four general categories of learning activities. It should be emphasized again that these categories do not exclude each other. For example, a learning activity that effectively develops information-processing and problem-solving skills may also help develop social attitudes.

Criteria for Selection and Development of Learning Activities

Feasibility and Economy Within Constraints of Program Needs, Resources, and Staff Capabilities

The educational goals of a school usually are determined by conducting an assessment of students' educational needs. These goals are then prioritized, objectives are identified, and types of learning activities are selected that are expected to help students achieve the goals and objectives. However, the availability of resources in the school also affects the selection of learning activities. In many cases, the selection of activities may be constrained by budgetary considerations. Another possible constraint is staff preferences and capabilities. The teaching style of the teacher will affect choice of learning activities. For example, a teacher who feels uncomfortable with an inquiry approach will not use learning activities reflecting this approach.

In order to offset these constraints, it is important to provide the teacher with alternative learning activities to meet the same goals and objectives. Many curriculum guides do provide such alternatives.

Match to Goals and Objectives

The position taken in this chapter has been that learning activities are categorized or identified according to the goals of education. The learning objectives that define those goals usually specify the conditions under which the student must demonstrate mastery of the behavior to be learned. These conditions should be appropriate for the learning activities. These conditions might include such variables as time allotted for demonstrating mastery, number of problems, type of setting, and so on.

The kind of behavior desired as a result of participating in the learning activity is also identified by the objective, along with its level of proficiency. The learning activity must provide an opportunity for the student to practice the kind of behavior implied by the objective (Tyler, 1975). If the objective is to acquire a basic skill, then the learning activity must offer opportunity to practice this skill at appropriate levels as the student's proficiency grows.

The content and concepts with which the learner must interact are also specified by the goals and objectives, and the selected learning activities should offer the student an opportunity to use this content and these concepts.

Match to Students

Learning activities should match the characteristics of the student population for whom they are designed. Developmental psychologists (Piaget, Erikson, Kohlberg) postulate that children's intellectual, moral, and social/emotional growth and development go through certain well-defined stages. Of course learning activities should be identified to match the capabilities of the students for whom they are chosen and stage of development is one individual difference that affects that choice. As an example, their stage of logical operations limits the problem-solving capabilities of children (Piaget, 1950; Flavell, 1963). Care is necessary in choosing activities in the information-processing/problem-solving category that the student is mature enough to perform successfully. Where more than one stage is represented among students in a class, a corresponding array of activities makes an appropriate match more probable.

In those cases where learning is sequentially structured, students must have already mastered behaviors prerequisite to the present objectives. The curriculum designer needs to consider the students' prior learning before designing learning activities.

Other student characteristics that should be considered in designing learning activities are learning style and interests. Given the range of individual differences in learning style that have been identified by researchers (Kagan, 1967; Harvey, Hunt and Schroeder, 1961; Witkin, Dyk, Faterson, Goodenough, and Karp, 1962; Cohen, 1976) and the paucity of evidence on treatment effects, self-choice may be the expedient method of matching. It might be neither practical nor even best for the students to suggest that every objective could be attained through a preferred learning mode. However, some attempts to match activities to style that could facilitate self-selection suggest such alternatives as programmed learning, multi-sensory instructional packages, and contract activity packages (Dunn and Dunn, 1979). Another and very promising procedure uses a cognitive style profile, which has accurately predicted academic achievement, to identify learning deficits (Letteri, 1980). This would then permit selection of learning activities that might remedy those deficits.

One of Tyler's (1975) five general principles that apply to the selection of learning activities is that the student should obtain satisfaction from carrying on the kind of behavior implied by the objectives. Selecting a range of activities known to be interesting to students of a given age and stage of development is helpful and permits the teacher, who will implement the curriculum and who knows the students, to select those which are likely to provide satisfaction.

Linking learning activities to out-of-school experiences provides a means of making the relevance of those activities apparent to the student. Such activities allow the student to work with practical problems, social problems, and personal issues. Permitting the student freedom of choice also provides an opportunity for examining the consequences of such choices, a valuable learning activity in itself. For students to think of themselves as learners, to think about their own learning, and to think of learning as useful and related to their needs can facilitate the development of responsible, self-directed learners.

Match to Subject Matter Continuity, Sequence, and Integration

The final criterion for selecting and developing learning activities is their match to subject matter. The structure of any discipline—its fundamental concepts, principles, generalizations, constructs and their interrelationships, and the discipline's methodology—provide a map or blueprint of the area the student will enter, explore, pass through, and reenter at a later date.

As Bruner (1960, p. 7) described it, "Grasping the structure of a subject is understanding it in a way that permits many other things to be related to it meaningfully." To learn structure, in short, is to learn how things are related. He pointed out that:

Though the proposition may seem startling at first, its intent is to underscore an essential point often overlooked in the planning of curricula. It is that the basic ideas that lie at the heart of all science and mathematics and the basic themes that give form to life and literature are as simple as they are powerful. To be in command of these basic ideas, to use them effectively, requires a continual deepening of one's understanding of them. That comes from learning to use them in progressively more complex forms (pp. 12, 13).

(Twenty years after publication of Bruner's *Process of Education*, that point still is overlooked in the design of many curriculum guides, though some of the curriculum products of the Reform Movement still survive.)

This "continual deepening of one's understanding" requires continuity, sequence, and integration (Tyler, 1975). Continuity is vertical organization. Sequence is building each experience on the preceding one more broadly and deeply. And integration is the horizontal relationship of experiences across subjects. Taba's "spiralling" (1967) and Gagné's (1965) hierarchies can be used to attain both continuity and sequence.

In this context, Gagné (1965) has pointed out the behaviors that demonstrate one has acquired the fundamental elements of a discipline. To demonstrate acquisition of a concept the student must be able to identify new examples of the concept not previously encountered. To demonstrate acquisition of a principle, the student must be able to apply the principle when appropriate. To demonstrate problem-solving ability, the student must be able to recall the relevant principles and apply them to the problem. When the student acquires problem-solving ability, he or she has acquired a higher order principle that can be generalized to a whole class of problems. Wherever possible, given the constraints of the school program, students should be encouraged to use the actual methods that sociologists, anthropologists, or biologists use when solving problems and processing information. The general approach to instruction taken by the curriculum materials or prescribed in teachers' manuals or guides should reflect these methods. Practical application of the knowledge and skills to be acquired should be provided by the learning activities selected and the students should have ample opportunity to practice these behaviors.

It is wise to select learning activities that draw on more than one discipline whenever possible. Students need to see the relationships between subject areas; linking subject areas together or pointing out relationships wherever appropriate helps to break down the artificial barriers between school subjects.

Procedures for the Development of Learning Activities

Systematic curriculum design and development procedures are not necessarily linear. Ordinarily, curriculum developers perform the operations described in the various chapters of this publication, but not necessarily in the order in which they appear. The sequence of procedures, and the emphasis on each design dimension for the stage of curriculum design at which learning activities are defined, would vary according to the category of learning activity being developed and the context of development. For example, for learning activities in the categories of knowledge acquisition and basic skills and of information processing, structure would be a critical dimension. The identification of objectives probably would be followed by an analysis of the concepts and the structure of the knowledge to be acquired or of the discipline within which problems are to be solved. This analysis would guide the hierarchical structuring of objectives and selection of appropriate methods, media, and strategies for the learning activities identified to facilitate goal attainment.

On the other hand, for some learning activities in the other two categories (self and social skills), and the learning environment that facilitates such goals, the identification of objectives might be followed directly by description of the environment and the identification of the methods, media, and strategies of the appropriate learning activities without prestructuring objectives in any kind of hierarchy. In some cases, student-centered activities would be self-selected by students.

Systematic procedures for curriculum development, such as those used by research and development centers and described or implied in the organization of this chapter, usually are not employed by curriculum development teams in schools unless they are designing curriculum packages including lessons or modules, tests, record forms, and so on.

The more typical process is the development of curriculum guides that provide the advantages of site-specificity with expediency since the student materials are assembled primarily rather than developed.

Resources for curriculum guides are mainly textbooks with supplementary audiovisuals (Stake and Easley, 1977). This is not surprising, since, for example, a survey of teachers in Pennsylvania, New Jersey, and Delaware revealed that almost nine out of ten of the teachers in the tri-state area use a basal text as their major instructional resource (Rouk, 1979, p. 1).

This preference for textbooks, and the objectives of the textbooks over those of the district (Rouk, 1979, p. 3), probably is a reflection on the failure of the usual curriculum guide to supply the teacher with the kind of support system provided by well-designed teacher's manuals or desk copies of texts.

A sense of ownership that comes from involvement in the development process would be helpful in achieving more widespread usage (Berman and McLaughlin, 1977). However, making the curriculum guide more usable for the teacher is the best way to ensure its use.

Components of a curriculum guide usually are the goals and explicit objectives and a rationale detailing what content, concepts, skills, methods, and strategies are included for whom and why. A scope and sequence chart is useful. The management system and record forms for keeping track of student progress as well as a description of the options for different categories of students should be explained clearly and, perhaps, graphically.

Any background information on content or on expectations of how different students will respond to the learning activities is also helpful information. The teacher who will use the curriculum guide should be given specific information on how to use these learning activities with the gifted and the handicapped.

Most curriculum guides include lists of resources which need to be analyzed for their appropriateness for the learning activities that have been identified. Guides will be more useful if specific sections and pages in source books are coded to the objectives they address. This simplifies the teacher's task of tailoring instruction to student needs. Television and film are most likely to be successful if they are integrated into the pattern of learning activities.

When complete curriculum packages are designed, student lesson materials usually go through several tryouts beginning with an in-house troubleshooting session with colleagues of the developers, a tryout with a few students followed by a pilot test with a larger group, and then a field test. This is immeasurably useful in validating the materials for their intended use. Usually, nothing comparable takes place with curriculum guides, probably because written student lesson materials are not the major component. If a run-through from the perspective of the student, anticipating possible student questions or problems and additional resources necessary to answer them or help students solve them, was followed by tryouts by several teachers with the range of students for whom the guides were designed, weaknesses could be uncovered and remedied.

We do know, from studies of innovations, that the majority of teachers cannot identify the essential features of an innovation they are working with (Gross, Giacquinta, and Bernstein, 1971). It would be helpful to the teacher-user if the critical elements of each learning activity were explicitly pointed out in the curriculum guide and the teacher and student roles for each activity clearly defined.

A final suggestion for optimizing the usefulness of curriculum guides for teachers so that they will be used is that they be formatted in loose-leaf style to make revision simpler; that forms be distributed throughout for teacher notes on possible future revisions, adaptations, or additional resources; and that a research update should be added at least once each year.

This research update suggestion stems from increasing value of research to practice, especially the meta-analysis results of recent studies (such as Glass and Smith, 1978). Implications for practice were formerly the weakest part of educational research. Today, no curriculum guide could be considered complete if it did not point out and emphasize the implications for defining learning activities of such studies as those by Carroll (1963), Wiley and Harnischfeger (1974), and Stallings (1980) on academic learning time; Rosenshine (1976; 1978) on direct instruction; and Walker and Schaffarzick (1974) on choice of content and content covered.

Future trends probably will include increasing emphasis on use of computers both to manage instruction and to provide learning activities. Increasingly, the array of learning activities offered will have to accommodate the needs of a broader range of students in age and prior learning as the out-of-school learning in museums, planetariums, industries, and other informal settings continues to grow and students drop in and out of school as needed. Students will have to learn how to gain access to information through computers, TV, and printed materials and how to evaluate the quality of what they see and hear.

Four categories of learning activities have been described that require different methods, strategies, and environments along with examples of learning activities in each category. Criteria are suggested for selection and development of learning activities, including feasibility, given local constraints, and match to goals and objectives, students, and subject matter. Since curriculum guides are locally-developed in schools more often than are complete packages which include student materials, general developmental procedures have been suggested with some specific guidelines for curriculum guide components and format.

References

Ausubel, D. P.; Novak, J. D.; and Hanesian, H. *Educational Psychology: A Cognitive View.* New York: Holt, Rinehart & Winston, 1978.

Bereiter, C., and Engelmann, S. *Teaching Disadvantaged Children in the Preschool.* Englewood Cliffs, N.J.: Prentice-Hall, 1966.

Berman, P., and McLaughlin, M. W. *Federal Programs Supporting Educational Change, Vol. 7, Factors Affecting Implementation and Continuation.* Santa Monica, Calif.: Rand Publishing, April 1977.

Bloom, B. S. "Learning for Mastery." *Evaluation Comment* 1,2 (May 1968).

Bloom, B. *Human Characteristics and School Learning.* New York: McGraw-Hill, 1976.

Brandt, R. "On Families and Schools: A Conversation with Urie Bronfenbrenner." *Educational Leadership* 36 (April 1979): 459–463.

Bronfenbrenner, U. "The Experimental Ecology of Education." *Review of Educational Research* (October 1976).

Bruner, J. *The Process of Education.* Cambridge: Harvard University Press, 1960.

Bruner, J. *Toward a Theory of Instruction.* Cambridge: Harvard University Press, 1966.

Bruner, J.; Goodnow, S.; and Austin, G. A. *A Study of Thinking.* New York: Science Editions, 1956.

Burns, N. B. "Mastery Learning: Does It Work?" *Educational Leadership* 37 (November 1979): 110–113.

Carroll, J. B. "A Model of School Learning." *Teachers College Record* 64 (1963): 723–733.

Cohen, R. A. "Conceptual Styles: Culture Conflict and Non-Verbal Tests of Intelligence." In *Design and Development of Curricular Materials,* Vol. 2. Edited by D. Gow. Pittsburgh: Center for International Studies Publications, 1976.

Combs, A. W., and Snygg, D. *Individual Behavior.* New York: Harper, 1959.

Dewey, J. *Experience and Education.* New York: Macmillan, 1938.

Dewey, J. *How We Think.* Boston: Heath, 1910.

Dunkin, Michael J., and Biddle, Bruce J. *The Study of Teaching.* New York: Holt, Rinehart & Winston, 1974.

Dunn, R., and Dunn, K. "Learning Styles/Teaching Styles: Should They . . . Can They . . . Be Matched?" *Educational Leadership* 36 (January 1979): 238–244.

Eisner, E. W., and Vallance, E. *Conflicting Conceptions of Curriculum.* Berkeley, Calif.: McCutchan, 1974.

English, F. W. *Quality Control in Curriculum Development.* Arlington, Va.: American Association of School Administrators, 1978.

Flanders, N. A. *Interaction Analysis in the Classroom: A Manual for Observers.* Ann Arbor: University of Michigan, 1960.

Flavell, J. H. *Developmental Psychology of Jean Piaget.* Princeton: Van Nostrand, 1963.

Gagné, R. M. *Conditions of Learning.* New York: Holt, Rinehart & Winston, 1965.

Getzels, J. W., and Jackson, P. W. *Creativity and Intelligence.* New York: Wiley, 1962.

Glaser, R. "Concept Learning and Concept Teaching." In *Learning Research and School Subjects*, pp. 1–38. Edited by R. M. Gagné and W. J. Gephart. Itasca, Ill.: Peacock, 1968.

Glass, V., and Smith, L. *Meta-Analysis—Research on the Relationship of Class Size and Achievement*. San Francisco: Far West Laboratory for Educational Research and Development, September 1978.

Gow, D. T. *Design and Development of Curricular Materials*, Vol. 1. Pittsburgh: Center for International Studies Publications, 1976.

Gow, D. T. "Intrinsic Analysis of Instructional Materials: An Aid to Site-Specific Tailoring of Instruction." *Educational Technology* 20 (May 1980): 7–15.

Gross, N.; Giacquinta, J.; and Bernstein, M. *Implementing Organizational Innovations: A Sociological Analysis of Planned Educational Change*. New York: Basic Books, 1971.

Harvey, O. J.; Hunt, D. E.; and Schroeder, H. M. *Conceptual Sytems and Personality Organization*. New York: Wiley, 1961.

Hersh, H.; Paolitto, D. P.; and Reimer, J. *Promoting Moral Growth from Piaget to Kohlberg*. New York: Longman, 1979.

Hyman, J. S., and Cohen, S. A. "Learning for Mastery: Ten Conclusions After Fifteen Years and Three Thousand Schools." *Educational Leadership* 37 (November 1979): 104–109.

Jackson, P. W. *Life in Classrooms*. New York: Holt, Rinehart & Winston, 1968.

Joyce, B., and Weil, M. *Models of Teaching*. Englewood Cliffs, N.J.: Prentice-Hall, 1972.

Kagan, J. "Impulsive and Reflective Children: Significance in Conceptual Tempo." In *Learning and the Educational Process*. Edited by J. D. Krumboltz. Chicago: Rand McNally, 1965.

Kagan, J. "Personality and the Learning Process." In *Creativity and Learning*, pp. 153–163. Boston: Houghton Mifflin, 1967.

Kohlberg, L. "Stage and Sequence: The Cognitive-Developmental Approach to Socialization." In *Socialization Theory and Research*, pp. 347–372. Edited by D. Goslin. Chicago: Rand McNally, 1969.

Kohlberg, L. "The Development of Children's Orientation Toward Moral Order: 1. Sequence in the Development of Moral Thought." *Vita Humana* 6 (1963): 11–33.

Letteri, C. A. "Cognitive Profile: Basic Determinant of Academic Achievement." *The Journal of Educational Research* 73 (March/April 1980).

Lippitt, R.; Fox, R.; and Schaible, L. *Social Science Resource Book*. Chicago: Science Research Associates, 1969.

Maslow, A. *Maturation and Personality*. New York: Harper & Row, 1954.

Maslow, A. *The Farther Reaches of Human Nature*. New York: Viking, 1971.

Massialas, B. G., and Cox, C. B. *Inquiry in Social Studies*. McGraw-Hill, 1966.

Massialas, B. G., and Hurst, J. B. *Social Studies in a New Era: The Elementary School as a Laboratory*. New York: Longman, 1978.

Oliver, D., and Shaver, J. *Teaching Public Issues in the High School*. Boston: Houghton Mifflin, 1966.

Piaget, J. *The Psychology of Intelligence*. London: Routledge and Kegan Paul, 1950.

Rogers, C. R. *Freedom to Learn*. Columbus, Ohio: Merrill, 1969.

Rosenshine, B. V. "Classroom Instruction." In *The Psychology of Teaching Methods*, pp. 355–371. Edited by N. L. Gage. 75th Yearbook of the National Society for the Study of Education. Chicago: University of Chicago Press, 1976.

Rosenshine, B. V. "Academic Engaged Time, Content Covered, and Direction Instruction." Paper presented at American Educational Research Association Annual Meeting, Toronto, March 1978.

Rouk, U., ed. "RBS Regional Exchange." In *Educational R&D Report*. St. Louis: CEMREL, 1979.

Schwab, J. J., Supervisor, Biological Sciences Curriculum Study. *Biology Teacher's Handbook*. New York: Wiley, 1965.

Stake, R. E., and Easley, J. A. "Design Overview and General Findings." In *Case Studies in Science Education*, Vol. 2. Washington, D.C.: National Science Foundation, 1977.

Stallings, J. "Allocated Academic Learning Time Revisited or Beyond Time on Task." *Educational Researcher* 9 (December 1980).

Stallings, J.; Needels, M.; and Staybrook, N. *How to Change the Process of Teaching Basic Reading Skills in Secondary Schools*. Menlo Park, Calif.: SRI, 1979.

Suchman, J. R. *Inquiry Box Teacher's Handbook*. Chicago: Science Research Associates, 1967.

Taba, H. *Teacher's Handbook for Elementary Social Studies*. Reading, Mass. Addison-Wesley, 1967, reprinted 1971.

Thelen, H. A. *Classroom Grouping for Teachability*. New York: Wiley, 1967.

Thelen, H. A. *Education and the Human Quest*. New York: Harper, 1960.

Torrance, E. P. *Guiding Creative Talent*. Englewood Cliffs, N.J.: Prentice-Hall, 1962.

Tyler, R. *Basic Principles of Curriculum and Instruction*. Chicago: University of Chicago Press, 1949, 1975.

Walker, D. F., and Schaffarzick, J. "Comparing Curricula." *Review of Educational Research* 44 (January 1974): 83–111.

Wiley, D. E., and Harnischfeger, A. "Explosion of a Myth: Quantity of Schooling and Exposure to Instruction, Major Educational Vehicles." *Educational Researcher* 3 (1974): 7–12.

Witkin, H. A.; Dyk, R. B.; Faterson, H. F.; Goodenough, D. R.; and Karp, S. A. *Psychological Differentiation*. New York: Wiley, 1962.

Chapter 10

Curriculum Implementation

Susan F. Loucks and
Ann Lieberman

People responsible for implementing new curricula voice many concerns:
"Here we go again, another mandate!"
"Teachers are already overloaded—how can we ask for their involvement?"
"The needs assessment indicates no one is teaching science. So, who's responsible for filling the need?"
"They say change really only happens at the school level, but I have the whole district to consider!"

These concerns are real and painful. There is never enough time. Expectations and roles are unclear. New laws and regulations constantly add to the already heavy burden. And does anyone really know how to make change occur in schools? Is it really just a "seat of the pants" operation?

Only in the last ten years has curriculum implementation become a major concern of our educational systems. This concern has resulted partially from the expenditure of millions of dollars on development and partially from the realization that relatively few new ideas make it "behind the classroom door." Now thousands of individuals—principals, coordinators, consultants—have implementation responsibilities, and they are just now asking such questions as: What conditions are necessary to ensure implementation? Who should do what? What expectations should we have for the process?

Findings from research in implementation are inconclusive and contradictory. It is not yet known what should be done to successfully implement new curricula in different settings, under different conditions. Philosophical debates rage. Different perspective and sets of experiences bolster different points of view.

Two fundamental questions are asked in this chapter. From the morass of dialogue and research: What are the key understandings that have emerged from research and experience in making curricular changes? And how can these new understandings be used to plan and carry out more effective curriculum implementation efforts. Three concepts will be noted and applied to different situations and their application in several instances described.

Some Perspectives About Curriculum Implementation

We define implementation as the actual use of a new practice, what the practice looks like when certain characteristics are actually in use in a social system. This differs from planned use or intended use and from the decision to use, which we would refer to as adoption (Fullan and Pomfret, 1977).

One barrier to understanding successful implementation has been a lack of description and discussion of improvement efforts from the perspective of the teacher and the school. The task in this section is to attempt to understand how new ideas actually get used at these levels and gather clues about how to act on our understandings.

Cutting across knowledge about schools and efforts at improvement are ways of thinking about innovations themselves. (In this chapter, the term "innovation" is defined broadly as any process, product, idea, or practice that requires new behaviors of the user.)

People tend to hold many different views of schools, of teachers, and of curriculum. And these views have a great deal to do with how one organizes resources, provides support, and deals with the complexities of social change. Ernest House (1979) offers three perspectives that begin to help us think about the problems and prospects of implementing new curricula in schools. Each perspective alerts us to ask different questions and focuses our attention on different parts of the implementation process.

The Technological View

By far the most prevalent view is the technological. Assumptions are held that education is technical, and teachers are technicians. Improvement is possible by training teachers in new and improved techniques.

This view is best illustrated by hundreds of districts that adopt "programs" and assume they will be implemented immediately. The process of involving school staff is linear; that is, it is assumed that people just need exposure and minimal training to implement these new and better ideas. The technological view focuses on the innovation itself and pays scant attention to the process of change, the politics, or the people. When improvement is viewed from this perspective, the idea is critical. We ask such questions as: Is the innovation well developed, with materials, activities, strategies that substantially change the teacher-pupil relationship? Is it a set of techniques to replace existing ones? Does it contain a new set of assumptions about how to work? These important questions help us consider change from the technological perspective.

The Political View

The focus here shifts to the organization, to what happens when the innovation meets the school. In this perspective, it is assumed that many groups are involved with schools; these groups have vested interests in different kinds of changes. Education is thus political, and innovations are value-laden as they are sponsored or ignored by different groups. They are often adapted and re-shaped, congruent with the groups' values, assumptions, and beliefs.

The most important understandings from this perspective have been those gained from the Rand Change Agent Study of Title III and Title VII (Berman and McLaughlin, 1978). It alerted educators to some critical factors regarding the implementation of innovations:

1. Activities and interactions that happen at the school level, regardless of the type or method of the innovation, determine the success or failure of implementation.

2. Mutual adaptation, the process by which project goals are formulated and teachers adapt what they do, is necessary for successful implementation. This process describes the dynamic interactions between the innovation and the practical realities of the classroom.

3. Strategies for accomplishing this mutual adaptation include: concrete teacher experiences, classroom assistance, teacher observation of other teachers, regular meetings with a practical focus, teacher participation in project decisions, local materials development, and principal participation in training.

For the first time, educators began to see what happens when ideas are put into an institutional context. The organizational influences on the innovation are at least as crucial as the innovation itself.

The Cultural View

More recently there has been a focus on the school itself and the people in it. How do teachers respond to constant pressure to make changes in the teaching of reading or math (Goodlad, 1975; Sarason, 1971)? How do they see their work? What does it look like when teachers are involved in innovative activity and the process is described from their perspective (Gibson, 1973; Wolcott, 1977)? The cultural perspective takes into account the complexity of classroom life and the implications of innovations for the individual classroom and the school. Although school people have a lot of experience, systematic study from this perspective has been meager (Hall and Loucks, 1978; Sieber, 1979; Smith and Keith, 1971).

Studies from these three perspectives have added to understandings of the impact of the new practice itself, of the interactions between the innovation and groups within the new setting, and of the dynamics of teachers as they confront and use the new ideas. If some learnings about the unique aspects of schools as organizations are added, we begin to get a sense of several key components that are critical to curriculum implementation.

Schools as Organizations

A critical part of understanding the implementation of innovations is recognizing some salient features about schools (Miles, 1979):

1. Goals for schools are vague and therefore lend themselves to many interpretations.

2. Since teachers learn their craft essentially from experience, many styles develop in the process of interpreting the vague goals of schooling (Lieberman and Miller, 1978; Lortie, 1975).

3. Teachers are both constrained by and autonomous of school leaders.

4. The school is actually an organization of loosely-tied classrooms. Therefore, there is little centralized control. This has both advantages and disadvantages for curriculum change. Mandating across-the-board changes is often ineffective. But pockets of innovation are easy to encourage and may flourish in spite of groups that are not open to improvement.

5. Each school is a unique culture. Generalization or "how to's" are often not specific enough because of these differences (Sarason, 1971).

6. Schools as organizations and teachers in their classrooms go through stages as they cope with new ideas (Hall and Loucks, 1978). But teachers' commitments at one stage do not guarantee commitment at another stage (Sieber, 1979).

If we look at the research focused on questions from the above three perspectives, and at how schools as organizations are known to function, we see the puzzle pieces begin to take shape. We begin to recognize some major understandings that cut across our growing knowledge about teachers, about innovations, about the process of change, and about the context within which new curricula begin to take hold. These understandings are based on three key concepts that have implications for our ways of thinking and ways of acting. They are: Developmentalism, Participation, and Support.

Key Concepts Related to Curriculum Implementation

Developmentalism

An important notion that helps us understand teachers and their responses to curriculum improvement efforts is *developmentalism*. Inquiry into the areas of adult development and, more specifically, teacher development, has shed light on how teachers change as they confront new ideas. Further, such research alerts us to what kinds of personal, material, and interactive support are needed at different stages in the change process.

Heath (1971, 1977), in his work on maturation during adulthood, has identified several principles through which teacher maturity may be encouraged. These include furthering multiple perspectives, increasing integration, and making learning more autonomous. Strategies for curriculum implementation that incorporate these principles include encouraging active involvement (experiential learning), creating a climate that encourages openness and trust, and appreciating and affirming strengths. Such strategies are sensitive to adults' needs to grow and expand their repertoires.

Oja and Sprinthall's (1978) work on moral and conceptual development suggests additional ways of working with teachers as new curricula are introduced and implemented. These include providing opportunities and support for role taking (trying new tasks), reflection (thinking about and learning from new experiences), and challenge.

Both Fuller (1969) and Field (1979) have addressed teacher development from the perspective of the preservice or beginning teacher. Their work, remarkably parallel, describes stages in the development of teachers that begin with personal, survival concerns, progress with growing confidence to concerns with classroom functioning, and finally reach a focus on the effects of their teaching on students, both as individuals and in the entire learning context.

These stages and the abilities congruent with them are inherently teacher-like. They again clue us into how we need to think about curriculum implementation. Both Fuller and Field suggest that typical staff development and supervisory activities are planned for teachers at the higher stages, and that they often appear irrelevant to teachers who are functioning at lower stages.

The most intensive and extensive research in the area of teacher development that is specific to curriculum implementation is that of Hall and Loucks and their associates at the Texas Research and Development Center for Teacher Education. Their study of the change process indicates that as individuals implement new curricula, they change in their feelings about and their skills in using new ideas. The concerns teachers feel about new curricula develop from more *self-oriented* early in the process (Can I do it? What will I have to do differently?), to more *task-oriented* as they begin use (It takes *so* long to prepare every day! Will I ever get the materials organized?). And, finally, when they have mastered a procedure that works for them, they can focus on the *impact* of the curriculum (Is this new curriculum working with all my students? Are there ways I can refine it so it will be better?). (For a more detailed description of the seven Stages of Concern identified through Texas research, as well as for measurement tools, see Hall and Loucks, 1978).

Similarly, teachers' behaviors in using new curricula are developmental: they first *orient* and *prepare* (attend training, acquire supplies); initial use is *mechanical*, where the unanticipated often happens and planning is largely day-to-day; curriculum use becomes *routine*, with few changes being made; and they then may *refine* or adjust the curriculum to better meet learner needs. (Again, more extensive information about the concept and measurement of Levels of Use can be found in Hall and Loucks, 1977).

Understanding the developmental aspects of change helps us design implementation efforts that are long-term and that anticipate teachers' questions and problems. For example, if we know that personal concerns occur early, we are certain to clarify expectations and plan for individual input and consultation. If we know management concerns accompany first use, we provide hands-on training, and stand by to answer questions, help solve problems, and provide continual material support and encouragement.

The developmental aspects of school improvement also allow curriculum people to set goals about how far to encourage teachers in their development. It is one thing to meet needs as they emerge; it is another to arouse concerns at higher levels. For example, teachers often establish a routine use of a curriculum and immediately their concerns are elsewhere (typically resulting from new expectations or innovations that have a higher priority for administrators). Do we wish to encourage teachers to refine their use of the new curriculum? Do we work to arouse their concerns about student impact? These questions arise from our understanding of "developmentalness," which we must consider in designing efforts to implement new curricula.

Participation

If we accept the fact that the majority of teachers have learned to teach by doing it, we come to understand that teacher style is idiosyncratic. Teachers also differ in skill, commitment, and in their sense of professionalism (Daft and Becker, 1978; Field, 1979). Because of these differences, a teacher's view of teaching and learning must be part of any innovative activity.

The engagement of teachers in new ideas that have relevance for their classroom activities calls upon curriculum staff to create opportunities for involvement. In many ways teachers are the experts, and their commitment to improvement depends heavily on involving them in shaping ideas to fit their style.

Research indicates that when teachers participate in decisions made during the process of implementation, the likelihood of successful implementation is increased (Berman and McLaughlin, 1978; Louis, 1980). What is not clear is when exactly teachers ought to be engaged, nor is it clear how much teachers should be involved. Characteristics of teacher style, commitment, and skill are critical to decisions about when participation should take place. School characteristics such as organizational structure, principal style, and student population must also be considered in the decisions about teacher participation. It remains clear, however, that without adequate participation, the chance of successful implementation greatly diminishes.

The pre-condition for real participation in improvement efforts must be a trust built between those responsible for facilitating implementation (principals, curriculum personnel, staff developers) and teachers. This is often not the case, since teachers in many districts have been asked to adopt new practices without the necessary support. So as a starting point there must be a significant level of trust among members of the school staff. Given this, there are many opportunities for teacher participation.

One possible strategy employed is the use of teachers as peer trainers or advisors. Teachers have always picked up ideas from other teachers, so the role of peer trainer is a natural one. A few teachers from a school might be given support to become experts in a new curriculum, with the responsibility for subsequently training other teachers in its use. The added benefit of this strategy is the ability of these new trainers to relate directly to the problems and conditions of implementing the curriculum in the particular classroom involved.

Another strategy is for teachers representing either schools or grade levels within schools to be part of a team charged with planning an implementation. Such a team can take responsibility for scheduling and facilitating training, for procuring and maintaining needed materials and equipment, and for convening problem-solving sessions as implementation unfolds. This direct involvement encourages ownership as well as accountability for the outcomes of the new curriculum.

These are but a couple of instances of how participation comes about. There are infinite combinations and strategies. The significance of teacher participation in school improvement has more to do with how the activities are handled than with the content of the improvement itself (Emrick and Peterson, 1978). Sensitivity to who the faculty are, their past experience with improvement activities, an accurate assessment of the social context (What are the pressures on the faculty?), and an understanding of the interpersonal relations among the staff—these are the factors that help determine how one organizes for participation.

Support

A final key concept to implementation is *support*. It has always been clear that certain financial and material support are needed to implement a new curriculum. There are, however, many more kinds of support that are important, and the kinds of support vary with where teachers are in the implementation process (Emrick and Peterson, 1978; Loucks and Hall, 1979).

One of our assumptions is that with an understanding of how change occurs and what influences it, it is possible to purposefully design and carry out a long-term, successful implementation effort. To do so, certain supportive arrangements must be anticipated and made in advance. Other arrangements are necessary while first implementation is in process, and still others for when the initial furor has subsided and maintenance must occur.

Material support, the most obvious, is of prime importance initially, when teachers are supplied with new materials and equipment. Nothing slows down an implementation effort more surely than late-arriving materials, or requirements to share beyond what is practical. In addition, one indicator that a curriculum is institutionalized is the regular, deliberate reordering and refurbishing of necessary supplies.

Human support is more often overlooked than physical support. The need for trusting relationships between administration and teachers was noted earlier. Both research and common knowledge indicate that the principal is a key element in the success of a change effort (Berman and McLaughlin, 1978; Mann, 1976). It is not entirely clear what behaviors of a principal are most supportive, but two are critical: reminders that use of the new curriculum is a school priority, and informal encouragement and interest. Principals are not often trained to understand teachers and how they experience change. Helping principals become aware of the developmentalness of change influences them to make their expectations more realistic, especially in the first year, and to be more supportive and understanding of personal and management concerns.

Another ingredient of human support is intentionally delaying the introduction of additional new curricula or programs during the first and second years of implementation. The all-too-common routine of overloading teachers with innovations has given school improvement a bad reputation and has soured many on trying anything new. Some districts have established priority inservices so that teachers will not be involved in too many new training experiences at the same time.

Time is a commodity as important to successful change as material and moral support. Research indicates that it takes three to five years to institutionalize a complex innovation. Before deciding to implement a new curriculum, a commitment is needed to take the time required to facilitate the process and ensure its continuance. Time is needed for teachers to plan, adapt materials, train, solve problems, and provide peer support. Released time is optional for at least some of this, since time spent at the end of a busy school day is rarely productive.

The support of peers is another form of support. Teaching is a lonely activity, particularly in schools with self-contained classrooms. Teachers spend the large majority of their time with students and have minimal interaction with other professionals. Improvement efforts are greatly enhanced when teachers are provided the time and encouragement to work together, sharing ideas, solving problems, creating new materials to enhance a new curriculum. This is especially true when the curriculum has been used for a time and their experiences have made teachers more aware of strategies for improvement.

A final source of support that is often not considered by the district level curriculum person is the national bank of validated programs and practices that are available through the U.S. Department of Education. The National Diffusion Network, just one of several such sources, combines expertise in the form of consultants and trainers, with packaged materials and activities upon which to base a sound school improvement effort. Research has indicated that assistance from individuals external to the district can have an important impact on curriculum implementation (Crandall and others, 1981; Havelock, 1973) as can the use of the validated programs themselves (Louis, 1980).

The curriculum person does not have to be the only support for teachers implementing a new curriculum. If these various kinds of support are considered and multiple sources such as principals, other teachers, and external resources are taken advantage of, a change effort is more likely to succeed.

Applying the Understandings

Common implementation issues faced by curriculum people are how to respond to new federal or state guidelines, how to make improvements where low achievement scores prevail, and how to use results of new research.

The key concepts we have delineated may not be applied with equal emphasis to all situations. For example, in a school responsible for its own curriculum, teacher participation may be at a maximum; with a federally-mandated program, less participation in decision making may be possible, while more emphasis may be placed on meeting developmental needs of teachers as they emerge.

Following are some common situations faced by those responsible for curriculum implementation. We have created scenarios that incorporate the major learnings and suggest some courses of action. Note that, at times, for the sake of clarity, we do not discuss all the ramifications of suggested actions. Clearly, each is part of the highly complex process of implementation and must influence every other step that is taken. Our object here is not to understand and anticipate every possible situation, but rather to suggest some general courses of action.

Local Problem Situation

Many studies of implementation indicate that the local school is where new ideas stop or start. Often these ideas arise from needs within the school. What might this look like? How do the key concepts look when a curriculum problem arises from the inside?

Experiences in a large metropolitan district, with typical big-city problems such as overcrowding, low student self-concept, and many "pull out" programs, provide several opportunities for looking at local situations. In one school, programs proliferated because of Title I funds, compensatory money, and additional district funds given because of double sessions. The principal met with representatives from each grade level and decided to take drastic measures. After assessing grade-level needs, the group found the school's key problem to be student progress, in spite of the many programs. The district had mandated a diagnostic-prescriptive reading program but because record-keeping proved to be too time consuming, the program was not being implemented. Initial participation in the school came from grade level coordinators and the principal acting as a team, with their views corroborated through grade-level meetings. Here the concepts of participation and developmentalism were apparent, with broad-based participation, and those in leadership positions considering where people start, where the frustrations are, and how people can participate in solving their own problems.

To follow this school's scenario, the team decided to take the reading program and dissect it to see why it was not working. They started from the beginning. What does the teacher need to do to make this reading program work? What are the barriers? Their initial findings were that "the program" was too mechanistic to be implemented as designed. The teacher and students were taking and correcting tests all day. Teachers needed help integrating this program into a larger language arts curriculum. Because teachers and students needed to see progress, the team broke up the program into four-week segments. Teachers decided what objectives were legitimate for *their* class in a four-week block of time. And aides were hired to help prepare materials and correct tests.

Both human and material resources from outside the classroom served as support for the teachers. The year-long program was broken up into small segments. After the first four weeks, the team synthesized pre- and post-test scores for each class. These were printed for all teachers, who were very enthusiastic about seeing their four-weeks' work bear fruit. Students had accomplished 75 percent of the objectives. The team then called the staff together to share their learnings. Teachers began to plan the next four weeks and discuss feedback for parents.

What had been a generally frustrating situation, manifested in disappointed parents, a proliferation of programs with few results, and worn out teachers, turned into an enthusiastic group of teachers defining their own problem. With their involvement the problem was defined, short-term goals were created, resources for support were organized, and both teachers and students began to see results. The team used their strategy and the results for their initial parent meetings. And parents responded not only to the raised achievement scores, but to an invitation to help their children by reinforcing the four weeks' worth of reading skills.

This scenario suggests that involving people (participation in definition of the problem), starting where the group wants to start and moving as they learn (developmentalism), and providing adequate support (both human and material) are possible. In such situations, the key concepts give dignity to the teachers' knowledge of the problems and provide clues to the strategies to deal with them.

Implementation of District Curricula

Some of our educational systems prefer districtwide curriculum, others schoolwide, and still others encourage curriculum created by each teacher for his or her classroom. Districtwide curricula are common, and in spite of opinions to the contrary, have many arguments in their favor. In our mobile society, students who change schools need consistency. Articulation between elementary, junior high/middle, and senior high schools is eased when students have had similar preparation and experiences. Assistance in the form of expertise and material resources can be more targeted and efficient if consistent districtwide. With ever-shrinking resources, it is difficult to provide each school the opportunity to select or create curricula in all the areas of schooling, in addition to acquiring appropriate materials and training.

In districts where curricula are implemented districtwide, special challenges present themselves. These deal with creating opportunities for teacher participation, conducting both extensive and intensive training, and providing adequate follow-up and support for ongoing use. Implementation at the district level requires systematic planning without losing sight of the teacher's need to be involved in the process and supported as his or her perceptions change.

In some districts, a sophisticated process of curriculum development has been used that involves teacher needs assessments, teachers and district personnel serving on writing teams, pilot and field testing, and revisions based on teacher input. Teacher participation is viewed as critical in curriculum development.

Implementation of such curricula begins then with some ground rules derived from the key concepts (Loucks and Pratt, 1979). The implementation process is expected to take time, with an investment of several years and adequate staff and material resources. The developmentalness of the process requires different activities as implementation unfolds (Pratt and others, 1980).

A sensitive issue in district curriculum is teacher adaptation. Clearly, teachers must make a curriculum usable in their classrooms. On the other hand, the "essence" of a program is often lost through adaptation. For example, in one district, a new science curriculum with a major environmental strand requires live organisms. To maintain these daphnia, crickets, or crayfish, certain procedures and equipment are needed which are sometimes messy and time-consuming. Teachers who accommodated and minimized the mess, and tolerated the extra time it took, discovered students loved the activities and learned a great deal. Those who "adapted" the activities before trying them, eliminating the live organisms, did not provide their students with such opportunity.

The relationship among curricula, teachers, and curriculum personnel is critical. First, the curriculum *must* "work"—the objectives and activities must be developed so that their possible impact is optimized. When children learn, teachers rarely object to the curriculum. Second, expectations for use of the curriculum must be clear. In cases of district-formulated curricula, a contract agreement may bind teachers to its use. A less authoritarian stance may be a mutual understanding among curriculum personnel and teachers that the curriculum is the best that is available and the teachers will try it until it is proven ineffective. Acknowledging that it takes time for implementation to occur and teachers are not expected to be experts overnight is also important. Third, the most important job of curriculum personnel is to facilitate use of the curriculum, to ensure that teachers have all the materials, training, facilities, time, and moral support they require to use it with the fewest problems and concerns.

Now that the ground rules are established, the sequence of events in an implementation effort can parallel the emergence of teachers' different concerns and increasing skills. Early information and self-oriented concerns are resolved with brief overview sessions and with opportunities for teachers to discuss how they will use the curriculum. At this time, individual and school discussions might evolve around adaptations for the particular physical or organizational settings, or the student population. As noted earlier, caution is in order, since adaptations made without first trying a new curriculum are often oriented more toward practicality than student need. An agreement to try the curriculum first "as is" may be in order.

"Support" in these early stages of implementation clearly has both affective and material connotations. Curriculum personnel know they should listen to teachers' concerns, but instead are often so enraptured with the new programs that they ignore those who are expected to use them. Teachers need to know that they are the acknowledged experts in their classrooms, that the curriculum is for their use, and that discussion about its effectiveness is encouraged. This alleviates some of the self-oriented concerns.

As the time arrives for use of the curriculum, management concerns begin to emerge and extensive, hands-on training is necessary. Involvement with the new procedures and materials is facilitated by providing teachers released-time, long enough to understand and explore what the curriculum involves. Merely delivering the teachers' guide and materials, and/or a single after-school inservice, is not an effective way to promote implementation.

The optimal situation is a series of released-time inservices spread over a semester or year. This acknowledges the developmentalness of the change process. As the early nitty-gritty learnings are incorporated into the classroom, concerns emerge from experience with students. These concerns may constitute the substance of later inservice sessions. Teachers who have used the new curriculum and understand adult learning can be used to conduct inservice sessions (Schiff, 1981).

During the first months of implementation, an effective strategy is what may be called "comfort and caring," where district curriculum people or teacher facilitators visit and "troubleshoot" in classrooms where the new curriculum is in use. At the same time, the support and participation of the school principal is particularly important. Teachers must know that the principal supports the curriculum, both substantively (by making certain supplies are available and schedules are accommodating) and psychologically (by encouraging teachers, acknowledging that it will take time to get the curriculum incorporated smoothly, communicating that it is clearly a priority).

Once the problems of initial implementation have been solved, and use of the new curriculum has smoothed out for teachers, it is timely to review the goal set for implementation. Was it to get this far and then maintain use? Or was it to assist and encourage teachers to continually refine the curriculum to meet particular student or class needs? Strategies for these two goals are clearly different. If use is to be simply maintained (although often not "simple"), attention is paid to how curricula become institutionalized. Certain behaviors are built into school and district functioning: new teachers are automatically oriented to the curriculum; supplies and replacements for equipment are ordered routinely; periodic visits to schools are made by curriculum staff. Without continued attention to these ongoing support functions, new curricula are soon lost.

If the goal is constant refinement of the curriculum by teachers, additional strategies are needed. One of these may be periodically convening teacher support groups to discuss successes and problems, new ideas and strategies. After sufficient time has passed since use of the curriculum became smooth, training teachers to do self-analysis, classroom observations, and student assessments can provide data for making changes in curriculum use. One school district has sponsored a curriculum improvement plan where principals and district staff make observations in teachers' classrooms, providing data for dialogues with teachers about what they need to make more effective use of the curriculum (Melle and Pratt, 1981). Advanced and sophisticated staff development techniques such as "interactive research and development in teaching," developed at Far West Laboratory (Ward and Tikunoff, 1975) may be in order at this point.

At this advanced stage of implementation, curriculum staff are clearly facilitators, with teacher participation and leadership the key ingredients. Providing opportunities for teachers to meet and to be exposed to new ideas through workshops and attendance at conferences is of utmost importance. Utilizing these strategies and points of view maximizes the possibilities for a curriculum to be most effective for each student.

Implementation of Mandates

Some of the most difficult challenges faced by curriculum personnel are mandates—usually federal or state—that require changes in what happens in schools and classrooms. Few argue with the intentions of such concepts as "least restrictive environment," competency testing, and equal opportunity. Yet the actual implementation of these ideas is far more time-consuming, costly, and energy-depleting than policy makers usually anticipate.

Those who mandate educational change most often have a purely technological view of the implementation process: "Decree it today, it will be implemented tomorrow with short, intensive training, and we can hold people accountable for its outcomes by the end of the school year." Rarely are adequate time and resources allocated. Resisting mandates, protesting that they are unrealistic, is one strategy for dealing with them. But this is rarely, if ever, effective. If a mandate is to be implemented, it should be possible to make it an opportunity for improvement, rather than a complete waste of energy.

Mandates can be seen as an opportunity because, like all other impetuses for change, they have the effect of unfreezing individuals and organizations. They cause introspection into present practice and movement toward behavior change. Such unfreezing is one of the most difficult challenges faced by the facilitator and, for this reason, mandates can help.

Once the unfreezing occurs, opportunities exist to shape what will happen in schools and classrooms. We often complain that mandates are not specific enough; they decree outcomes, but it is unclear how to get there. However, the lack of specificity allows for local definition, which provides opportunities for creation of unique programs targeted at the specific settings. Mandates can take as many forms as there are teachers or schools, if the past is any predictor. No two plans for desegregation are alike; districts implement P.L. 94-142 using widely different strategies; and bilingual education is implemented in different ways in different schools.

Mandates can be implemented using strategies similar to those described for local problem situations and districtwide implementation. Which of these strategies is chosen, however, depends on the answers to two interrelated questions:

1. Where is the flexibility for defining what will happen as a result of the mandate?

2. Where will responsibility for the major design and decision making lie?

The first question recognizes that mandates dictate different kinds of policies and activities. A competency testing mandate may decree that a specific test be given to students in a certain grade, but not what materials or strategies will be used for teaching. A school improvement mandate may define a certain process to be undertaken, resulting in a concrete plan for action, but not which areas should be the focus for improvement. A bilingual education mandate may specify precisely which students must receive instruction in their first language, but not what and how they will be taught. None of these mandates may dictate how the implementation will occur, who should be involved in its planning and evaluation, and what strategies might be used. So although certain areas are well defined, others are left entirely to the discretion of local districts and schools. Identifying where this flexibility lies is a critical first step in designing the implementation for a mandate.

Finding the flexibility is related to deciding the next question: where does the major responsibility for implementation reside? Certain mandates clearly dictate a districtwide approach, desegregation, for instance. Here a district plan is required as is a unified approach to the community. Other mandates allow more decision making to reside at the school level. For example, competency testing may require districtwide test administration, but the instructional and curricular approaches taken to ensure student success on the tests may be an individual school decision. Clearly, the responsibility is rarely either wholly at the school or at the district level. But an important ingredient in mandate implementation, perhaps even more important than for nonmandates, is designation of who is responsible for what, and establishment of clear lines of communication between the different parties.

The three key concepts of curriculum implementation—developmental-ism, participation, and support—can be helpful in dealing with mandates and their implications for classroom instruction. Some mandates require a district approach, while others require a school-level approach; others can be defined wherever appears appropriate. For example, districts with a statewide mandate for citizenship education might adopt and implement a districtwide curriculum, or may leave the area to individual schools to develop. Depending on the level at which the major implementation effort occurs, it is possible to draw strategies from the two previous sections: Local Problem Situations and Implementation of District Curricula. Some of the key concepts, however, lend themselves more appropriately to mandate situations than others.

What is known about teacher development can guide how a mandate is handled in its early stages. Teachers naturally will feel less comfortable, more anxious, and need more information about a new program when they have not participated in the decision to use it. Special attention must be paid to these early concerns. As in district implementation, one way is to be very clear about what is involved, that teachers are expected to use the program, and that they will be given all the moral and physical support they require to do so. Another way is to identify the flexibility open at the classroom level and allow for teacher input into and adaptation of all but the most essential components. Participation in molding what is actually to happen in their classrooms will alleviate some early anxieties and adequacy concerns. Again, participation often leads to ownership and successful implementation, so that wherever teachers can be involved in shaping the new program, or in planning the process of implementing it, the effort is more likely to lead to positive results.

Support is critical to mandates since teachers rarely "go the extra mile" for something they did not choose. They can, however, get hooked on something if it is not impractical to use and it appears to influence their students positively. Our experience is that ownership can be developed after the fact when something is mandated; both teachers and support staff agree that "if we can't beat 'em, join 'em," and adequate support is provided to make it all possible (Crandall and others, 1981). At times, the support may need to take unique forms, such as providing clerical assistance for paperwork, released time for extra planning or team meeting, and rewards for participation (course credit, stipends). The combination of adequate support, attention to teacher developmental needs, and clear and explicit expectations for use of a new program provides greatest potential for successful implementation.

References

Berman, P., and McLaughlin, M. *Federal Programs Supporting Educational Change, Vol. VIII, Implementing and Sustaining Innovations*. Santa Monica: Rand, 1978.

Crandall, D., and others. *Findings from a Study of Dissemination Efforts Supporting School Improvement*. Andover, Mass.: The NETWORK, 1981.

Daft, R., and Becker, S. *The Innovative Organization*. New York: Elsevier, 1978.

Emrick, J., and Peterson, S. *A Synthesis of Findings Across Five Recent Studies in Educational Dissemination and Change*. San Francisco: Far West Laboratory, 1978.

Field, K. *A Study of the States in Development of Teachers*. Brookline, Mass.: Brookline Teacher Center, 1979.

Fullan, M., and Pomfret, A. "Research on Curriculum and Instruction Implementation." *Review of Educational Research* 47 (January 1977): 33–39.

Fuller, F. "Concerns of Teacher: A Developmental Conceptualization." *American Educational Research Journal* 6 (February 1969): 207–226.

Gibson, T. *Teachers Talking, Aims, Methods, Attitudes to Change*. Great Britain: Allen Love, 1973.

Goodlad, J. *The Dynamics of Educational Change*. New York: McGraw-Hill, 1975.

Hall, G., and Loucks, S. "A Developmental Model for Determining Whether the Treatment is Actually Implemented." *American Educational Research Journal* 14 (March 1977): 263–276.

Hall, G., and Loucks, S. "Teacher Concerns as a Basis for Facilitating and Personalizing Staff Development." *Teachers College Record* 80 (January 1978): 36–53.

Havelock, R. *The Change Agent's Guide to Innovation in Education*. Englewood Cliffs, N.J.: Educational Technology Publications, 1973.

Heath, D. *Humanizing Schools: New Directions, New Decisions*. New York: Hayden, 1971.

Heath, D. *Maturity and Competence: A Transcultural View*. New York: Gardner, 1977.

House, E. "Three Perspectives on Innovation: The Technological, the Political, and the Cultural." Prepared for program on Research and Education Practice. Washington, D.C.: National Institute of Education, 1979.

Lieberman, A., and Miller, L. "The Social Realities of Teaching." In *Staff Development: New Demands, New Realities, New Perspectives*. New York: Teachers College Press, 1978.

Lortie, D. *School Teacher*. Chicago: University of Chicago Press, 1975.

Loucks, S., and Hall, G. *Implementing Innovations in Schools: A Concerns-Based Approach*. Austin, Tex.: University of Texas Research and Development Center for Teacher Education, 1979.

Loucks, S., and Pratt, H. "A Concerns-Based Approach to Curriculum Change." *Educational Leadership* 37 (March 1979): 212–215.

Louis, K. *Findings from the Study of the R & D Utilization Program*. Cambridge: Abt, 1980.

Mann, D. "The Politics of Training Teachers in Schools." *Teachers College Record* 77 (March 1976): 323–338.

Melle, M., and Pratt, H. *Documenting Program Adaptation in a District-Wide Implementation Effort: The Three-Year Evolution from Evaluation to an Instructional Improvement Plan.* Austin, Tex.: University of Texas Research and Development Center for Teacher Education, 1981.

Miles, M. "Common Properties of School in Context: The Backdrop for Knowledge Utilization and School Improvement." Prepared for program on Research and Educational Practice. Washington, D.C.: National Institute of Education, 1979.

Oja, S., and Sprinthall, N. "Psychological and Moral Development for Teachers: Can You Teach Old Dogs?" In *Value Development . . . As the Aim of Education.* Edited by N. Sprinthall and R. Mosher. New York: Character Research Press, 1978.

Pratt, H.; Melle, M.; Metzdorf, J.; and Loucks, S. *The Design and Utilization of a Concerns-Based Staff Development Program for Implementing a Revised Science Curriculum in Eighty Elementary Schools.* Austin, Tex.: University of Texas Research and Development Center for Teacher Education, 1980.

Sarason, S. *The Culture of the School and the Problem of Change.* Boston: Allyn and Bacon, 1971.

Schiff, S. *Training Teachers as Inservice Leaders for Implementation.* Arvada, Colo.: Jefferson County Public Schools Staff Development Academy, 1981.

Sieber, S. "Incentives and Disincentives for Knowledge Utilization in Public Education: A Synthesis of Research" Prepared for program on Research and Educational Practices. Washington, D.C.: National Institute of Education, 1979.

Smith, L., and Keith, P. *Anatomy of an Educational Innovation.* New York: Wiley, 1971.

Ward, B., and Tikunoff, W. *An Interactive Model of Research and Development.* San Francisco: Far West Laboratory, 1975.

Wolcott, H. *Teachers vs. Technocrats.* Eugene, Oreg.: Center for Educational Policy and Management, University of Oregon, 1977.

Chapter 11

Curriculum Research and Evaluation

Frederick A. Rodgers

Throughout the second half of this century there have been a number of large-scale curriculum development activities conducted in many countries with very different socioeconomic and political circumstances. In the developing countries, the availability of new educational systems suggested the need for major curriculum revisions. In developed countries, support for curriculum change was fueled by widespread dissatisfaction with existing educational programs and practices. These various movements led directly to increased activity in the field of curriculum development across the whole spectrum of problems associated with the area. Specifically, there was increasing agreement about the compelling need to revise instructional materials and methods of teaching to deal more precisely and effectively with the changing characteristics of students, the accumulation of new knowledge and ways of combining content, emerging social issues, the environmental context of learning, and the variety of social and personal practices characterizing contemporary living.

Many of the educational critics of the 50s and 60s were concerned and many times opposed to either the nature of the content and its organization or to how the content was taught. In many instances critics thought that both content and instructional approaches needed a radical overhaul. On the basis of the concerns of critics and professional educators alike changes in the way the curriculum is selected, organized, and presented to students have been made and established as part of accepted practice. The establishment of new curriculum practices has led to the need to provide knowledge of the effects of the revised practices in helping students acquire the knowledge and learning experiences needed to attain the educational goals of the nation.

As curriculum development activities expanded, demand for systematic research and evaluation of educational programs increased. Greater demands were made by funding agencies and consumers alike to make available acceptable evidence on the effectiveness of the new programs for bringing about expected results. There is a need for better information (1) attesting to the relevance of the new programs to meet the needs of society and diverse learners, (2) establishing the scientific significance and validity of new instructional materials, (3) outlining the extent to which certain teacher and student behaviors are elicited, and (4) certifying the actual outcomes resulting from the use of a given set of instructional materials.

Attempts to find answers to specific questions suggested by these four areas have led curriculum evaluators to design models of curriculum components and outline guidelines and methods for generating, collecting, summarizing, and analyzing data required to arrive at conclusions about key educational questions. The need to learn more about educational programs as contrasted with learning more about students or teachers exclusively has led to the creation of the field of curriculum evaluation.

The Systematic Practice of Curriculum Evaluation

As resources were made available for public and private sources to revise, develop, and implement curriculum materials and activities, there were increased demands for accountability and judgments of value and effectiveness. The call for more systematic evaluation of curriculum activities by funding agencies and consumers alike began to parallel the growth in curriculum development and implementation that characterized the score of years between 1960 and 1980.

The proliferation of educational programs dictated a need for data and information that could be used as evidence to judge the value of the materials and suggested teaching methods in relation to expected educational and social outcomes. Answers were being sought concerning the social and educational relevance for different kinds of learners, worth and validity of content and materials, impact of programs on the behavior patterns of teachers and learners, and measured outcomes resulting directly from the use of selected instructional materials. According to Lewy (1977) curriculum evaluation was being asked to provide specific answers to (or at least some insight into) the following questions:

Is it worthwhile to devote time to learning the materials included in the program?

Do the educational materials reflect recent developments and contemporary ideas dominant in a given field of intellectual or scientific behavior?

Are the study materials free from obsolete concepts and ideas?

Under the prevailing system of teaching-learning conditions can the new program be successfully implemented?

Will the students master certain skills as a result of the program?

Will the students acquire certain desired attitudes and values?

Will the teachers accept the major tenets and objectives of the program?

Is the new program an economic means of obtaining certain desired goals?

What unintended or unforeseen outcomes may emerge as a result of utilizing a given program?

To that list should be added these questions:

Was there a plan or design for implementing the curriculum program?

Were teachers given the time and training necessary to understand and master the content and major components of the curriculum program?

Were teachers afforded an opportunity to observe and practice the delivery approaches called for in the curriculum program?

To what extent was the curriculum program implemented according to the design suggested by the developers?

Do user groups require any prerequisite learnings or experiences to use the materials effectively?

How complete and independent is the new curriculum program as a total learning experience?

Are there provisions for making changes in the program's design and implementation or strategies?

It is obvious that the pursuit of answers to these questions requires a system for selecting, collecting, analyzing, summarizing, and making judgments about relevant data. Some systematic approaches or models used for evaluating curriculum programs have evolved and will be discussed later in the chapter.

Curriculum evaluation is concerned with making judgments about educational materials and practices. Since the range and number of combinations possible for educational materials and practices are far-reaching, complex, and diverse, it is necessary to restrict one's thinking to major categories of concerns that characterize curriculum development, design, materials, and implementation strategies. Given this problem, we must set the stage for our converts on curriculum evaluation by briefly outlining major categories that guide the curriculum making process. The categories to which I refer are program focus, medium of instruction, organization of material, teaching strategy, classroom management, and teacher role.

The program focus establishes a boundary for related knowledge in a given field of study. Some scholars in the field refer to it as subject matter, a discipline, or established knowledge in a given field. Knowledge accumulated in a particular field is labeled in accord with traditional areas such as mathematics, biology, chemistry, history, geography, and physics. This approach to grouping and labeling curriculum does not eliminate the possibility of grouping related knowledge according to social problems such as inflation, conservation, energy, democracy, or recreation. The point to be made here is that program focus is a way of determining knowledge selecting boundaries and structure. Curriculum evaluation should take into account the program focus as one basis for selecting and guiding the approaches.

The medium of instruction is primarily concerned with how the program is packaged for delivery. It is concerned with whether the material is in print form, pictures, flyers, filmstrips, or records, and the types of equipment required to present the packaged materials. Presently the medium of instruction is discussed in terms of software (format) and hardware (equipment). The medium of instruction plays a crucial role in the development and delivery of curriculum programs and, accordingly, shapes the nature and approach to curriculum evaluation.

Another area of concern for curriculum evaluation is the organization of material. Curriculum materials may be tightly structured and sequentially presented to intended users or they may be thought of as resource materials to be selected at the discretion of teachers and students. Materials may be organized to achieve stated behavioral outcomes determined by the developer, or to achieve outcomes determined by users with a number of different purposes in mind. The organization of curriculum materials determines in part the approach to evaluation.

The teaching strategy suggested in most curriculum materials concentrates on how the teachers conduct the instructional patterns (interactions with pupils and interactions of pupils with materials), how to deal with selected content, and how to determine expected outcomes. Teaching strategies are specific techniques teachers employ to foster learning and understanding of content and skills. The nature of teaching strategies involved suggests types of curriculum evaluation approaches and questions that might be employed.

Classroom management deals with how the teacher controls the interactions of learners, materials, methods, and schedule of events. How children are grouped according to selected characteristics (needs, abilities, interests, sex, race, experience, and so on) and matched with content, skill, and attitude requirements is a major concern of classroom management. Another aspect of classroom management is the structuring of time and resources for efficient, effective, and balanced use for each child. Classroom management helps set the pattern for curriculum evaluation.

The final area of concern is the role played by the teacher in using the curriculum materials with learners. The role can vary from interpreting the developers' instructions, revising materials, providing prerequisite skills and learnings, motivating students to practice, and assisting students to work independently. Since the teacher often plays a number of different roles, the evaluation approach must be flexible enough to capture the impact of the teacher in different environmental contexts.

Models and Approaches for Curriculum Evaluation

The literature deals with curriculum evaluation in terms of models and approaches. It is important to establish the distinction between models and approaches when applied to curriculum evaluation. In a strict sense a model is:

a description of a set of data in terms of a system of symbols, and the manipulation of the symbols according to the rules of the system. The resulting transformations are translated back into the language of the data and the relationships discussed by the manipulations are compared with the empirical facts (English and English, 1958, p. 326).

Using this definition, patterns of curriculum evaluation are not easily classified as models. Those patterns of curriculum evaluation so classified as models focus on selected features of evaluation, highlight unique functions, and outline procedural patterns. Models used in curriculum evaluation do not always reflect discrete alternatives toward evaluation and are often complementary to one another. In fact, different evaluators often shift the focus of particular evaluation models until they appear to be different from the stated intent of the evaluation model.

There are three major models that dominate the field of curriculum evaluation. These models can be classified on the basis of their concern with (1) achievement of desired outcomes, (2) assessment of merit, and (3) decision making.

The Achievement of Desired Outcomes Model is used primarily to evaluate the achievement level of individual students and/or groups of students. The curriculum evaluator employing this model is interested in the extent to which students are performing in accord with expected behavior. This model seeks to answer the question: "What is the nature of the relationship between educational objectives and student achievement?"

The Assessment of Merit Model of curriculum evaluation is primarily concerned with the examination of the merit of a given entity. The evaluator employing the Merit Model is interested in determining worth of a given entity according to a standard. This model can also concern itself with stages in the curriculum process when certain evaluative questions are raised. The stages refer to functions studied at both the formative and summative periods of the implementation of a curriculum program.

The Decision-Making Model of curriculum evaluation is primarily concerned with future actions based in the evaluation results. This model seeks to sort out alternatives to assist in decision making. While the three models of evaluation briefly discussed are the most prevalent in the field of curriculum, they are usually not mutually exclusive when they are employed. In practice, components of each model may be combined to get at all the different kinds of questions a curriculum evaluator might be asked to handle.

The ways evaluators combine components of various evaluation models have created a number of approaches that are better suited to dealing with specific problem areas than would be the case when using any one of these three models.

Approaches to curriculum evaluation are generic patterns of combining models of evaluation to achieve specific purposes required by selected educational programs. The use of approaches to curriculum evaluation appears to be better suited to the kinds of problems curriculum developers have to solve and to the types of questions that are posed by users and potential users of educational materials. According to Stoke, there are nine approaches that can be employed to conduct educational evaluations. Stoke does not claim that all nine approaches are mutually exclusive both in terms of elements used or applications practiced by evaluators. The nine approaches to which Stoke refers are shown in Figure 1.

How to Conduct a Curriculum Evaluation

Before one can focus a curriculum evaluation study, the evaluator must define the primary audiences and identify critical issues. A second step for the evaluator is to identify information that is relevant to each issue variable and the best sources for obtaining the necessary information. The third step should focus on determining how much information should be collected, summarized, and organized to analyze. A fourth step should involve the selection of appropriate instruments and procedures for gathering and analyzing required data. The final step in the sequence involves interpreting data and comparing results with appropriate standards to support conclusions about value and effectiveness. Components of the various steps are shown in Figure 2.

Reporting Curriculum Evaluation Results

A major consideration in curriculum evaluation is how the results will be reported to the user groups. Since different people have different information needs and different tolerance levels for dealing with certain types of material, the format, style, and technical aspects of an evaluation report must appeal to its intended audience. The curriculum evaluator must remember that different people use a variety of different criteria to judge programs based on the meaning they derive from the data as presented. Figure 3 shows some of the areas that might be considered in reporting curriculum evaluation results.

Figure 4 shows an outline of an evaluation proposal in terms of the dynamic processes associated with implementation and operation (formative evaluation) and the observed results of content and activities of the performance of participants (summative evaluation). The evaluator is responsible for gathering data in process patterns as suggested by the elements shown under "process" in Figure 4. The primary function of the process section of the evaluation is to obtain an accurate description of early development, implementation, and operation of the project's programs and activities.

The program focus of the evaluation is primarily concerned with the effectiveness of the total curriculum program's effort to promote positive changes in achievement performance, attitudes, behaviors, and instructional response patterns of target populations. Protocols for collecting different kinds of data must be matched with the various program elements to be studied. After program data are collected, analyzed, summarized, and formatted for presentation, the different intended audiences should be able to decide the worth, effectiveness (cost and achievement performance), and revisions required of a curriculum program.

Figure 1. Nine Approaches to Educational Evaluation*

Approach	Purpose	Key Elements	Purview Emphasized	Protagonists	Cases, Examples	Risks	Payoffs
Student Gain by Testing	to measure student performance and progress	goal statements; test score analysis; discrepancy between goal and actuality	Educational psychologists	Ralph Tyler Ben Bloom Jim Popham Mal Provus	Steele Womer Lindvall-Cox Husen	oversimplify educ'l aims; ignore processes	emphasize, ascertain student progress
Institutional Self-Study by Staff	to review and increase staff effectiveness	committee work; standards set by staff; discussion; professionalism	Professors, teachers	National Study of School Evaluation Dressel	Boersma-Plawecki Knoll-Brown Carpenter	alienate some staff; ignore values of outsiders	increase state awareness, sense of responsibilities
Blue-Ribbon Panel	to resolve crises and preserve the institution	prestigious panel; the visit; review of existing data & documents	Leading citizens	James Conant Clark Kerr David Henry	Flexner Havighurst House et al. Plowden	postpone action; over-rely on intuition	gather best insights, judgment

Transaction-Observation	to provide understanding of activities and values	educational issues; classroom observation; case studies; pluralism	Client, audience	Lou Smith Parlett-Hamilton Bob Rippey Bob Stake	Macdonald Smith-Pohland Parlett Lundgren	over-rely on subjective perceptions; ignore causes	produce broad picture of program; see conflict in values
Management Analysis	to increase rationality in day to day decisions	lists of options; estimates; feedback loops; costs; efficiency	Managers, economists	Leon Lessinger Dan Stufflebeam Marv Alkin Alan Thomas	Kraft Doughty-Stakenas Hemphill	over-value efficiency; undervalue implicits	feedback for decision making
Instructional Research	to generate explanations and tactics of instruction	controlled conditions, multivariate analysis; bases for generalization	Experimentalists	Lee Cronbach Julian Stanley Don Campbell	Anderson, R. Pella Zdep- Joyce Taba	artificial conditions; ignore the humanistic	new principles of teaching and material development
Social Policy Analysis	to aid development of institutional policies	measures of social conditions and administrative implementation	Sociologists	James Coleman David Cohen Carol Weiss Mosteller-Moynihan	Coleman Jencks Levitan Trankell	neglect of educational issues, details	social choices, constraints clarified

Goal-Free Evaluation	to assess effects of program	ignore proponent claims, follow checklist	Consumers, accountants	Michael Scriven	House-Hogben	over-value documents & record keeping	data on effect with little co-option
Adversary Evaluation	to resolve a two-option choice	opposing advocates, cross-examination, the jury	Expert, juristic	Tom Owens Murray Levine Bob Wolf	Owens Stake- Gjerde Reinhard	personalistic, superficial, time-bound	info. impact good; claims put to test

Of course these descriptive tags are greatly over-simplified. The approaches overlap. Different proponents and different users have different styles. Each protagonist recognizes one approach is not ideal for all purposes. Any one study may include several approaches. The grid is intended only to show some typical, gross differences among contemporary evaluation activities.

*Prepared by R. Stake, CIRCE, September 1974

Figure 2. Steps in Conducting a Curriculum Evaluation

Steps	Things to Consider
1. Identifying Primary Audiences	Program Sponsors; Program Managers and Administrators; Program Participants; Program or Product Consumers; Content Specialists; Lay Citizens; Politicians; Lawmakers
2. Identifying Critical Issues	Outcomes (Expected and Unexpected); Processes; Costs (Resource and Opportunity); Consequences; Justifications; Establishing Standards
3. Identifying Data Sources	People (Teachers, Students, Parents, Developers, etc.); Existing Documents; Available Records (Dynamic and Static); Related Evaluation Research Studies; Competitors
4. Identifying Techniques for Collecting Data	Standardized Tests; Informal Tests; Samples of Student Work; Interviews; Scales (Rating and Attitude); Historical Inquiry; Observation Schedules; Participant Observations; Checklists (Student and Teacher); Behavior Analysis; Anecdotal Records; Interaction Analysis; Utilization of Biographic Data
5. Identifying Techniques for Establishing Standards	Statements by Selected People (Program Personnel, Content Experts, Scholars and Opinion Makers); Reports/Recommendations by Boards, Commissions, or Other Study Groups; Statements by Regulatory Agencies; Survey of Social Values
6. Identifying Techniques for Data Analysis	Content Analysis; Statistics; Graphic Interpretations; Value Comparisons; Logic

Figure 3. Components of Curriculum Evaluation Reporting

Types of Reports   Written; Oral; Progress Reports; Final Reports; Summary Reports; General; Specific; Technical; Nontechnical; Descriptive Only; Graphic Only; Evaluative and Judgmental; List of Recommendations

Modes of Display   Case Studies; Portrayals; Graphs and Charts; Test Score Summarizations; Scenarios; Questions/Answers; Dialogues/Testimonies; Multimedia Representations; Product Display; Simulations

Figure 4. Focus Components of Evaluation Plan

| Process | | Program | | | |
Developmental	Administrative	Objectives	Activities	Performance	Attitude Change
A. Needs assessment	A. Existing administrative organization and procedures	A. Process	A. Student	A. Student achievement	A. Students
B. Curriculum program design	B. Organizational structure and administrative procedures required by new programs	B. Content	B. Staff	B. Staff development	B. Staff
C. Implementation design and strategies	C. Design and operation of program management approach	C. Attitude	C. Administrators	C. Communication	C. School personnel
D. Participant involvement	D. Design and operation of communication pattern		D. Parents	D. Management	D. Community members

References

Beatty, Walcott H., ed. *Improving Educational Assessment and Inventory of Measures of Affective Behavior*. Washington, D.C.: Association for Supervision and Curriculum Development, 1969.

Davis, Joseph L., Conference Director. *Educational Evaluation, Official Proceedings of a Conference*. Columbus, Ohio: State Superintendent of Public Instruction, 1969.

English, Horace B., and English, Ava C. *A Comprehensive Dictionary of Psychological and Psychoanalytical Terms, A Guide to Usage*. New York: Longman, Green, 1958.

Lewy, Arieh, ed. *Handbook of Curriculum Evaluation*. New York: Longman, Inc., 1977.

Patton, Michael Quinn. *Utilization-Focused Evaluation*. Beverly Hills: Sage, 1978.

Rutman, Leonard, ed. *Evaluation Research Methods: A Basic Guide*. Beverly Hills: Sage, 1977.

Chapter 12

Curriculum as a Field of Practice

Elizabeth Vallance

Nothing about curriculum is simple. Indeed, it is not even clear what we mean by "the curriculum": is it a course of study? a document? an academic discipline of its own? What are "curriculists," anyway, and how do they contribute to the enterprise of schooling? And what intellectual and practical skills do curriculists most need in order to do their jobs well? The questions are fairly basic, and they demand a response by each succeeding generation of curriculum professionals; they underlie each of the chapters of this Yearbook, with greater or lesser degrees of emphasis.

It is curiously reassuring that the questions cannot be addressed simply. While the answers proposed here accumulate in a rich tapestry of related viewpoints and arguments, they do not present a simple set of instructions on how to do curriculum. There are numerous common threads and they define a refreshingly coherent overall approach to understanding curriculum problems; but the answers offered to the basic questions are perhaps most interesting for the diversity of theoretical and practical viewpoints they represent. It is in this very diversity that the real richness of the curriculum discipline may lie. Certainly it is this diversity that has attracted such a wide spectrum of scholars and practitioners to accept, explicitly or by implication, the frustratingly vague label of curriculist. Curriculum as a field of study demands complex responses to complicated problems, and only gradually and occasionally does the discipline look as though it offers any kind of consensus on how to deal with its practical problems. This Yearbook is an effort to marshall some illuminating and useful responses to specific basic questions about the curriculum and to present them as guides to practice. As such it necessarily presents a slice of the curriculum field itself and offers it to public scrutiny.

While many of the interesting questions facing curriculists are too complex and subtle for simple formulas, they can be approached intelligently and systematically, and they are amenable to productive deliberation. This Yearbook attempts to define some of the boundaries of such discussions, and in the process to identify in a modern context those problems that have vexed educators for centuries. In the end, this practical art—and its products—is in the hands of its practitioners. Regardless of the rules and prescriptions handed across in any book, those who work with and shape the forms the curriculum takes— curriculum developers, textbook authors, curriculum committees, school boards, and teachers (to name a few)—will create it. They will do so whether or not a Yearbook such as this exists; they have obviously done it with great gusto up to now. But a guide to practice should at least help curriculum workers to phrase their questions well, to ask them of the right people, to know what background is pertinent to their own situations, to be sensitive to the intellectual and political forces claiming legitimacy in their decisions, and to make curriculum decisions grounded in practical reasoning.

Curriculum problems are commonly thought to have both theoretical and practical components and much ado is also made about the alleged split between theory and practice in the dialogues and concerns of professional curriculum workers. It is revealing that this Yearbook, explicitly concerned with providing practical answers to very practical questions having to do with the design, development, implementation, and evaluation of curricula, regularly demonstrates the importance of model-making and theorizing in this practical area. Virtually every chapter attacks its appointed problem by first sketching at least a simple model describing the definitions and boundaries of the concepts it is treating; chapter after chapter acknowledges, implicitly at least, the importance of distinctions that might well be considered "theoretical" in nature—distinctions between content and form, societal and other sources of objectives, and between varying conceptions of "curriculum." The very task of thinking clearly about curriculum problems seems to demand first a methodical analysis of the concept of "curriculum" and a mapping of its salient components in the context at hand. That the breakdowns of the concept offered in the various chapters here do not precisely parallel one another is less important than that they do cumulatively form a clear picture of the basic questions in curriculum-making.

Consider briefly the various distinctions and descriptive models that the various chapters offer us. Beauchamp acknowledges three meanings of "curriculum" and identifies four "levels" of curriculum planning. Unruh identifies three levels of political influence on the curriculum, levels later reflected in Loucks' and Lieberman's analysis of curriculum implementation. Tyler and Brandt cite several sources of curriculum goals and objectives and three types of goals useful to schools. Smith discusses several different ways in which the content of a culture can be conceptualized in terms accessible to inclusion in a curriculum. Gow and Casey identify four "types" or functions of learning activities to be derived from available content in accordance with the goals of the curriculum.

Major Questions and Common Threads

Our examination of the curriculum development process has addressed a number of questions, both explicitly and implicitly. The questions addressed explicitly in our chapters are questions essential to curriculum development: curriculum development cannot proceed without at least tacit responses to them. Thus, an individual engaged in building a curriculum at any level must either address these questions directly or be prepared to face the charge that the resulting curriculum embodies responses to them, intended or not. Any curriculum necessarily reflects a position on these basic questions.

· What ideologies, theories, or philosophies are we communicating—deliberately or not—in our dialogues about curriculum problems? How do we know? What constraints do these values place on our deliberations?

· What political forces are most pertinent to this curriculum project, and how does this political context shape our priorities and our decisions?

· What are our major goals, where do they fall on a socialization-individual development continuum, and how do we know these goals are the most appropriate?

· In what terms do we define our educational "needs" and on what basis do we assess the importance of different needs?

· In what terms do we describe the content of the curriculum (concepts? values? goals?), and on what basis do we organize it?

· What is the role of planned "learning activities" in our curriculum, and what is their relationship to students, to subject matter, and to purpose?

· At what levels will the curriculum be implemented, and what historical and political realities will foster and encumber the implementation process?

· What, ultimately, is the purpose of evaluation and how can we know how best to use it? What can evaluation tell us in addition to addressing the explicit questions on which the curriculum was based?

Some commonalities underlie the various points of view on the curriculum reflected in these chapters. Six in particular stand out:

1. "The field" of curriculum practice is broad and embraces all those whose work allows them to influence the content, form, and impact of learning programs. This includes administrators, curriculum developers, writers, teachers, managers, and others.

2. Curriculum practitioners operate within a set of regular and identifiable constraints which shape their decisions and their actions. These constraints are imposed by the subject-matter disciplines, the practical climate, fiscal limitations, existing mandates, time, and local and cultural understandings of the role of the school in society. Some constraints will be more salient than others in some situations. None can be ignored.

3. Though the school curriculum is usually our focus, it cannot be considered outside the total context of the family, community, work roles, and other educative forces that shape a child.

4. There are nonschool curricula equally needing systematic attention—the curricula of industrial training programs, lifelong learning programs, community centers, trade unions, and others.

5. Every practitioner involved in curriculum development faces a fairly regular set of decision points involving easily identifiable groups: deliberations

with state boards, legislatures, district administrators, building principals, parents, teachers, and students all result in levels of decisions essential to continued progress.

6. There is a commonly accepted orderly sequence to be followed in constructing a curriculum. Lately the sequence refers to the importance of evaluation in terms of goals and is embodied in the much-overworked "Tyler rationale" (goal identification/selection of learning experiences/sequencing of same/evaluation). In future generations it may be different. But the field of curriculum accepts a basic grammar that its practitioners and students are expected to have mastered. They have, and this book uses it.

These commonalities are partially embodied in the established set of "curriculum knowledge" that is available to us in the works of Tyler, Schwab, Huebner, and others. The set of logical steps outlined in Ralph Tyler's famous syllabus (1950) over three decades ago has been embraced, questioned, quantified, made the basis of an educational movement, and revisionistically examined—but they are still with us, more or less intact. Schwab's (1969, 1971, 1973) principles for understanding curriculum work as a practical art, and his principles of deliberation and of sensitivity to the commonplaces of curricular issues, are basic to most of our thinking. Huebner's (1966) important work placing curriculum questions into conflicting but concurrent value systems has remained with many of us a reminder of the many practical dimensions of any curricular decision. Eisner and Vallance (1974) offer a kind of map of five alternative ways of conceptualizing the important questions in the curriculum field.

The ultimate value of these conceptual analyses, however, is in the extent to which they inform and improve upon practice. This test is rendered especially difficult by the fact that the practical world of curriculum-making is itself complex, shifting, and rarely takes the same form twice. No simple rules, models, or deliberative techniques can easily be applied to all curricular situations with anything like the same results. The problems of selecting textbooks vary from community to community, and from year to year; the needs of third graders in Detroit are not the same as the needs of third graders in Austin; the curricular problems faced by planners of a vocational continuing education program in industry are not the same as those of a building principal in a rural elementary school. That much seems obvious, and it means that any book claiming to address recurring curriculum decisions must seek the generic and most common kinds of problems addressed by all curriculists; it must attempt to provide rules applicable to this wide variety of contexts.

There is also a second rank of questions appropriate to any curriculum-making endeavor but only tangentially addressed here. These are questions that are addressed almost by default in real curricular situations but that rarely assume a sufficiently tidy form to invite chapter headings. These second-rank questions raise themselves in the process of practical curriculum work, and they will influence our approach to the more directly practical questions.

One such question is: "To what extent *is* it possible to be systematic in developing a curriculum?" Many standard curriculum texts describe the curriculum development process as a logical step-by-step procedure. A cursory reading of some of the chapters might suggest that the goals of the curriculum, derived in part from a systematic needs assessment, may be applied to the accepted body of content in a way that results in specific learning activities: needs assessments can clarify our goals, which in turn will tell us how to select among the learning activities available to us for teaching the content in its various forms. In fact, of course, the process is never so simple, and the logical steps implied by each of these chapters become significantly muddled when we add the context demands of philosophy and politics. These can confuse the best-laid plans, and the confusion demands resolution before the curriculum can be implemented.

Thus, *does* goals identification always precede the definition of learning activities? Is format decided when learning activities are selected, or before, or sometimes after? What role does needs assessment actually play in the identification of goals or of the "culture content" of the curriculum? The answers to these questions may vary with each situation, but the curriculum developers will at least tacitly address them as they determine how and when to answer the explicit and unavoidable questions.

Also at play in any curriculum decision-making situation is the developers' tacit understanding of whether "curriculum" is primarily a body of content or a logical structure and process: What *is* the curriculum, and which aspects of it are we most intent on shaping in the course of our deliberations? Several chapters skirt the question, and several incorporate it into other arguments. On the whole, their answer is "both": the curriculum is both a body of content and a systematic organization of its specific forms. The problems of curriculum-making are both of selecting the right content and of presenting it in a fashion accessible to students. The problems are of both substance and form, though one or the other aspect may predominate at various stages in the curriculum-making process. Thus, for example, parents, the public, special interest groups, and others may be especially concerned with the content of what is taught in schools, and may phrase their arguments in those terms. Arguments for consumer education, vocational education, drug abuse education, "equal time" for creationist theories, and the like tend to emphasize the content that is to be communicated in these curricula. Others in the dialogue may be more concerned with the process or attitude by which knowledge is conveyed to students—concerns with "discovery learning," "mastery learning," "contract learning," and "lifelong learning" stress the kind of involvement offered to students rather than the specific material they will address.

The confusion between content and structure emerges at several levels of discussion in curriculum making. Some of the decision points identified focus on content questions, others pertain more to structure, and the emphasis necessarily shifts in the course of developing a complete curriculum. This Yearbook accommodates the shifts without explicitly addressing them; any practitioner will need to address the distinction and resolve it periodically.

Finally, some assumptions are incorporated into the present model of curriculum development, and it is appropriate for curriculists to test the validity of these assumptions against their own situations. For example, the model presented here presumes that the planned-for goals of a curriculum, as its most important outcomes, are those most deserving of evaluation and revision. Little has been said of the unintended but regular consequences of schooling such as political socialization, obedience training, value formation, and the like. The developer may well ask whether this assumption of the centrality of planned-for and measurable objectives is warranted in any given situation—or whether long-term emerging effects such as students' remembered images of schooling or the community's pride in a program might be as important. A second assumption inviting questioning is that curriculum development skills can somehow be separated from teacher training programs and dealt with as a set of problems in their own right. The question will be faced separately in each situation: are the curricular problems at hand problems that can be solved by curriculists not based in classrooms, or is the implementation process so central that instructional principles and the teacher's role are as critical as the other relatively clear decision points treated here? Is it justifiable to assume that roughly the same curriculum development skills are required of all persons involved in the process, or will some individuals' roles require broader or more intensive training?

One other assumption embodied in this Yearbook is, of course, the upbeat belief that educators are to some extent free to analyze and revise what is taught in school and elsewhere. Obviously we are, to some extent. But it is worth wondering just how much of our effort to do what this Yearbook claims to help us do is limited by circumstances; addressing this implicit question should help us to appreciate the real possibilities and limits of our task and to gear our efforts realistically within that framework.

Curriculum as a Field of Practice

The curriculum field is by no means clear; as a discipline of study and as a field of practice, "curriculum" lacks clean boundaries, and despite the tidy titles defining the concerns in each of the chapters, muddy issues remain. These issues are different from the direct practical "questions" already cited. The issues are dilemmas, and while they are periodically addressed by curriculum theorists and other reflective types, they do not demand resolution in every practical situation. They can be ignored, but they never completely disappear. Most of us live with them in a kind of peaceable truce. They merit at least a quick sketch.

One enduring issue in the field of curriculum refers to the ever-present possibility that in developing and implementing a curriculum we are also doing a lot of other things. That is, we may be creating a kind of hidden curriculum that teaches rules and principles of social and political conduct but whose outcomes we neither anticipated nor sought to measure. In many cases we can't know this for some time, if ever. But it is likely that we are having an effect on classroom atmosphere, on community feelings toward education, on students' feelings toward their school and toward learning in general, on teacher morale, and the like. A substantial curriculum change may well color the images of schooling that students carry with them into adulthood, and these images may subtly enter the mainstream of American culture without our having realized it, certainly without our having planned for it. It seems prudent to be sensitive to these peripheral effects of curriculum change and to our ethical responsibility for them, though we may be quite unable to control them. The issue—of how much we can influence education through influences on the curriculum—is an ethical one and an important one. We can hope that through thoughtful and deliberative experience with curriculum development, over time, we can come to better understand such subtleties.

A related issue is the question of which parts of the curriculum really are susceptible to change by deliberate action. In principle, of course, since curriculum is an artifact like many others, it can be wholly revised by direct effort. In fact, however, portions of it have become so ensconced in tradition that the curriculum as a whole may be only variously susceptible to change depending on which portion we are considering. This Yearbook presumes that anything in the curriculum, from goals to evaluation criteria, is subject to revision; in real life these may operate only as trade-offs against each other. The possibilities and limitations of curriculum change are defined in part by the broader role of the school in society, and by the curriculum's role within the school. The enduring issues in the field of curriculum as a practical art are shaped in large part by these relationships: the curriculum in American schools has never yet been used as a tool for deliberately overthrowing established majority tradition. Schooling and learning have since colonial times been directed toward the development and maintenance of the social structures that had created the country: the family, the small community, the coherence of the dominant culture. Thus, while the curriculum has been employed to "Americanize" immigrants and to instill traditional American values in generations of school children (and has seemed to perform these functions extremely effectively), it has not generally been the tool of revolution and dramatic change (though Paulo Freire's work may change this). Some reformers—Dewey and Rugg, to name two—have argued the need to revise the curriculum so as to teach political values *not* currently in vogue among most educators, but on the whole the curriculum seems to have played a relatively conservative role.

This apparent commitment to the transmission of culture has placed the school squarely in the role of socializing agent, a role it must steadily balance with the goals of individual growth and development which it so explicitly fosters. The balance between socialization and individual growth is fairly even; neither has ever fully overridden the other, and it seems safe to say that no substantial curriculum change is likely to occur that espouses either at the expense of the other. Thus, any curriculum development effort must take account of this traditional role, and either overtly uphold it or try to revise it. Curriculum development is necessarily constrained by the school's political, social, and ethical commitments to the society that supports it. It is this fact more than any others that irrefutably defines curriculum-making as a practical art and demands the application of rational deliberative skills. Curriculum change is always something of a bootstrap operation; the extent to which any specific situation limits or liberates its change agents is a question to be acknowledged in the application for any curriculum development skills.

The content-oriented view of the curriculum would hold that underlying all curricular problems is that of selecting the appropriate culture content, the question with which curriculum development begins and ends. We ask "What knowledge is of most worth?" several times in each generation. The question shapes the way we seek to identify our goals, it shapes our goals themselves, and the debates it provokes are fundamental to educators' deliberations at all levels and in all eras. Any given curriculum, whether structured around content or around method, obviously embodies some responses to the question; every curriculum at some point attempts to teach x and y, devotes a chapter to a and none to b, applies the newest teaching to c content and not to d. The curriculum—the curriculum developers—select from the realm of the possible. The curriculum presented to children as a result of these deliberations embodies answers to the question. The creation of a curriculum tacitly acknowledges that yet another answer has been provided to yet another generation of students. An acknowledgment that the answers are always temporary, however, may enable curriculum developers to address the issue with some humility and in a historical context that sees its own limitations. "What knowledge is of most worth?" is an issue unresolved by this Yearbook or by any other; a set of mechanisms for getting at an answer, however, has been provided in some of the chapters.

The unknowns facing the curriculum field seem sometimes reassuringly stable. The identification of parts of the curriculum that are susceptible to change; the working out of an acceptable relationship among theory, research, and practice; the identification of the boundaries describing what curriculum change really affects besides the curriculum itself; the constraints and possibilities imposed by the enduring function of the school as socializer and as liberator; the perpetual need to determine what students need to know—all are issues that can be traced back through generations. In a sense we are dealing with little that is new, yet in another sense we are addressing standard problems with new and evolving practical skills that were not available to our forebears.

Implications for the Training of Curriculum Practitioners

Curriculum practitioners are a diverse group. They include teachers (those ultimate curriculum implementers), commercial and district curriculum developers, superintendents, community education directors, directors of curriculum, building principals, textbook writers and editors, directors of education in a variety of settings other than K-12 schools, and college professors attempting to train all of the above. All these individuals, and others, have direct and observable impacts on what is taught in school; it is they who distill from the surrounding culture the goals of schooling and attempt to communicate them through a program of study. Through their efforts they attempt to answer the unavoidable questions identified earlier in this chapter, and throughout this Yearbook.

But a Yearbook alone cannot educate curriculists, and it cannot train educators of widely varying backgrounds to share a common view. We may well wonder, then, what the implications of this Yearbook and its practical approach to curriculum development are for the long-term training of practitioners. What training *is* of most worth to the curriculum practitioner, and what does this Yearbook suggest for the curriculum of curriculists?

There would seem to be three common requirements among curriculists in their training, as reflected and expressed in chapters of this Yearbook. There is, first, a clear need for some how-to-do-it *skills and rules* of the sort proposed in several of these chapters, and there is especially a requirement for a means of integrating these various skills into a coherent body of practical knowledge. Most of us are trained in some of the skills outlined here; few have covered all of them. Second, and in order to make this compilation of knowledge useful, there is a requirement for developing a solid *conceptual grasp* of the regular variables, of the philosophical arguments behind a given curriculum or proposals for curriculum change, and of the various configurations that curriculum change can take. That curriculum development is a practical art does not mean the developer can successfully muddle through without some broader sense of the context in which he/she operates. Some grasp on conceptual analysis seems essential. And third, it seems not tautological to say that curriculum developers require *experience*. The experience might take the form of full-time immersion or only peripheral involvement in a curriculum project. In either case it seems imperative for the curriculum developer to acquire a fund of experience that will enrich the meaning of the various principles and theoretical constructs gleaned from Yearbooks such as this and from other formalized curricula for curriculists.

The task of providing even the rudiments of such a common education to curriculists is tremendous, for though we work together on common problems in our various curriculum development projects, there is almost nothing that our various backgrounds hold in common as a starter. Many of us are trained as teachers, which may be our single most common denominator; it is not, however, universally shared. Curriculists come from many directions: teaching as well as scholarship in the disciplines; school settings as well as industrial, post-secondary, and community settings; and practical as well as research orientations. How can professionals from these diverse backgrounds ensure that the common language they share as curriculists is truly common? How can the requirements for practical skills, conceptual clarity, and experience be nurtured in professionals from different fields who must come together in curriculum projects?

The usual sources of the three basic requirements identified above are familiar: we provide practical skills in the "methods" courses offered by schools of education; we attempt to foster conceptual clarity through courses on philosophy and research methods; rich experience comes in the sink-or-swim quality of most of our jobs, and it is intensive and effectual. Those not trained in traditional "education" professions, however, will perforce miss the first (the methods course), and may well miss the second unless their "other" disciplines emphasized conceptual rigor. And there are some professional curriculists well trained in research who have little or no experience in curriculum development itself. The training commonly available to us in schools of education does not guarantee that we will all possess the essential tools.

While there are no guarantees, it seems reasonable to suggest that the lessons offered by this Yearbook encourage and reward various *different kinds* of backgrounds. The practical skills covered in the Yearbook *are* in a sense generic: needs assessment and goals selection are hardly unique to curriculum, nor are problems of organization and formatting, nor are the trials of implementing approved changes. We encounter similar problems in selecting organizational goals, in preparing grant proposals and final reports, in accepting any new organizational responsibilities. Identifying purpose and organizing materials around it may be central to curriculum development but it is scarcely peculiar to it: any good research or writing project demands the same talents, and most decisions to spend money imply some sense of organizational purpose and priority. Because curricular questions are so highly charged with notions of community purpose and cultural transmission, curriculum implementation takes on a coloration that is intense and sensitive; the implementation of most new projects, however—from downtown redevelopment to wholesale shifts in political party power—require many of the same practical skills as curriculum development. Needs assessments, sensitivity to philosophical and political bases, selecting and sequencing of major content materials, evaluation, reassessment— the same skills are called upon, though they take different forms.

Likewise, the conceptual skills of analysis, identification of context, and intellectual rigor are available in a number of backgrounds. Many of the traditional "disciplines" require these skills of their students; good writing requires them; so does good editing; so does effective management, at many levels. And the experience relevant to curriculum development may be available in a variety of settings besides those typically considered curricular—research projects, staff training, and program administration in many areas may afford opportunities for acquiring experiences in decision making and program planning essential to curriculum planning per se.

None of which is to argue that the education of curriculists can effectively be conducted piecemeal or that good curriculists can come from simply anywhere. But it does suggest that the components of good training in curriculum may be available both in and outside schools of education, and that the educators of curriculists—including the curriculists themselves—are well advised to capitalize on this.

A Yearbook such as this one can provide a compendium of the major decisions to be made; it can suggest the major variables in these decision points and provide some techniques for assessing them. The real training of curriculists, however, must come in their respective professions, with practical and conceptual skills developed in a variety of deliberative situations and honed in the peculiar contexts of developing educational programs for others.

References

Eisner, Elliot, and Vallance, Elizabeth. *Conflicting Conceptions of Curriculum*. Berkeley, Calif.: McCutchan, 1974.

Huebner, Dwayne. "Curricular Language and Classroom Meanings." In *Language and Meaning*. Edited by J. B. Macdonald and R. R. Leeper. Washington, D.C.: Association for Supervision and Curriculum Development, 1966.

Schwab, Joseph. "The Practical: A Language for Curriculum." *School Review* 78 (November 1969):1–23.

Schwab, Joseph. "The Practical: Arts of the Eclectic." *School Review* 79 (August 1971):493–542.

Schwab, Joseph. "The Practical: Translation into Curriculum." *School Review* 81 (August 1973):501–522.

Tyler, Ralph. *Basic Principles of Curriculum and Instruction*. Chicago: University of Chicago Press, 1950.

1983 Yearbook Committee and Authors

FENWICK W. ENGLISH, Editor and Chairperson of 1983 Yearbook Committee

Currently Superintendent of Schools, Northport-East Northport Union Free School District, Long Island, New York. Formerly a Partner in the firm of Peat, Marwick, Mitchell & Co. in the Washington, D.C. office, and past Associate Director of the American Association of School Administrators. Recipient of the AASA-NASE Distinguished Professor Award in 1973 and the ASCD-NCSI Outstanding Consultant Award in 1981. He received his B.S. and M.S. from the University of Southern California and Ph.D. from Arizona State University.

GEORGE A. BEAUCHAMP

Professor Emeritus of Education, Northwestern University. Author of numerous books in the curriculum field and of the Fourth Edition of *Curriculum Theory* published by F. E. Peacock. A U.S. Delegate to the Third and Fourth International Curriculum Conferences and formerly Secretary, Division B, AERA, 1969–1972. He earned his A.B. degree from Eastern Michigan University, M. Ed. from Wayne State University, and Ph.D. from the University of Michigan.

RONALD S. BRANDT

Executive Editor of Publications for the Association for Supervision and Curriculum Development. From 1970 to 1978 he was Associate Superintendent for Instruction for the Lincoln, Nebraska, Public Schools. He has also been a teacher, junior high principal, staff member of a regional educational laboratory, and director of staff development for the Minneapolis Public Schools. In the mid-1960s he spent 18 months teaching in a teacher training college in Nigeria, West Africa.

TOMMYE W. CASEY

Course Designer for CIGNA Corporation which was formerly the Insurance Company of North America, Inc., in Philadelphia. Prior to this she was an educational consultant specializing in instructional design and research and evaluation to Research for Better Schools, Inc., Community College of Philadelphia, and other such institutions.

ROGER A. KAUFMAN

Professor of Educational Research and Development and Director, Center for Needs Assessment and Planning, Florida State University. He has served as President of the National Society for Performance and Instruction, as a member of the Secretary of the Navy's Advisory Board on Education, and on the Training and the Education Committees of the U.S. Chamber of Commerce. He received his M.A. from Johns Hopkins University and his Ph.D. from New York University.

DORIS T. GOW

Associate Professor in the Curriculum and Supervision Program, School of Education, University of Pittsburgh. She has been a secondary school social studies teacher, curriculum designer, curriculum consultant to schools and universities, and Research Associate at the Learning Research and Development Center.

ANN LIEBERMAN

Associate Director of the Horace Mann Lincoln Institute, Teachers College, Columbia University, New York.

SUSAN F. LOUCKS

Currently on the staff of The Network, Inc., in Andover, Massachusetts, where she directs projects in the areas of evaluation, training, program validation research, and technical assistance. She recently moved from Austin, Texas, where she spent nine years at the Research and Development Center for Teacher Education, conducting research on the change process and training in applications of research to schools. She received her B.A. in geology from the State University of New York at Binghamton and her M.A. and Ph.D. in curriculum and instruction from the University of Texas at Austin.

FREDERICK A. RODGERS

Chairperson and Professor of Elementary Education, University of Illinois, Urbana. Rogers was editor of the Research Supplement and Research in Review columns in *Educational Leadership* and has been an elementary teacher and instructor of geography at the college level. He received both an M.Ed. and Ed. D. from the University of Illinois.

B. OTHANEL SMITH

Professor Emeritus, University of Illinois and University of South Florida. He is currently working with the Florida Beginning Teacher Program, Coalition for the Development of a Performance Evaluation System. He has been a teacher of science, high school principal, and instructor at the University of Florida, University of Illinois, and University of South Florida.

ARTHUR W. STELLER

Assistant Superintendent of Schools, Shaker Heights City School District, Ohio. He has an extensive background in planning and in 1980 published *Educational Planning for Educational Success*, Phi Delta Kappa. Formerly he was Coordinator of Special Projects and Systemwide Planning for the Montgomery County Public Schools, Rockville, Maryland. He received his B.S., M.A., and Ph.D. from Ohio University.

RALPH W. TYLER

Director Emeritus of the Center for Advanced Study in the Behavioral Sciences. He began his teaching in 1921 in the high school of Pierre, South Dakota. He served on the faculties of the Universities of Nebraska, North Carolina, Ohio State, and Chicago. Since his retirement in 1967 he has been teaching part time in a number of universities and consulting on curriculum and evaluation projects in the United States and abroad.

GLENYS G. UNRUH

Recently retired as Deputy Superintendent of the School District of University City, Missouri. Her major career has been in curriculum development in the public schools. She was President of the Association for Supervision and Curriculum Development in 1974–75, and has served on various national and state advisory committees and on overseas teams at international conferences on education. She is the author of several journal articles and books related to curriculum development.

ELIZABETH VALLANCE

Director of Academic Outreach and Assistant Professor in Kansas State University's Division of Continuing Education. She received her Ph.D. from Stanford University and has published in the areas of curriculum theory, the hidden curriculum, aesthetic criticism and qualitative evaluation of curriculum, and the relationship of curriculum theory to problems of post-secondary education. She has published in curriculum journals abroad and was co-editor (with Elliot Eisner) of *Conflicting Conceptions of Curriculum*.

Board of Directors

Board Members Elected at Large

(Listed alphabetically; the year in parentheses following each member's name indicates the end of the term of office.)

MITSUO ADACHI, University of Hawaii, Honolulu (1983)

GENE RAYMOND CARTER, Norfolk Public Schools, Norfolk, Virginia (1985)

C. LOUIS CEDRONE, Westwood Public Schools, Westwood, Massachusetts (1983)

GLORIA COX, Board of Education, Memphis, Tennessee (1984)

ELAINE MCNALLY JARCHOW, Iowa State University, Ames (1985)

LOIS HARRISON-JONES, Richmond City Schools, Richmond, Virginia (1986)

JOAN D. KERELEJZA, West Hartford Public Schools, West Hartford, Connecticut (1983)

MARCIA KNOLL, New York City Public Schools, Forest Hills (1984)

K. JESSIE KOBAYASHI, Public Schools, San Jose, California (1986)

ELIZABETH R. LANE, Shelby County Schools, Memphis, Tennessee (1986)

MARIAN LEIBOWITZ, Teaneck Public Schools, Teaneck, New Jersey (1986)

BETTY LIVENGOOD, Mineral County Schools, Keyser, West Virginia (1985)

ELIZABETH S. MANERA, Arizona State University, Tempe (1983)

GLORIA MCFADDEN, Oregon College of Education, Salem (1984)

E. GAYE MCGOVERN, Miami East School District, Casstown, Ohio (1985)

MARVA GARNER MILLER, Houston Independent School District, Houston, Texas (1983)

ANN CONVERSE SHELLY, Bethany College, Bethany, West Virginia (1986)

CLAIRE H. SULLIVAN, Secondary School Services, Clearwater, Florida (1984)

LAUREL TANNER, Temple University, Philadelphia, Pennsylvania (1985)

MILDRED M. WILLIAMS, State Department of Education, Jackson, Mississippi (1984)

Unit Representatives to the Board of Directors

(Each Unit's President is listed first; others follow in alphabetical order.)

Alabama: PEARL JACKSON, Public Schools, Moulton; MILLY COWLES, University of Alabama, Birmingham; JIM GIDLEY, Public Schools, Gadsden

Alaska: DENICE CLYNE, Public Schools, Anchorage; DONALD MCDERMOTT, University of Alaska, Anchorage

Arizona: ANNA JOLIVET, Public Schools, Tucson; PAT NASH, University of Arizona, Tucson; ELLIE SBRAGIA, Arizona Center for Law Related Education, Phoenix

Arkansas: JIM ROLLINS, Public Schools, Springdale; PHILLIP BESONEN, University of Arkansas, Fayetteville

California: HELEN J. WALLACE, Public Schools, Cotati; REGINA CAIN, Public

Schools, Tustin; RICHARD EHRGOTT, Public Schools, Visalia; CAROL BARNES, California State University, Fullerton; DORIS PRINCE, Santa Clara County Office of Education; MARILYN WINTERS, California State University, Sacramento

Colorado: DONNA BRENNAN, Public Schools, Englewood; CILE CHAVEZ, University of Northern Colorado, Greeley; TOM MAGLARAS, Public Schools, Aurora

Connecticut: BERNARD GOFFIN, Public Schools, Monroe; EDWARD H. BOURQUE, Public Schools, Fairfield; ARTHUR ROBERTS, University of Connecticut, Storrs

Delaware: WILLIAM McCORMICK, Public Schools, Dover; MELVILLE F. WARREN, Public Schools, Dover

District of Columbia: BARBARA T. JACKSON, Public Schools, Washington; ROBERTA WALKER, Public Schools, Washington

Florida: MARY GIELLA, Pasco County Schools, Land O'Lakes; JEAN MARANI, Council of Secondary Education, Tallahassee; MARY JO SISSON, Public Schools, Fort Walton Beach; HILDA WILES, Public Schools, Gainesville

Georgia: ANN CULPEPPER, Bibb County Board of Education, Macon; SCOTT BRADSHAW, Georgia Department of Education, Atlanta; JOE MURPHY, Augusta College

Hawaii: LARRY McGONIGAL, Mid-Pacific Institute, Honolulu; CLAIRE YOSHIDA, Hawaii State Department of Education, Honolulu

Idaho: GARY DORAMUS, Public Schools, Caldwell; DAVID CARROLL, Public Schools, Boise

Illinois: RODNEY M. BORSTAD, Northern Illinois University, DeKalb; PATRICIA CONRAN, Public Schools, West Chicago; ALLAN DORNSEIF, Public Schools, Matteson; RICHARD HANKE, Public Schools, Arlington Heights; KATHRYN RANSOM, Public Schools, Springfield; SYBIL YASTROW, Educational Service Region, Waukegan

Indiana: CHARLES MOCK, Public Schools, Bloomington; DONNA DELPH, Purdue University, Hammond; MARJORIE JACKSON, Public Schools, Indianapolis

Iowa: DOUGLAS SCHERMER, Public Schools, Maquoketa; BETTY ATWOOD, Heartland Area Education Agency, Ankeny; HAROLD HULLEMAN, Linn-Mar Community Schools, Marion

Kansas: HAROLD SCHMIDT, Public Schools, Salina; JIM JARRETT, Public Schools, Kansas City

Kentucky: RANDY KIMBROUGH, Kentucky State Department of Education, Frankfort; JUDY MINNEHAN, Oldham County Board of Education, LaGrange; TOM TAYLOR, Public Schools, Owenton

Louisiana: JOHN M. LEE, Public Schools, New Orleans; JULIANNA L. BOUDREAUX, Public Schools, New Orleans; KATE SCULLY, Public Schools, Kenner

Maine: LYNN M. BAK, publisher, Falmouth; RICHARD BABB, Public Schools, Auburn

Maryland: DENNIS YOUNGER, Anne Arundel County Public Schools, Annapolis; Thomas R. Howie, Calvert County Public Schools, Prince Frederick; Thelma M. Sparks (retired), Public Schools, Annapolis

Massachusetts: C. Burleigh Wellington, Tufts University, Medford; Gilbert Bulley, Public Schools, Lynnfield; Morton Milesky, Public Schools, Longmeadow; Robert Munnelly, Public Schools, Reading

Michigan: Dixie Hibner, Public Schools, Saline; Rita Foote, Educational Center, Southfield; James House, Public Schools, Wayne; James W. Perry, Public Schools, Muskegon; Virginia Sorenson, Western Michigan University, Kalamazoo

Minnesota: John Butts, consultant, Minneapolis; Merill C. Fellger, Public Schools, Buffalo; Arnold Ness, Public Schools, St. Anthony

Mississippi: Juliet P. Borden, Public Schools, Plantersville; Bobbie Collum, State Department of Education, Jackson

Missouri: Geraldine Johnson, Public Schools, St. Louis; Frank Morley (semi-retired), Public Schools, Webster Groves; Pat Rocklage, Public Schools, St. Louis County

Montana: Jim Longin, Public Schools, Havre; Henry N. Worrest, Montana State University, Bozeman

Nebraska: Don Dahlin, Kearney State College, Kearney; Dorothy Hall, Public Schools, Omaha; Edgar Kelley, University of Nebraska, Lincoln

Nevada: Fred Doctor, Public Schools, Reno; Melvin Kirchner, Public Schools, Reno

New Hampshire: Jean Stefanik, Public Schools, Amherst; Frederick B. King, Public Schools, Exeter

New Jersey: Judith Zimmerman, Rutgers University, New Brunswick; Paul Braungart, Public Schools, Moorestown; Ruth Dorney Crew, Public Schools, Randolph; Frank Jaggard, Public Schools, Cinnaminson; Paul Manko, Public Schools, Mt. Laurel

New Mexico: Jack Bobroff, Public Schools, Albuquerque; Delbert Dyche, Public Schools, Las Cruces

New York: Dorothy Foley, State Department of Education, Schenectady; Anthony Deiulio, State University College, Fredonia; Stephen Fisher, Foxlane Campus, Mt. Kisco; Donald E. Harkness, Public Schools, Manhasset; Gerard Kells, Public Schools, Henrietta; Timothy M. Melchior, Public Schools, Valley Stream; Arlene Soifer, Nassau BOCES, Westbury

North Carolina: Robert C. Hanes, Public Schools, Charlotte; Lucille Bazemore, Bertie County Board of Education, Windsor; Mary Jane Dillard, Jackson County Board of Education, Sylva

North Dakota: Richard B. Warner, Public Schools, Fargo; Glenn Melvey, Public Schools, Fargo

Ohio: Ronald Hibbard, Summit County Board of Education, Akron; Robert L. Bennett, Public Schools, Gahanna; Eugene Glick (retired), Public

Schools, Medina; ROBERT H. HOHMAN, Public Schools, Avon Lake; ARTHUR E. WOHLERS, Ohio State University, Columbus

Oklahoma: JERRY M. HILL, Central State University, Edmond; JAMES ROBERTS, Public Schools, Lawton; NELDA TEBOW, Public Schools, Oklahoma City

Oregon: TOM LINDERSMITH, Public Schools, Lake Oswego; JEAN FERGUSON, West Oregon State College, Monmouth; REA JANES, Public Schools, Portland

Pennsylvania: ROBERT F. NICELY, JR., The Pennsylvania State University, University Park; DAVID CAMPBELL, State Department of Education, Harrisburg; ROBERT FLYNN, Public Schools, Lemoyne; ANTHONY LABRIOLA, Public Schools, McVeytown; THERESE T. WALTER, Public Schools, Edinboro; JEANNE ZIMMERMAN (retired), Public Schools, Lancaster

Puerto Rico: RAMON M. BARQUIN, American Military Academy, Guaynabo; RAMON CLAUDIO, University of Puerto Rico, Rio Piedras

Rhode Island: JAMES TURLEY, Rhode Island College, Providence; GUY DiBIASIO, Public Schools, Cranston

South Carolina: CEICLE HEIZER, Public Schools, Greenville; EDIE JENSEN, Public Schools, Irmo; CECIL WARD, Public Schools, Florence

South Dakota: JOHN BONAIUTO, Public Schools, Brookings; JANET JONES, Public Schools, Martin

Tennessee: MARSHALL C. PERRITT, Public Schools, Memphis; JOHN LOVELL, The University of Tennessee, Knoxville; MARGARET PHELPS, Tennessee Tech University, Cookeville

Texas: ANN L. JENSEN, Public Schools, Garland; ROBERT ANDERSON, Texas Tech University, Lubbock; WAYNE BERRYMAN, Region VII Education Service Center, Kilgore; CAROL KUYKENDALL, Public Schools, Houston; DEWEY MAYS, Public Schools, Fort Worth

Utah: JO ANN SEGHINI, Public Schools, Sandy; CORRINE P. HILL, Public Schools, Salt Lake City

Vermont: LARNED KETCHAM, Public Schools, Charlotte; GEORGE FULLER, Public Schools, Orleans

Virgin Islands: MAVIS BRADY, State Department of Education, St. Thomas; LINDA CREQUE, Sibley Public Schools, St. Thomas

Virginia: EVELYN P. BICKHAM, Lynchburg College, Lynchburg; CLARK DOBSON, George Mason University, Fairfax; DELORES GREENE, Public Schools, Richmond; NANCY VANCE, State Department of Education, Richmond

Washington: BOB VALIANT, Public Schools, Kennewick; JOE FLEMING, Education Service District 114, Port Townsend; MONICA SCHMIDT, Department of Public Instruction, Tumwater

West Virginia: JOYCE CLARK WAUGH, University of West Virginia, Institute; HELEN SAUNDERS, State Department of Education, Charleston

Wisconsin: JOHN KOEHN, Public Schools, Oconomowoc; ARNOLD M. CHANDLER, State Department of Public Instruction, Madison; ROLAND J. CROSS, Public Schools, Oregon

Wyoming: ALAN G. WHEELER, State Department of Education, Cheyenne; DONNA CONNOR, University of Wyoming, Rawlins

International Units:

Germany: RUSS FIRLIK, Mainz American Elementary School

ASCD Review Council

ASCD Headquarters Staff

Gordon Cawelti/Executive Director

Ronald S. Brandt/Executive Editor

Ruth T. Long/Associate Director

Diane Berreth/Associate Director

Sarah Arlington, John Bralove, Joan Brandt, Anne Dees, Dolores Dickerson, Anita Fitzpatrick, Jo Ann Irick, Jo Jones, Teola Jones, Jacquelyn Layton, Indu Madan, Deborah Maddox, Barbara Marentette, Clara Meredith, Frances Mindel, Nancy Modrak, Nancy Olson, Gayle Rockwell, Robert Shannon, Carolyn Shell, Charlotte Stokes, Betsey Thomas, Barbara Thompson, Al Way, Colette Williams

DATE DUE

DEMCO 38-296